Coaching Modern Basketball

Matt James

Coaching Modern Basketball

Hints, Strategies, and Tactics

William F. Stier, Jr.
State University of New York,
Brockport

Allyn and Bacon
Boston   London   Toronto   Sydney   Tokyo   Singapore

Series Editor: Suzy Spivey
Senior Editorial Assistant: Amy Braddock
Manufacturing Buyer: Suzanne Lareau

Library of Congress Cataloging-in-Publication Data

Stier, William F.
    Coaching modern basketball : hints, strategies, and tactics /
William F. Stier, Jr.
        p.   cm.
    Includes bibliographical references and index.
    ISBN 0–205–15935–4
    1. Basketball--Coaching.   I. Title.
GV885.3.S75   1997   96-38719
796.323'07'7--dc20   CIP

Printed in the United States of America

10 9 8 7 6 5 4 3 2   01 00 99 98

To my wife, Veronica Ann, and to our loving family members
Missy Ann
Barbara Ann
Lori Ann
Reba Ann
Mary Joann
Missie Ann
Samantha Ann
Katie Lee
Joshua
Jessica Bree
Mark
Mikey
Mic
Michael
Patrick
Will III
for loving encouragement and continuing support.

Contents

SECTION TWO

The Defensive Side of Coaching Basketball   25

Chapter 2   Quarter-Court Zone Defenses   27

Chapter 3   Man-to-Man Defense   45

Chapter 7   Combatting Presses: Zones and Man to Man   137

SECTION FOUR
Special Situations   155

Chapter 9   The Proper Use of Drills   181

Preface

This book, *Coaching Modern Basketball*, has been written for coaches by a coach. I have successfully coached basketball and served as athletic director at the junior high, high school, and university levels for over 20 years.

Whether you are a neophyte or a highly experienced mentor, *Coaching Modern Basketball* will prove to be an invaluable source of important and timely information and knowledge. If you are not yet a coach or are a relatively inexperienced coach, this book will help you become well versed in all of the essential areas of the sport, including the current tactics and strategies utilized in practices and game situations in today's hectic and fast-paced world of competitive basketball. If you are an experienced coach, this book will assist you in remaining current, at the cutting edge, in terms of your own knowledge base and in respect to your understanding of the prevailing trends in coaching basketball now and in the foreseeable future.

A unique feature of this book is the inclusion of 223 **Coaching Hints** covering every facet of the game, including offense, defense, special situations, use of drills in practice, and other essential aspects of coaching and playing the sport of basketball. These Coaching Hints include suggestions regarding what to do as well as what not to do if coaches are to experience consistent success at any level. In addition to the strategies and tactics involving the Xs and Os of the sport, an entire chapter (10) is devoted to the mental/psychological aspect of coaching basketball.

Coaching Modern Basketball was written to help you become a better coach, a more knowledgeable coach, and a more successful coach. In Chapter 1, you are advised to become a discriminating reader, learner, and consumer of the sport. This means that you should make judgments in terms of what strategies and tactics might fit with your coaching philosophy, your coaching style, your preferences, your experiences, and the skill level and abilities of your athletes.

As you read the book, ask yourself what could work for you and your team. View each of the offensive and defensive series, special-play situations, practices suggestions, and the Coaching Hints in light of your own current or future coaching situation. Critically assess the wealth of information presented in the book to see what might be applicable for use in your own coaching methods. What information might serve to meet your needs and the needs of your athletes, now and in the future? What might be suitable to utilize in your existing arsenal of offensive and defensive attacks? What meshes with your thinking as a basketball coach? What might be appropriate to use with your team, perhaps with some minor modification or adaptation?

Good luck in your efforts to improve yourself and to remain at the cutting edge as a coach in the exciting and ever-changing sport of basketball. Enjoy the read.

ACKNOWLEDGMENTS

This book is dedicated to my wife, Veronica, and to our extended family. To Veronica, who sacrificed so much during our 20 years of coaching, and whose ever-present support and loving encouragement provided the motivation for the completion of this book, I thank from the bottom of my heart. To my children, who also understood and accepted the necessity of the long and late hours involved in coaching basketball during these two decades, I appreciate your understanding and to you I dedicate this book.

Thanks also to the countless coaches, staff members, and athletes with whom I have worked during my tenure as a coach on the junior high, high school, and collegiate/university levels. I have learned much from my peers, my assistant coaches, and my players. Special mention must be made of Robert Davidshofer, former coach at Aquin High School, Cascade, Iowa; Mauro Panagio, former basketball coach at SUNY Brockport and now head coach within the CBA professional league; Gale Daughtery, former men's basketball coach and now athletics director at Ohio Northern University; and Gayle Lauth, women's basketball coach, also at Ohio Northern University. To these outstanding coaches and former colleagues, I also dedicate this book.

Special thanks should be given to Karen Rupp, Kim Scott, and Norman Frisch, graphic designers, and to Richard Black, Director of Design and Production, SUNY, Brockport. I also extend my gratitude to James Dusen, Manager Photographic Services, SUNY, Brockport, for the photographs. In addition, I thank my former secretary, Gale Player, for her years of faithful collaboration and support. Thanks, too, to the following reviewers of my manuscript for their helpful suggestions: Thomas Ball, Northern Illinois University; Ross Friesen, University of Idaho; Michael Mondello, University of Florida; and Michael Scareno, University of Alabama.

Finally, I gratefully acknowledge the memory of two of the best basketball coaches with whom I have had the pleasure to work: the late David L. Carrasco, who, at the time of his death, was director of the El Paso Job Corps Center, and who has previously enjoyed a successful career as basketball coach and athletic director at The American University as well as at Bowie High School in El Paso, Texas; and the late Constancio Cordoba Alvarez, who, at the time of his death, was the president of the National Coaching School in Mexico City (Escuela Nacional de Entrenadores Depotivos) and who is considered the most famous basketball coach of all time within the Republic of Mexico.

Overview of This Book

Welcome to the world of coaching basketball. A truly American sport, basketball has captured the fancy and the imagination of sport enthusiasts the world over. Whether one is a spectator or a participant, whether a player or a coach, basketball is a challenging and exciting sport—one that is enjoyed by individuals of all ages, from the youth sport level to the professional level.

HOW THIS BOOK IS ORGANIZED

The book is organized into four major sections. The first section presents an *overview* to the book as well as an introduction to coaching the sport of basketball. The second section deals with the *defensive aspects* (strategies and tactics) of coaching and playing basketball—that is, limiting the scoring opportunities of one's opponents.

The third section is devoted to the *offensive side* of the sport, obtaining high percentage scoring opportunities against a variety of defensive alignments. The fourth and last section deals with *special situations* that every coach will face, such as the fast break, special stunting defenses, out-of-bounds plays, last-second plays, stalling or freezing tactics, and jump balls. The last section also focuses on drills that enhance the teaching and learning of the various skills, competencies, and maneuvers necessary to successfully compete in the sport of basketball as well as an overview of the psychological or mental dimension of coaching basketball.

Throughout the book are *Coaching Hints*. In fact, there are 223 such coaching hints. These are suggestions and guidelines that highlight and emphasize the more important teaching concepts associated with the sport of basketball. Pay close attention to these important coaching points in an effort to master the learning of specific coaching strategies or teaching tactics.

EXPLANATION OF DRAWINGS AND DIAGRAMS WITHIN THE BOOK

Throughout the book are diagrams that help illustrate offensive and defensive tactics and maneuvers as well as various drilling situations. To better understand these diagrams, the reader should be familiar with the explanations provided below.

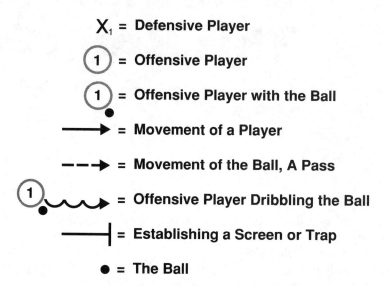

X_1 = **Defensive Player**

(1) = **Offensive Player**

(1) = **Offensive Player with the Ball**

⟶ = **Movement of a Player**

– – ➤ = **Movement of the Ball, A Pass**

(1) ∿➤ = **Offensive Player Dribbling the Ball**

⊢ = **Establishing a Screen or Trap**

● = **The Ball**

1

Understanding the Sport of Basketball

THE CHANGING FACE OF THE SPORT OF BASKETBALL

Basketball has undergone significant changes since Dr. James Naismith, at age 30, invented the game in December of 1891 in Springfield, Massachusetts, at the International YMCA Training School (later to become Springfield College). The game was invented in an effort to keep 18 young and active men busy in a physical education class during the long, winter months.

Who would have thought that this simple game (with a mere 13 basic rules) would have evolved into an international sport with over 250 million people competing in some type of organized form (Wolff, 1991). The 13 original rules are depicted in Figure 1–1 (*Basketball Was Born Here,* 1990). Of course, the game is no longer played with a peach basket with nine players on a side participating at the same time. Today, there are break-away rims and glass backboards. Also, not only has the two-handed set shot disappeared but more and more athletes are "playing the game" at or above the rim.

Other Changes in the Game of Basketball

Numerous other changes have taken place in the sport of basketball. Female basketball has now moved away from the more conservative 6-on-6 game (involving 3 against 3 at each end of the court) to the same aggressive, fast-paced, full-court, 5-on-5 method of play seen in male basketball. The states of Iowa and Oklahoma were the last two states to offer 6-on-6 competitive basketball for high school girls. Iowa converted to 5-on-5 play in the fall of 1994 ("Iowa Benches," 1993). Oklahoma became the last state to abandon the 6-on-6 style of play at the secondary school level when it decided to move to the 5-on-5 play with the advent of the 1995–1996 school year (Oklahoma Secondary School Activities Association, personal communication, September 29, 1994). In fact, the last sanctioned 6-on-6 game played in the United States took place in Oklahoma

FIGURE 1–1 ORIGINAL THIRTEEN RULES OF BASKETBALL

The goals are a couple of baskets or boxes about fifteen inches in diameter across the opening and about fifteen inches deep. If the field of play is large the baskets may be larger, so as to allow of more goals being made. When the field is 150 feet long the baskets may be thirty inches in diameter. These are to be suspended, one at each end of the grounds, about ten feet from the floor. A neat device for a goal has been arranged by the Narragansett Machine Company, by which the ball is held and may be thrown out by pulling a string. It is both lasting and convenient.

The object of the game is to put the ball into your opponents' goal. This may be done by throwing the ball from any part of the grounds, with one or both hands, under the following conditions and rules:

The ball to be an ordinary *Association* foot ball.

1. The ball may be thrown in any direction with one or both hands.
2. The ball may be batted in any direction with one or both hands (never with the fist).
3. A player cannot run with the ball. The player must throw it from the spot on which he catches it, allowance to be made from a man who catches the ball when running if he tries to stop.
4. The ball must be held by the hands, the arms or body must not be used for holding it.
5. No shouldering, holding, pushing, tripping, or striking in any way the person of an opponent shall be allowed; the first infringement of this rule by any player shall count as a foul, the second shall disqualify him until the next goal is made, or, if there was evident intent to injure the person, for the whole of the game, no substitute allowed.
6. A foul is striking at the ball with the fist, violation of Rules 3, 4, and such as described in Rule 5.
7. If either side makes three consecutive fouls it shall count as a goal for the opponents (consecutive means without the opponents in the mean time making a foul).
8. A goal shall be made when the ball is thrown or batted *from the grounds* into the basket and stays there, providing those defending the goal do not touch or disturb the goal. If the ball rests on the edges, and the opponent moves the basket, it shall count as a goal.
9. When the ball goes out of bounds, it shall be thrown into the field of play by the person first touching it. He has a right to hold it unmolested for five seconds. In case of a dispute the umpire shall throw it straight into the field. The thrower-in is allowed five seconds, if he holds it longer it shall go to the opponent. If any side persists in delaying the game the umpire shall call a foul on that side.
10. The umpire shall be judge of the men and shall note the fouls and notify the referee when three consecutive fouls have been made. He shall have power to disqualify men according to Rule 5.
11. The referee shall be judge of the ball and shall decide when the ball is in play, in bounds, to which side it belongs, and shall keep the time. He shall decide when a goal has been made, and keep account of the goals, with any other duties that are usually performed by a referee.
12. The time shall be two fifteen minute halves, with five minutes' rest between.
13. The side making the most goals in that time shall be declared the winner. In the case of a draw the game may, by agreement of the captains be continued until another goal is made.

Reprinted with permission from Basketball Hall of Fame. "Basketball Was Born Here," Fall, 1990, pp. 10, 11.

at the end of the 1994–1995 season when Stigler High School beat Meeker High 63–37 in the Class 3A state championship game ("Deep Six-on-Sixed," 1995).

Eliminating the center jump ball following made baskets, widening of the lane, adopting the goal-tending rule, adding the 3-second lane and the 10-second midcourt rules, prohibiting and then permitting dunking of the ball, adding the shot clock, eliminating jump balls (except to begin games and to start the overtime period), and adding the 3-point shot are just some of the major alterations that have taken place over the years that have contributed to changing the face and the pace as well as the attractiveness of the sport.

These and other rules of the game of basketball have changed, evolved over the years, in response to two major factors. The first factor centers around the ever-increasing abilities and skill levels of those players, both female and male, who compete in the sport of basketball. The second factor is the desire or need to provide a more entertaining, challenging, and interesting competitive situation for both spectators and players alike.

Increased Parity in the Sport

Another area where there has been great change in recent years has been in the leveling of the so-called playing field of competition throughout the world. At one time, the United States dominated amateur basketball, at every level in international competition, but this is no longer the case today. Many other countries have also developed superior amateur teams (for men and for women) that have been able to more than hold their own in international competition against U.S. amateur squads. The United States is no longer sitting on top of the basketball world, alone. Today, it has company.

True parity at the international, amateur level—although not yet a reality—is closer than it has ever been in the past, and the gap is rapidly closing. In 1996, some 202 countries had national federations, under the auspices of the Olympics, in the sport of basketball. More are sure to follow.

CURRENT BASKETBALL SCENE IN THE UNITED STATES

At the present, basketball continues to be one of the most popular, competitive sports played in the United States, at all levels, from youth sports to the professional teams. In 1991, more boys and girls in this country, ages 7 to 17, played organized basketball than any other sport (Wolff, 1991). In 1993, it was the *number one team sport* in terms of number of participants. In fact, over 40.4 million Americans, age 6 and over, participated in the sport during 1993. Only bowling (49.6 million participants) and freshwater fishing (44.1 million) had more people involved ("Basketball Leads," 1994). As a result, the demand for quality coaches remains high as the popularity of the sport continues to grow.

Questions for Would-Be Coaches

How does one become a competent basketball coach? What does one have to do and know to become a highly skilled or superior coach in the sport of basketball? What body of knowledge should a skilled basketball coach possess—that is, what specifically should a competent coach know and what special skills or talents should a qualified coach possess in terms of coaching the sport and being able to relate to and motivate players? What are the current strategies and tactics of which coaches must be aware? What particular style or brand of basketball should a coach employ in an effort to get the most out of the athletes playing on the team? And, how does one remain at the so-called cutting edge as a coach of basketball?

These are just some of the questions that both beginning and experienced coaches must ask themselves in the constant search for excellence. If there is one thing that is certain in coaching basketball, it is the fact that the process of learning and improving as a coach is a never-ending one.

Coaches Are Like Physicians

Coaches are like physicians in three important ways. First, just as physicians find themselves constantly striving to stay abreast of new innovations and developments in medicine, and to stay current in their specialty field(s), basketball coaches also need to remain current and stay abreast of innovations, new trends, and changes in their sport. Second, just as physicians diagnose illnesses and prescribe appropriate courses of action for their patients, coaches are involved in identifying problems and diagnosing errors with individual players and the team as a whole (both in practices and in actual competition) and then suggesting appropriate corrective remedies. Third, physicians and coaches are required to make strategic decisions in the "heat of battle"—while under extreme pressure.

THE ART AND SCIENCE OF COACHING

Coaching basketball can be considered both a science and an art (Fuoss & Troppmann, 1981). As a science, there are fundamental, scientific principles and a body of knowledge that are applicable to and associated with coaching basketball at all levels, whether in youth sports, junior and senior high schools, colleges, or even at the professional level (see Figure 1–2). "These foundational principles hold true and are applicable regardless of the setting in which coaches or athletes find themselves" (Stier, 1995, p. 38).

However, coaching basketball is also an art. It is an art because the manner in which an individual mentor actually coaches can be significantly influenced and enhanced through each individual coach's ingenuity, resourcefulness, creativity, innovation, and the ability to adapt. The creative and innovative use (ingenious adaptations) of coaching principles (guidelines) and the body of knowledge (strategies and tactics) underlying the coaching of basketball can have a significant effect on the ultimate success that the team, the players, and the coach(es) experience in actual competition.

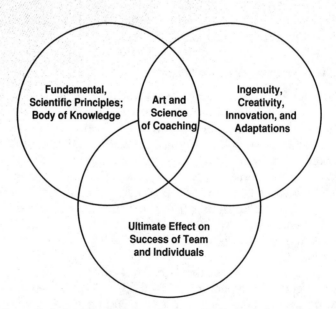

FIGURE 1–2 THE ART AND SCIENCE OF COACHING BASKETBALL

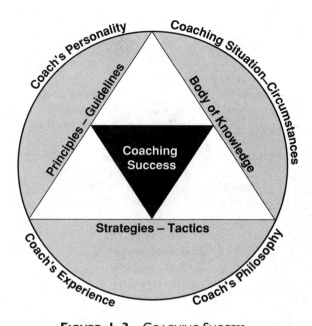

FIGURE 1–3 COACHING SUCCESS

BEING SUCCESSFUL AS A COACH

The eventual level of success that any individual coach might experience as a basketball mentor will depend on three major factors (see Figure 1–3). First is the extent to which the person understands and has mastered various coaching principles and the body of knowledge comprising the sport of basketball. Second is the individual's ability and willingness to use, adapt, and adjust various teaching/coaching principles, strategies, tactics, and knowledge in light of one's own particular coaching situation and one's own personality, ability, and experience. And third is the actual coaching situation or circumstances in which the individual mentor finds oneself.

> **Coaching Hint 2**
> Knowledgeable coaches have a better chance for success.

DEVELOPING A PARTICULAR STYLE OR APPROACH TO COACHING

Each mentor develops a unique approach or style of coaching. This is because each mentor coaches in light of his or her personality, prior experience, training, and knowledge. Knowledge is absolutely essential for coaching success. Of course, knowledge must be based on reality, facts, and up-to-date information. In reality, no two coaches are exactly alike. Yes, there are similarities among coaches in terms of coaching styles, approaches, and methods, as well as preferences in specific strategies and tactics. However, in reality, each coach is truly unique, just as each individual athlete is unique.

> **Coaching Hint 3**
> Coaches should be themselves—they shouldn't try to imitate (copy) someone else.

The manner in which one coaches—that is, the decisions made as well as the strategies and tactics employed, both in practices and actual competition—are dictated by a number of different factors. For example:

1. The coach's formal coaching education
2. Prior athletic experiences (as an athlete and/or as a coach)

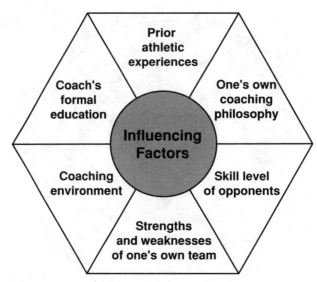

FIGURE 1–4 FACTORS AFFECTING A COACH'S APPROACH TO COACHING

3. One's own individual coaching philosophy or preference(s) coupled with one's biases and prejudices
4. The characteristics and skill levels of opponents
5. The ability (strengths) and shortcomings (weaknesses) of one's own team
6. The circumstances or environment in which the individual works as a basketball coach

All of these elements can play a significant role in shaping the way an individual mentor acts and make decisions as a coach. This is true both in terms of the selection of coaching strategies and teaching tactics as well as the manner in which a coach interacts (interpersonal relations) with individual athletes, the team as a whole, and others (see Figure 1–4).

DEVELOPING A PHILOSOPHY OF COACHING

An individual's coaching philosophy is a reflection of that person's personality, experiences, and environment(s) combined with his or her skills and competencies (Stier, 1995). A coach's philosophy refers to how he or she views all aspects of the coaching process. Thus, it is imperative that coaches take stock of their feelings toward every aspect of the sport that they coach, including the type of relationship(s) that should exist between themselves and their players; the expectations that they as coaches have of their own athletes, both on and off the field; the manner in which athletes are to be treated, motivated, and disciplined; and, of course, the specific style of "ball" that the players would be expected to execute in competition. How a coach views these and other components of the game of basketball will affect his or her philosophy of coaching. A coach's philosophy will, in turn, have a direct effect on his or her decisions and actions.

THREE DISTINCT STYLES OF COACHING

In the sport of basketball, there has traditionally been three schools of thought relative to the style of coaching and playing the sport of basketball. The distinguishing factor among all three styles is the movement or tempo of the game itself. The playing (coaching) of basketball can be viewed as existing on a continuum, involving (1) a very, very slow or conservative tempo, (2) a more moderate or so-called normal rate of play, and (3) a very quick or fast tempo or pace. All three styles (see Figure 1–5) of play can be equally effective in varying circumstances. There is no one "right" or "correct" style of play.

The ultimate success of any particular style or tempo of play depends on the skill and conditioning levels of the teams involved, the experience of the athletes, and the competency of the coach(es). The determining factors in utilizing one style over another are based on efforts to take advantage of the strengths of one's own team while exploiting specific weaknesses of opponents.

The Upbeat, Fast-Break Style of Playing Basketball

At one end of the spectrum is the upbeat, fast-break style of basketball. This style is characterized by the quick transition from defense to offense and vice versa. Upon obtaining possession of the ball, the true fast-breaking team attempts to aggressively push the ball up the floor as quickly as possible (sometimes seemingly at almost breakneck speed and with reckless abandon). This is accomplished every time (almost) the team obtains possession of the ball.

This is done in an attempt to obtain an offensive advantage in the transition phase of the game, moving from defense to offense. The emphasis in this style is to move the ball into the offensive end of the court as soon as possible, before the opponents have had adequate time to regroup and exert meaningful defensive pressure, and to score as a result of a high percentage field goal attempt within a minimum amount of time.

This style of play places severe pressure on the opponents in making the transition from offense to defense immediately after losing possession of the ball. A fast-breaking team forces the opponents always to remain cognizant of the necessity of getting back quickly on defense if they are to be successful at negating the opponent's fast-break tactics. Any time a team, while on offense, has to worry inordinately about its own defensive capabilities to such an extent that its offensive efficacy is reduced, the team is in deep, deep trouble.

> **Coaching Hint 4**
> Fast-breaking teams force opponents to think about getting back on defense, even when the opponents have possession of the ball.

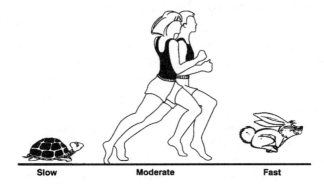

Slow   Moderate   Fast

FIGURE 1–5   THREE STYLES OF COACHING

The Conservative, Slower Style of Playing Basketball

At the opposite end of the spectrum is what is commonly referred to as the conservative or slow-down approach to playing the game. This style is noted for its distinctly slower tempo. In this instance, the fast break is only a very rare event, if it occurs at all. The team playing this style of basketball attempts to slow down the pace of the contest (thereby controlling the tempo or rhythm of the game) by taking its time both in moving the ball to its offensive end of the court and in working for a shot.

Conservatism is the watchword for this style of play, especially in respect to protecting and retaining possession of the ball. Similarly, disciplined shot selection and an emphasis on obtaining the highest percentage field goal attempt is paramount in this style. This type of team will continue to work very hard, very diligently, for the so-called good shot, the high percentage field goal attempt—all the while protecting its possession of the ball by not taking any unnecessary risks.

This type of effort, this "milking the clock" type of approach, keeps the ball away from the opponents. The thinking is that opponents cannot score when they do not have the ball. This style also forces opponents to work hard at playing defense and is marked by very conservative efforts on behalf of the offensive team in terms of risk taking and executing field goal attempts.

Teams employing such conservative tactics take few chances with turning the ball over by bad passes, violations, or poor shots. In fact, loss of possession is tantamount to a mortal sin. Turnovers are a key to victory in many games and thus must be kept to a minimum.

Implications of the Shot Clock   The day when a team could "sit" on the ball for minutes at a time while working for a shot is a thing of the past for those teams playing with the shot clock. Nevertheless, the shot clock has not precluded teams (or coaches) from controlling the tempo of the game by slowing the pace of the contest. Slowing the tempo of the game down is still possible by deliberately taking care of the ball while on offense and working for the highest percentage shot within the limitations of the shot clock.

Similarly, on defense, conservative teams are usually noted for hard-nosed defense (man to man, zone, and/or combination type defenses). Such defense is executed in such a fashion as to force (or invite) the opposing offensive players to be more reckless and anxious in terms of handling and protecting the ball and in taking quick, less opportune field goal attempts.

The Moderate or Middle-of-the-Road Style of Basketball

Somewhere in between these two extremes might be classified the so-called moderate style of playing (coaching) the game of basketball. Although not as upbeat and aggressive in terms of using the perpetual fast break, this style is not as conservative in terms of being superpatient in working (milking) the clock for every available second, all the while seeking to create the very highest percentage shot. This style is more closely identified with taking advantage of fast-break opportunities *if and when they are present,* but not playing at a breakneck speed in an effort to get a fast-break opportunity at every possession. Yes, the ball is quickly moved up court when there is a change of possession, but it is done at a more natural, controlled pace. The team employing this type of tactic or style of play is not really concerned with slowing down the tempo of the game, nor is it concerned with always taking the quick field goal attempt. Rather, this style dictates that the fast-break attempt be taken whenever the opportunity is avail-

---

Coaching Hint 5
If you want to keep the ball away from the opponents, utilize the slow-down style of play.

Coaching Hint 6
To turn the ball over without a high percentage shot is tantamount to committing a mortal sin.

able. However, if such a situation is not available, is not created, the players are quite content to implement their regular quarter-court offensive attack against their opponents. The team is concerned with the clock only insofar that there not be a violation of the shot clock.

Of course, there are an infinite number of variations of each of these three main styles or approaches to coaching (and playing) basketball. That is what makes coaching basketball truly unique for each individual coach—being able to make individual and unique decisions, in practices and game situations, in light of any number of different variables and circumstances.

It is up to each individual mentor to decide for oneself the particular style of play to employ in various situations and under different circumstances. The objective is to select the style of play that takes advantage of any weaknesses of the opponent as well as one's own strengths. Recognizing and exploiting the deficiencies of the opponent is a mark of a highly competent coach.

When deciding on a particular style of play to implement, coaches should choose a style to fit not only their players' temperaments and abilities (taking into account both their strengths and deficiencies) but also their own. Coaches must feel comfortable and confident with the particular style of play they intend to implement. In addition, they must be knowledgeable in all of the nuances and intricacies associated with that particular style (or have other coaches on staff who are).

> **Coaching Hint 7**
> Choose a style of play that enhances your team's strengths and exposes the weaknesses of your opponent.

> **Coaching Hint 8**
> A coach must feel comfortable with and have confidence in the style of play chosen for his or her athletes.

DECISION MAKING BY THE COACH

The strategies and tactics described in this book can be successful at all levels of competition, regardless of the particular style and tempo of basketball played. The offensive and defensive maneuvers and special plays presented herein are suitable whether the team primarily employs fast-break tactics, or the more moderate, middle-of-the-road approach to playing the sport, or even the most conservative, slow-down style.

It is up to the individual coach to determine which of the various offensive strategies, defensive tactics, and special plays described in the following pages might be most appropriate and suitable for his or her own team. Such decision making, of course, must be made in light of the individual's own particular situation and circumstances.

Selecting Appropriate Tactics and Strategies for the Athletes

When deciding what specific tactics to employ as a coach, it is important to choose those tactics and strategies that are appropriate for the age, experience, and talent level of the athletes. In many instances, it is not the specific offensive or defensive tactics or strategies that are the key to emerging victorious in competition. Rather, success is dependent on the appropriate selection of activities in light of the abilities, maturity, and experience level of the athletes as well as the actual execution and implementation of specific tactics. In short, coaches must not ask their players to perform activities that are inappropriate for the skill level of the athletes. In order to be successful, those skills and tactics to be performed must be performed accurately and precisely.

There is an old story of a famous university coach who, during a coaching clinic, showed a film of college athletes performing a specific offensive maneuver. The film showed the basketball players executing the play to perfection. The result was a high percentage shot taken and two points scored. The coach then

> **Coaching Hint 9**
> Don't ask athletes to do that which they are not capable of doing.

Coaching Hint 10

The skill level of players will determine the success of a specific play or tactic.

Coaching Hint 11

Precision and accuracy in the execution of specific tactics and skills is often the difference between success and failure in competition.

Coaching Hint 12

Coaches need to be careful that their plays, strategies, and tactics really work in competition and not only on paper.

Coaching Hint 13

There are no magic "bullets" or secrets in basketball.

showed the identical offensive maneuver being performed by high school athletes. However, in this instance, the film revealed that the defense was not only able to prevent the high percentage shot but was able to completely befuddle the offensive players. The confusion was so great that the offense turned the ball over. The result was a fast-break situation and a successful lay-up by the opponents at the other end of the floor.

The moral of this story is that it is not the specific offensive or defensive maneuver or tactic that is the key to winning basketball games. Rather, the key is to select the appropriate maneuvers, strategies, and tactics that one's players are able to successfully and adequately implement in the heat of battle, in actual competition. The ability and skill level of one's athletes will determine, for the most part, whether a specific play or tactic will be successful.

Thus, coaches need to be ready, willing, and able to make some adjustments in various offensive and defensive maneuvers as well as strategies and tactics to fit the abilities and limitations of their athletes. They also must insist on attention to detail and precision in the execution of skills, plays, and tactics. Proper execution is an absolute must in performing any maneuver, play or tactic.

Whoever Has the Chalk Last Wins

Another important concept for coaches to know is that "whoever has the chalk last wins." This refers to the common practice of coaches examining different offensive and defensive strategies and maneuvers in an effort to find one that is highly effective. In reality, almost all such strategies and tactics are highly effective—at least on paper or on the chalkboard. However, the game of basketball is not played on paper nor on the chalkboard. It is played on a basketball court, usually in front of hundreds, if not thousands, of spectators.

If two opposing coaches were to go to a chalkboard and start to diagram various offensive and defensive plays, the "winning" coach would always be the one who would have the chalk last. This is because, on paper or a chalkboard, almost every play, every stratagem, every maneuver looks great, like it will succeed. That is, until an opposing coach draws on the same piece of paper or chalkboard a countermove negating the supposed advantage(s) of the previously drawn play.

The point is simple. Coaches need to employ those strategies and tactics that work in real life, in those situations in which they currently find themselves, rather than what looks great on paper. The game of basketball is played on a court between opponents whose objective is to negate the efforts of each other. The plays must work on a court against a real opponent—not a paper opponent.

The author—as a young, inexperienced, 22-year-old head basketball coach on the high school level—sought to "discover" a secret offense or a secret defense that would not only surprise or shock opponents but would result in numerous victories. It did not take long (thank goodness) before it became abundantly clear that there were no supersecrets (or even minor secrets) in terms of offensive or defensive tactics or strategies in the sport. Teams have won championships using zone defenses. Teams have won championships using man-to-man defenses. Teams have won championships using combination-type defenses. Similarly, championships have been won by fast-breaking teams as well as by slow-down teams. In fact, there have been relatively few really new things surfacing in the sport of basketball insofar as offensive or defensive strategies or tactics in the past 30 years. Yes, there have been variations and adaptations, but there are few totally new inventions or creations.

Establishing Good Interpersonal Relationships with the Players

If there is one essential element in coaching basketball today, it is being able to work well with one's own players. A coach must be able to have meaningful, professional relationships with individual players and with the team as a whole. The reason that two different coaches can employ similar defensive and offensive tactics and yet end up with widely different win-loss records is because of the teaching, coaching, and interpersonal skills of the coaches and the resulting relationships and communication channels that exist (or that do not exist) between each coach and each player. Thus, it is imperative that a coach does not overlook or lose sight of the need to provide a bridge between the sterile Xs and Os (plays and strategies) and the humanistic, interpersonal relationships that should exist between a coach and individual team members.

> **Coaching Hint 14**
> Coaches must establish and develop good personal relationships with players.

Keep It Simple, Short, and Succinct

Basketball coaches sometimes have a tendency to get too complicated, both in terms of the complexity of their offensive and defensive tactics and in terms of the number of things they ask their athletes to master. Frequently, simplicity is best. Keeping things simple, rather than overly complex, aids in the learning and mastery of that which is to be learned and the execution of the physical skills (in actual competition) involved in the sport of basketball.

Use of Basketball Coaching Playbooks

In an effort to expedite and facilitate the teaching and the mastery of the various offensive and defensive maneuvers as well as special play situations involved in the sport of basketball, coaches may elect to create a basketball playbook. A playbook, in its simplest form, can be merely a collection of pages in a notebook that contain descriptions and diagrams of various offensive, defensive, and special plays as well as a breakdown and explanation of various drills to be mastered.

A playbook might also contain additional nontechnical information such as team rules; an explanation of the coach's philosophy; expectations of athletes and coaches; various procedures, policies, and practices associated with the basketball team; schedule of practices and games, motivational sayings and slogans; conditioning hints and suggestions; and the list could go on and on.

On the positive side, playbooks can become effective teaching tools when properly utilized by competent coaches and teachers. On the negative side, playbooks can become crutches that coaches rely on, often to the detriment of their teaching and coaching efforts. Also, if playbooks contain "secrets" in terms of a team's strategies, tactics, and actual defensive and offensive plays, and if they fall into the hands of opponents, playbooks can prove to be really damaging to some programs and teams. Thus, it is up to the individual coach whether to create a playbook, what to include in the playbook, and to whom it should be distributed.

> **Coaching Hint 15**
> Use playbooks to facilitate the athletes' learning of the knowledge and skills necessary for competition.

Some coaches do not include any of their so-called secrets (specific offensive or defensive tactics, strategies, or plays) in their playbooks in case the documents fall into the hands of opponents. Other coaches include such information and rely on the integrity of those to whom the handbooks are loaned to ensure that the contents of the handbooks are not compromised.

SOURCES OF COACHING INFORMATION AND KNOWLEDGE

Do not be too proud to borrow, beg, steal, or adapt ideas, strategies, or tactics from other coaches and/or teams. Borrowing ideas from others is the sincerest form of flattery. Ideas can also be obtained by watching other coaches and teams in action, including those against whom your own team is competing.

That is also why there are numerous basketball coaching clinics and camps held throughout the United States with thousands and thousands of coaches in attendance. Coaches who attend clinics and camps are seeking to reaffirm their current thinking and philosophy as well as to get new ideas on how to become better coaches and strategists, thus remaining at the cutting edge of their sport. These clinics host highly successful coaches who share ideas and tactics with which they have experienced success.

Nothing is wrong with having your team use what other teams and coaches are using. Just be sure that what you would like to incorporate into your existing repertoire of tactics and plays will work with your players, in your situation, against your opponents. It is interesting to note that whenever a particular team wins the National Collegiate Athletic Association (NCAA) Division I basketball championship using a particular zone defense, the incidence of zone defenses increases throughout the nation at all levels of amateur competition.

Whenever the national championship team uses the full-court press throughout their games, the number of high schools and other colleges that begin to use similar full-court presses the next season increases. There is nothing inherently wrong with this. However, the important thing to keep in mind is that merely adopting a strategy, tactic, or style of play from someone else is not sufficient. One must have the players who are capable of performing such skills and implementing such tactics. One must also have a very good reason for changing to such tactics and must have a complete understanding of the new strategies.

Choosing Appropriate Offensive, Defensive, and Special Plays

When reading the rest of this book, view each of the offensive and defensive series, special-play situations, and Coaching Hints in light of your own current (or future) coaching situation. Ask yourself: What might work now or in the future for me, my individual players, and my team? What will be the most appropriate stratagem under the circumstances in which my athletes must practice and play? What might be suitable to use in my existing arsenal of offensive or defensive plays or series? What might be appropriate to use, with some modification, alteration, or adaptation?

Being Educated about Basketball

Being an educational and discriminating consumer of basketball knowledge and information is a sign of a competent coach. Examine the remaining coaching suggestions and hints in this book with an eye to possibly adopting or adapting part of what you read into your current or future coaching efforts. No one would seek to adopt all of the information gleaned from any book (or any clinic presentation), lock, stock, and barrel. Rather, be a discriminating reader, learner, and consumer. Select those items, those tactics and hints, that fit your coaching philosophy, your coaching style, your preferences, and the abilities of your athletes.

Your coaching style, your coaching philosophy and your coaching knowledge will evolve as you continue to study, read, observe, listen, think, analyze, and synthesize. The end result will be that you will become a more effective and efficient mentor for your charges. Your players deserve that—and so do you.

There is always the danger of continually bouncing, almost on a whim, back and forth from one coaching style or tactic to another or from one coaching philosophy or strategy to another. Do not be a zone convert, only to switch the very next week to being exclusively a man-to-man defensive coach. Do not be a full-court press advocate one week and then, following a loss to a 1-3-1 quarter court zone defense, switch allegiance and swear by the 1-3-1 zone, thereby forsaking the full-court press.

Rather than jump from one focus to another, successful coaches develop their philosophies over time. They develop and refine a specific style of coaching (even though it might embrace varied ingredients) and, generally speaking, they stick to it. Time and effort is spent in refining and perfecting one's philosophy, one's strategies, and one's tactics. Significant changes in one's philosophy or in the very essence of coaching strategies usually do not happen overnight or even very frequently. The basic concept is that there must always be a very good reason for making significant changes.

Developing a Plan of Action for Everything—Before the First Practice

Coaches need to know what they are going to do in terms of practices and actual competition well in advance of the first day of official practice. This has as much to do with one's philosophy of coaching as it does with one's ability to make advance practice and game plans and to establish priorities.

Coaches need to be able to establish daily coaching plans, weekly and monthly coaching plans, as well as entire season plans. They must be organized *and* give the impression of being organized to their players, to parents, to their superiors, and even to the public. Of course, this does not imply that coaches will know exactly what they and their athletes will be doing every single minute in every single practice throughout the entire season. There must be opportunities to make modifications and take into consideration individual differences while adjusting to the unexpected.

However, it does imply that coaches should be capable of making plans and other coaching decisions well in advance of the time that these same plans must be carried out and decisions made. For example, once the team members have been evaluated and selected, coaches should decide on or confirm—at least in general terms—what they will be teaching their charges throughout various parts of the upcoming basketball season. Such planning should be broken down into preseason, inseason, and postseason time segments.

Successful coaches should be able to outline or plan in advance the general objectives of their preseason practice schedules and begin to put on paper the weekly and daily coaching (lesson) plans. Naturally, these plans and strategies are subject to change whenever necessary, in terms of any number of factors and events that might affect the team or players.

The Daily Practice Plan

The daily practice plan or schedule is really nothing more than a chronological (time) list of *who* (coaches and athletes alike) will be doing *what* during a specific practice session, and *when* (on which particular date). The content of a

Coaching Hint 19
Don't accept everything you read or hear—discriminate in your decision making.

Coaching Hint 20
Don't be constantly changing coaching philosophies, strategies, and tactics; rather, select a style of play and a philosophy of coaching and develop them to the fullest.

Coaching Hint 21
Be sure to plan in advance what you (as the coach) will do and what your athletes will be required to do (learn).

daily practice plan can include everything and anything that the coaches desire. It can be simplistic in design or very detailed. There is no one correct way to create a practice plan or schedule. The final version of the daily practice plan is usually firmed up the day before the practice session is to take place, at the conclusion of the previous day's practice session. This allows for last-minute changes in light of what took place during the last practice.

Such a plan can include conditioning activities, drills, introduction of new material, reinforcement of skills previously presented, game-like scrimmages, and opportunities for individual one-on-one work. At the end of each daily practice, and following an evaluation of that day's activities and efforts by the coaches, the next day's practice plan can be created or adjusted, taking into account what has been accomplished and what has not been accomplished in the practice session just concluded.

Some coaches prefer to have a rather detailed time schedule of exactly how each and every minute will be spent by those involved in practice. This consists of putting down on paper every activity that will take place during every minute of practice. In other words, each minute is accounted for, in advance. Other coaches prefer to have a more loosely organized daily practice schedule and will merely sketch in a general topic (such as "offensive" or "defensive work") for a general time period (e.g., 20–25 minutes).

Those coaches who prefer to account for each and every minute of practice time do so because, to them, time is so valuable. They may also do so to impress upon their athletes that there is no time or place for foolishness or the wasting of time during practice. Figure 1–6 is an illustration of a daily practice schedule that provides for a rather detailed accounting in terms of both time and the planned activities for a typical high school or college basketball team.

The important point in creating a daily practice plan, in advance of the practice date, is that the coaches are attempting not only to prevent wasting the time and effort of those involved in practice but also to put each and every available minute to good use in terms of providing opportune learning experiences for the athletes, individually and collectively. One of the major goals of any daily practice plan is to put the available time (and the available facilities and equipment/supplies) to the best, possible use. Since there is only so much time available for practice, it is imperative that the available time be well utilized. To do otherwise is foolish, if not criminal.

A second objective of preplanning one's daily practices is to ensure that what takes place in such practices is justifiable and appropriate in light of the goals and objectives of the team. The question that must be asked, in terms of any activity that might comprise a specific day's practice, is: Will this activity enable the athletes to become more proficient in those skills and competencies that are necessary in order to be competitive in the sport? In other words, will the activity help the athletes? Will the planned activity be beneficial?

The Weekly Coaching Plan

More advance planning is necessary when coaches attempt to create a weekly coaching schedule. This type of advance planning involves writing down on paper those activities that will comprise the following week's practice session. In this instance, a coach attempts to plan, at least in a general way, those activities that will take place over five, six, or seven days of practice. As a result, this type of practice plan is far less specific than the daily coaching plan in terms of how the time is to be spent on any specific learning (practice) activity. Nevertheless, the weekly plan does include all of the major components of each day's

FIGURE 1–6   A SAMPLE DAILY (DETAILED) PRACTICE PLAN

Daily Practice Plan

Date: December 4   *Day of Week:* Wednesday
Next Game: December 10—Westside High School

Time: **Activity:**

2:30 P.M.   Individual warm-up period (with and without the ball)—players report from class
2:40 P.M.   Team warm-up activities—official start of practice

Conditioning drills:
Go-go drill—4 minutes
Sprint & stop drill—5 minutes
Circle lay-up drill—5 minutes

2:52 P.M.   Each player to shoot 3 consecutive free throws—all 10 baskets
2:54 P.M.   1-3-1 half-court zone defense (no offense)
3:01 P.M.   1-3-1 half-court zone defense (add offensive players)
3:10 P.M.   Transition to fast-break tactics from the zone—walk through and full speed
3:17 P.M.   Man-to-man, half-court defense, breakdown drills (prevent ball from being passed into the wings)
3:27 P.M.   Whole court, fast-break drill—all players (full speed)
3:33 P.M.   Individual free throw shooting—3 attempts and rotate off line
3:40 P.M.   1-4 offense, half-court, rotation of 8 players against defense
3:55 P.M.   1-3-1 offense against half-court zone (2-1-2 & 1-3-1 front)
4:10 P.M.   Whole-court scrimmage—gold squad playing man-to-man defense and blue squad executing zone defense—no fast breaking allowed for first five minutes, then both teams to attempt the fast break (Coach Muzic to officiate, call 'em close)
4:20 P.M.   Individual free throw shooting—3 attempts and rotate off line
4:30 P.M.   Dribbling and shooting drill—full court
4:35 P.M.   Individual free throw shooting—10 consecutive attempts and rotate off line and work on individual field goal shooting
4:45 P.M.   Cool-down activities:

Jumping and tipping drill
Pass and dribble drill
Alley-oop drill
Field goal spot shooting drill
Precision dribble drill

5:00 P.M.   Official close of practice: Close on a positive note; share brief summary of today's practice; give a glimpse of tomorrow's activities.

Reactions & comments _____

_____

_____

---

practice session for that week. An example of a weekly practice plan is shown in Figure 1–7.

This is not to say that specific time allocations cannot or should not be included in a weekly practice schedule. However, the weekly coaching plan usually does not involve as much detail as the daily plan, either in terms of describing the actual practice activities or specifying the exact time when these activities will be conducted, and their duration. The weekly practice plan is not merely a compilation of five to seven individual daily practice plans. It is more global in scope. It lacks, by design, the specificity of the daily practice plan.

Figure 1–7 A Sample Weekly (Generalized) Practice Plan

Weekly Practice Plan
Dates: October 15 through October 19—Monday through Friday

Monday	Tuesday	Wednesday	Thursday	Friday
Conditioning Drills	Free Throw and Field Goal Drills	Conditioning Drills	Conditioning Drills	Conditioning Drills
Free Throw Drills	Half-Court Zone 1-3-1	Free Throw and Field Goal Drills	Free Throw and Field Goal Drills	Free Throw and Field Goal Drills
Field Goal Drills	Fast-Break Drill	Fast-Break Drill	Individual Defense Drills	Fast-Break Drills
Introduce 1-3-1 Zone	Man-to-Man Half-Court Defense	1-3-1 Zone Defense	Individual Offense Drills	Half-Court Zone
Combine Fast Break & Shooting Activities	Breakdown Drills, Individual Work	Man-to-Man Half-Court Drills	Half-Court Offense Against Zone	Half-Court Man-to-Man
Repeat Zone Drills	Zone Drills	1-4 Man-to-Man Offense	1-4 Man-to-Man Offense	Half-Court Scrimmage
1-3-1 Offense Against Zones	Introduce 1-4 Man-to-Man Offense	Individual Man-to-Man Drills	Half-Court Scrimmage Zone Defense	Full-Court Scrimmage
Cool-Down Drills	Cool-Down Drills	Half-Court Scrimmage, Man-to-Man Defense	Cool-Down Drills	Cool-Down Drills
	Chalk Talk Motivation	Cool-Down Drills	Chalk Talk Transition	Chalk Talk Positive Achievements and Things to Work on in Future
		Chalk Talk Half-Court Press		

It is from the weekly practice plans that the specific daily practice schedules or plans are created. Since the weekly schedule plans are made well in advance (sometimes two or more weeks) and involve activities that will be included within the upcoming week's practices, there is greater likelihood of change and adaptations when it comes time to actually establishing a specific daily practice plan. This is because of what might have taken place (or not taken place) between the time when the weekly schedule was created and when the more detailed daily plan is actually established.

Nevertheless, the weekly plan serves as an excellent tool in helping the coach design or sketch, well in advance and in general terms, those activities that will make up the practices in the upcoming week(s). Typically, a weekly practice plan is created at the end of a week or over the weekend and will cover the next five to seven practice days of the following week. Some coaches, however, might choose to establish a two-week (or more) practice schedule or plan. It must be emphasized that the weekly practice schedule forms the foundation or basis from which the coaches will be able to create individual, daily coaching or practice plans for each day of the subsequent week.

The Monthly or Multiweek Coaching Plan

Many coaches, especially when planning for the preseason (the time between the first official practice and the first official contest), prefer to write down on paper everything they intend to cover with their athletes during this all-important time period. This is done in an effort to ensure that everything that should be taught to the players will, indeed, be dealt with sometime during the preseason time frame. Of course, such monthly or multiweek practice schedules are not limited merely to the preseason but can cover any time of the year, or even the entire season.

Naturally, the earlier the plans are made (in terms of time between when the plans are made and when the actual practices take place), the greater the likelihood of change when the actual day of practice arrives. This fact, however, does not detract from the valuable benefits that such advance planning can provide for the coaches, the individual athletes, and the team as a whole. An example of a month-long practice plan is provided in Figure 1–8.

In Figure 1–8, the coaching staff has created a chart on which the next 20 practice days (four weeks) are numbered with the numbers placed horizontally along the top of the page, as shown. Along the left side of the sheet, vertically, is provided all of the major activities (offenses, defenses, drills, special situations, etc.) that the staff intends to have the team members, individually or collectively, work on during this time period.

Note that everything the players need to be exposed to in terms of being prepared to compete at the end of the 20 days is included along the left side of the multipage chart. When horizontal and vertical lines are then drawn on the page, as shown, boxes are created. Into these boxes are placed check marks, indicating that that particular activity is scheduled to be included in that particular day's practice schedule. Sometimes, coaches may elect to insert the actual number of minutes they hope or anticipate spending on a particular activity on a particular day.

The use of daily, weekly practice plans and/or monthly (or even multimonthly, i.e., the entire season) practice charts can accomplish three major objectives. First, their use aids the coaching staff in thinking through all of the necessary activities and skills that are to be included in the plan for that particular time span. Omission of important activities or aspects of the game can be easily detected and corrections can be made, well in advance. Second, the use of such a chart, if shared with the players, can help instill among the players confidence in their coaches and their coaches' planning and organizational skills. This is not an unimportant factor when it comes to developing the all important interpersonal relationships between coaches and athletes.

Coaching Hint 22
Be well organized and give the impression that you are well organized to others.

Third, if one's superiors (the athletic director, the principal) become aware of the use of such practice plans and practice charts, their estimation of the coach's adeptness in preplanning and organizational skills (and overall competency) will most likely be increased. It never hurts to make other people aware of one's talents, skills, competencies, and accomplishments.

Would-be coaches as well as experienced coaches should be aware of the principle that it is, indeed, important what others think of them as coaches. Yes, coaches must be organized. However, it is important that others, both those directly associated with the basketball team and the general public, are aware of this fact. Thus, it is important that coaches nurture their reputations as being a well-organized, competent, effective, efficient, knowledgeable mentors. The use of written practice plans, as outlined here, can go a long way toward realizing this important objective.

Figure 1–8 A Sample Monthly Practice Plan

Monthly Practice Plan

To Be Mastered	Practice Days																				
	1	2	3	4	5	6	7	8	9	10	11	12	13	14	15	16	17	18	19	20	
Half-Court Offenses Against Man-to-Man																					
1-4																					
2-1-2																					
Baseline																					
Motion																					
Half-Court Offenses Against Zones and Combination Zones																					
The Wheel																					
1-3-1																					
2-1-2																					
Match-Up																					
Whole-Court Offenses Against Man-to-Man Presses																					
1-3-1 Spread Offense																					
Long Pass—Bomb																					
Clear and Dribble																					
Whole-Court Offenses Against Zone Presses																					
1-3-1 Streak Offense																					
Long Pass (Lob)																					
Short Pass Attack																					
Half-Court Offenses Against Zone Press																					
1-3-1 Spread																					
2-1-2 Passing Attack																					
Half-Court Offenses Against Man-to-Man Press																					
2-1-2 Spread																					
Clear and Drive																					
Baseline																					
Half-Court Defenses— Man-to-Man																					
Box & One																					
Diamond & One																					
No-Switch																					
Switching																					
Swarm																					
Sagging																					

FIGURE 1–8 *(Continued)*

Monthly Practice Plan

To Be Mastered	Practice Days																				
	1	**2**	**3**	**4**	**5**	**6**	**7**	**8**	**9**	**10**	**11**	**12**	**13**	**14**	**15**	**16**	**17**	**18**	**19**	**20**	
Half-Court Defenses— Zones																					
1-3-1																					
2-1-2																					
Match-Up																					
1-2-2 Revolving																					
Corner Trap																					
Whole-Court Defense Man-to-Man Press																					
Switching Press																					
Trapping Press																					
"Token" Press																					
Whole-Court Defense Zone Press																					
1-2-1-1 Press																					
2-2-1 Press																					
1-3-1 Press																					
"Token" Press																					
Drills—Offensive																					
Alley-Opp																					
Screening																					
Cutting																					
Passing																					
Shoot and Tip																					
Pregame Warm-Up																					
Drills—Defensive																					
Rebounding																					
Block-Out																					
Slide																					
Break-Out																					
Step-Out																					
Conditioning																					
Sprint-Stop																					
Zig-Zag																					
Flexibility																					
Jumping																					
Agility																					
Pass-Shoot																					
Shot-Rebound																					
Go-Go																					
Warm-Up Shoot Around																					

(Continued)

FIGURE 1–8 (Continued)

Monthly Practice Plan

To Be Mastered	Practice Days																				
	1	2	3	4	5	6	7	8	9	10	11	12	13	14	15	16	17	18	19	20	
Shooting Drills																					
Round Robin																					
Drill Spot Shooting																					
Pivot																					
Perimeter																					
Corner																					
21																					
Shoot and Rebound																					
Screen and Shoot																					
Dribble and Shoot																					
Free Throw																					
Competitive F-T																					
Blindfold F-T																					
Scrimmage Time																					
Whole Court																					
Half Court																					
Special Plays Out-of-Bounds, Offense																					
Under Basket																					
From Sideline																					
From Endline																					
Out-of-Bounds, Defense																					
Under Basket—Zone																					
Under Basket— M/M																					
From Sideline																					
From Endline																					
Last-Second Offensive Plays																					
Against Zones																					
Against Man-to-Man																					
3 Seconds Left																					
10 Seconds Left																					
Defending Last-Second Plays																					
3 Seconds Left—Alert Defense																					
10 Seconds Left—Zone																					
10 Seconds Left—M/M																					

Adapted from Stier, 1995, pp. 388–390.

REFERENCES

Basketball leads all team sports in participation. (1994, January). *Journal of Physical Education, Recreation and Dance, 65* (1), 15.

Basketball was born here. (1990, Fall). Springfield, MA: Naismith Memorial Basketball Hall of Fame, pp. 10, 11.

Deep six-on-sixed. (1995, March 20). *Sports Illustrated, 82* (11), 15.

Fuoss, D. E., & Troppmann, R. J. (1981). *Effective coaching—A psychological approach.* New York: John Wiley & Sons.

Iowa benches 6-on-6 games. (1993, February 5). *Democrat and Chronicle* (Rochester, NY), p. 8D.

Stier, Jr., W. F. (1995). *Successful coaching—Strategies and tactics.* Boston: American Press Publishers.

Wolff, A. (1991, December 2). Happy Hundredth, Hoops. *Sports Illustrated, 75* (24), 104–108, 110, 111, 113–116, 119.

The Defensive Side of Coaching Basketball

GENERAL COMMENTS ABOUT DEFENSE

Defense can be a great equalizer in the sport of basketball. Excellent defense can be played and executed by average (but highly motivated) athletes. Defense is considered by many coaches as being more consistent than offense. For example, many teams and individuals are subject to an occasional "off night" in terms of the offensive aspects of the game—that is, being able to score. With defense, however, there are fewer instances of such "off nights." Thus, defense is considered to be more reliable and consistent than the offensive side of the sport.

Consequences of an Effective Defense

Defense can control the tempo of the game and can dictate what the offense is able to do. In other words, defense can "take the game" to the opponents. However, this is not to say that offense is unimportant or is of only secondary or minor importance. No matter how effective and efficient one's defense is, a team must still score points if it is to emerge victorious over an opponent. Nevertheless, many successful coaches place a *great deal of emphasis on the defensive aspects of the sport.*

Time Spent on Defense

It is important for coaches to remember that although a great deal of emphasis might be placed on a certain aspect of the game, such as defense, *this does not mean that the majority of time must be spent on defensive tactics in each and every practice session.* It is quite possible for a coach to emphasize defense as the most important part of the game but, at the same time, to actually spend more time during practices working on other phases of the game, including the

> **Coaching Hint 23**
> Defense can be more consistent than the offensive side of the sport.

offensive dimension of basketball. The key is how the head coach communicates (by words and actions) the importance of defense to the overall success of the team, not merely by how much time is spent practicing a specific phase of the game.

DECISIONS CONCERNING DEFENSES

When considering the defensive dimensions of basketball, one must take into consideration and make decisions in terms of (a) the actual type of defense, (b) where on the court the defensive players will position themselves, and (c) the amount of pressure that the players are exerting against the offensive personnel.

In respect to the *type of defense*, the coach must decide whether the team will execute a man-to-man type of defense, a zone defense, or some type of combination or match-up zone defense. In terms of the *positioning of the defensive players,* the coach must determine whether the athletes will execute the defense as part of a regular quarter-court formation or whether they will be extended to half-court, three-quarter court or even full court.

And, in reference to the *amount of pressure exerted* by the defense, the coach must decide: Will the defensive players attempt to prevent the ball from being passed into play? Will they exert extreme pressure (attempting to cut off passing lanes) once the ball is put into play? Will only token pressure be exerted? What passes will be contested (potential pass receivers overplayed)? Will trapping be part of the defense, and, if so, where on the floor?

The answers to these questions will depend on the coach's philosophy, the abilities and skill level of the players, and the caliber of the opponents to be faced in the upcoming season.

2 Quarter-Court Zone Defenses

Although there has been significant emphasis on the so-called pressure game in basketball involving man-to-man defense, there is currently a resurgence of interest focusing on that "old reliable" defense, the quarter-court zone. This is not to imply that the zone concept has been seriously neglected in recent years, for it has not. Zone defenses have been consistently utilized with great success at all levels of amateur competition. However, in recent years, the attention given to and the emphasis placed on zones and zone-type defenses have been refocused and revitalized.

REASONING BEHIND THE RESURGENCE IN ZONE DEFENSES

Some coaches, having taken notice of the overwhelming popularity of the man-to-man type defenses among their opponents, have rediscovered the advantages of zones. These same coaches have gone contrary to the mainstream of coaches in their particular locale and have instituted a zone defense or a variation of the zone in their repertoires.

An Advantage to Being Unique

The reasoning behind the move to zone defenses, when the majority of opponents employ man-to-man tactics, is one of uniqueness. That is, the coach forces the opponents to confront a type of defense (zone) in which they have had little experience attacking on a regular basis. As a result, the opponents are forced to use valuable practice time working to prepare for a type of defense that they will meet only infrequently (i.e., when competing against those teams using the zone-type defense).

The author has known coaches who have "allowed" the opponents to determine the type of defense that their own teams would play by simply utilizing the defense that their opponents *did not use*. That is, if the league was predomi-

Coaching Hint 24
It may be to a coach's advantage to be in the minority in terms of employing specific tactics.

Coaching Hint 25
Being out of the mainstream in terms of strategies and tactics forces opponents to make special preparations to combat your atypical approach to the game.

nantly man-to-man defense oriented, the coach would throw up a zone defense, and vice versa.

These coaches believe that if one would compete against a team noted for its outstanding man-to-man defense, perhaps one should zone that particular team. The reasoning being that the opponents would (or should) have perfected their man-to-man offensive capabilities to a very high degree as a result of practicing against their own superior man-to-man defense.

Thus, the popularity of man-to-man defenses has, in an indirect way, contributed to the revitalization of zones. This revitalization, in turn, has necessitated a renewal in an emphasis or resurgence in the methods of attacking various types of zone defenses. And so it goes. One might liken the change in strategy to a pendulum that has made one complete swing and is beginning its return swing. The message is clear: *Zones are back.*

> **Coaching Hint 26**
> Exploit opponents' weaknesses—never play to their strengths.

TYPES OF ZONE DEFENSES

Zone and zone-type defenses come in various types. The major differences between all these various defenses revolve around (a) the initial positioning of the players on the court, (b) the initial movement of the players comprising the zone in response to the movement of the ball by the offense, and (c) the amount of pressure being exerted by the defensive players against the ball and the offensive players themselves. Some of the more common zone defenses include:

Quarter-Court Zones

1-2-2 Regular Zone

1-3-1 Regular Zone

2-3 Regular Zone

3-2 Regular Zone

2-1-2 Regular Zone

Match-Up or Combination Zone from the 1-3-1 or 2-1-2 set

Half-Court Zones

3-2 Zone Press

1-3-1 Zone Press

1-2-1-1 Zone Press

Three-Quarter and Full-Court Zones

1-2-1-1 Zone Press

1-3-1 Zone Press

2-2-1 Zone Press

3-2 Zone Press

SPECIAL COMBINATION OR STUNTING QUARTER-COURT ZONE DEFENSES

There are also several different stunting or combination-type zone defenses that have gained increasing popularity in recent years. These stunting or special defenses are discussed in detail in Chapter 8. The more popular of the stunting defenses include:

> Diamond-and-One Special Zone
>
> Box-and-One Special Zone
>
> Triangle-and-Two Special Zone

WHEN TO USE QUARTER-COURT ZONE DEFENSES

Before contemplating a specific zone to teach to the players, a coach should first understand the strengths and weaknesses of the various types of zone defenses that are available. Coaches must have a reason for selecting a specific type of zone to use in any game situation.

Several factors can play a role in any particular zone being chosen to be implemented. These include (a) the caliber of players one has on the team, (b) the caliber of the team's opponents, and (c) the specific objective being sought by the defense (besides preventing the opponents from scoring).

> **Coaching Hint 27**
> Have a specific, substantial reason for selecting a defense—don't just pick a defense "out of the air."

COMMON ADVANTAGES OF ZONES

All regular-zone defenses have several things in common. Some of the advantages of using a zone or zone-type defense include:

1. A zone defense typically slows down the tempo of the game. This is because the offense must, by necessity, take more time to attack the zone once it has been set up. If the zone is executed properly, and the offense is not able to get a high percentage shot off prior to the defense setting up, the offense must take additional time to force the zone to overshift.

2. A zone defense usually distorts or disrupts a set offensive series that revolves around the theory of screening and working one on one. Zones usually necessitate that the offensive team have a distinct and separate offensive series or attack to use against the zone. Although offensive series that can be used against both man-to-man defenses and zones, do exist, rarely are they equally effective against both types of defenses. As a result, teams usually employ different offensive attacks for both types of defenses.

3. A zone defense, once set up, often clogs the immediate scoring area near the basket, thus preventing the crib (lay-up) shot or making it extremely difficult to obtain. An ideal consequence of a zone is to force the opponent to take the long shot (while being pressured or harassed by a defender) rather than allowing the higher percentage, in close, field goal attempt.

4. The fast break can be facilitated by the zone defense. This is because the placement of defensive personnel can more or less be predetermined on the court, thus expediting the potential outlet passes and subsequent filling of the lanes.

5. Rebounding may be enhanced due to the placement of the zone's taller players and/or better rebounders close to the basket.

6. Offensive dribbling to the basket is held to a minimum. It is difficult to pitch one offensive player against only one defensive player. This is

because defensive players in the zone are able to assist teammates in the zone and render additional defensive pressure against the dribbler.

7. A zone defense, properly executed, minimizes the possibility of the offensive players gaining an advantage through the creation of a mismatch situation involving a single defensive player.

8. Trapping, double teaming, sagging, and pressure tactics can easily be incorporated in all zones.

9. Different "fronts" or "looks" can be presented to the offense, at various times, while essentially keeping the basic movements of the defensive players the same.

10. A zone can sometimes hide a particularly weak defensive player or shield a player who is in foul trouble.

11. The likelihood of committing excessive fouls is usually diminished by playing a zone.

COMMON DISADVANTAGES OF ZONES

Some of the disadvantages that accompany the use of zone or zone-type defenses include:

1. The defensive team is especially vulnerable until the zone is completely set up by all five players. Thus, the zone is susceptible to fast-breaking tactics by opponents.

2. Accurate long-range shooting can devastate zones, especially with the advent of the 3-point shot. Zones are vulnerable against quality outside shooting.

3. Superior passing, coupled with quick overshifting of offensive personnel, can result in the overloading of the defense by the offensive players. The result can place one or two defensive players in a position of guarding two or three offensive players, thereby causing a mismatch in terms of numbers.

4. Zone players can have difficulty shifting against a quick and effective passing attack.

5. Zones have a tendency to break down or experience a decrease in effectiveness against opponents who are patient and exhibit excellent ball handling (passing) skills.

6. Some players become lazy or fail to take charge for their proper responsibilities in the zone, leaving it up to a teammate.

7. Zones require a great deal of teamwork, dedication, motivation, and coordination—zones are not a lazy player's panacea.

STRENGTHS AND WEAKNESSES OF SPECIFIC ZONE DEFENSES

Weaknesses of all zones have been traditionally characterized as those areas on the court not occupied by a defensive player in the initial defensive alignment. For example, the vulnerable areas on a 2-1-2 zone defense would, naturally, be at the top of the key and in the wings. Similarly, the strengths of this particular zone defense lies in the protection afforded the pivot slot and under the basket (see Diagram 2–1).

Likewise, the weaknesses of the 1-3-1 zone (see Diagram 2–2) would be along the baseline on each side of the basket as well as on either side of the

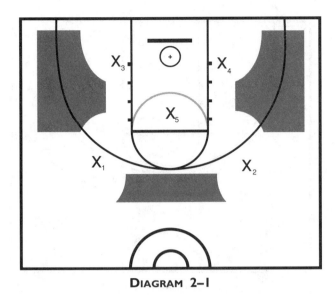

DIAGRAM 2–1

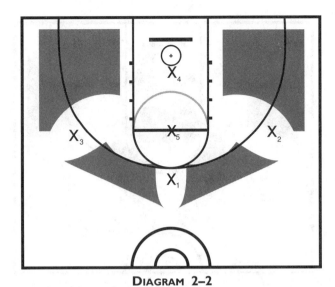

DIAGRAM 2–2

point guard above the free throw line extended. Diagrams 2–3, 2–4, and 2–5 illustrate the obvious weaknesses of other common zone defenses, the 3-2 zone, the 2-3 zone, and the 1-2-2 zone.

The 1-2-2 and 3-2 zones are very similar, as are the 2-1-2 and the 2-3 zones, in that the basic shifting responsibilities are almost identical. The major difference between the 1-2-2 and the 3-2 zones as well as between the 2-1-2 and the 2-3 zones is in the placement of the personnel in the initial or "home base" alignment of each zone.

SIMILARITY OF ALL QUARTER-COURT ZONES

An important factor to be aware of is that each zone, regardless of the initial positioning of the personnel, will have nearly the identical alignment once the players have shifted to compensate for an offensive thrust to either of the

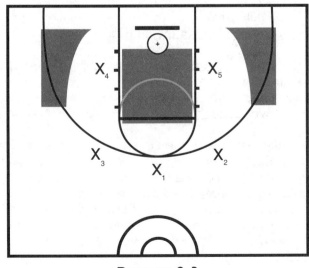

DIAGRAM 2–3

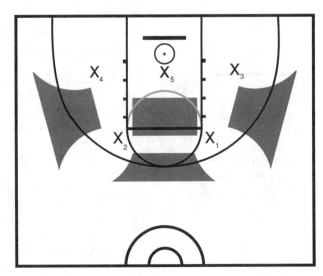

DIAGRAM 2–4

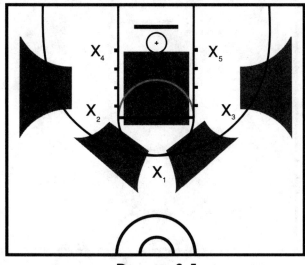

DIAGRAM 2–5

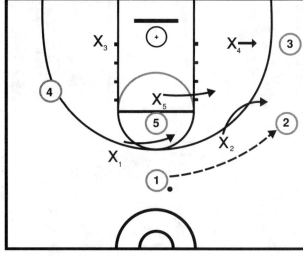

DIAGRAM 2–6

wing slots or to either baseline area. An example will illustrate this fact. Diagrams 2–1 and 2–2 depict the standard initial alignment of the 2-1-2 and the 1-3-1 zone defenses, respectfully.

Diagram 2–6 shows the shift and the resulting alignment of the players in the 2-1-2 once the ball has been moved to the wing slot. Diagram 2–7 depicts the shift accompanying the ball being passed from the wing to the baseline.

The defensive adjustments by the 1-3-1 zone defense in response to a pass to the wing area is shown in Diagram 2–8. This defensive shift to the wing is identical to that made in the 2-1-2 zone shift. Diagram 2–9 illustrates the resulting shift and alignment of the defensive personnel once the ball has been passed from the wing to the right corner. Note that the shifting of the defenders in this 1-3-1 zone in response to the movement of the ball to the wing or to the baseline results in an identical concluding alignment of personnel as found in the 2-1-2 zone.

The basic philosophy of shifting in response to the movement of the ball from the top of the key to the wing and to the corners generally remains the same whether the zone has a 2-3, 3-2, 1-2-2, 2-1-2, or 1-3-1 initial formation. That is, the concluding formation of the defensive personnel in response to a pass to the wing or the baseline is the same regardless of the initial alignment of defensive personnel.

In any regular quarter-court zone, when the ball is in a corner, there are essentially three defensive players between the ball and the basket, as shown in Diagrams 2–7 and 2–9. Whenever the ball is in a wing, there should be three defensive players in the zone "between" the ball and the basket (see Diagrams 2–6 and 2–8).

It is now obvious that the traditional classification of specific weaknesses for the various zone defenses are applicable *only when the defensive personnel are situated in or near their original alignment* on the floor. For example, attacking the 1-3-1 zone defense by exploiting the weak baseline slots (Diagram 2–2) can best be effected when the zone is situated in the 1-3-1 formation or when the players are moving or shifting in or out of the 1-3-1 alignment. This is true whether the zone has just been set up or whether the zone has been caught during its transitional shift in an effort to combat the ball being passed around the "horn."

Coaching Hint 28
Once the ball has been moved to the wing or baseline areas, most zone defenses shift into a similar defensive position.

Coaching Hint 29
Make sure the athletes understand the similarities in player movement in all quarter-court zones in response to the ball being moved to the wings and to the corners.

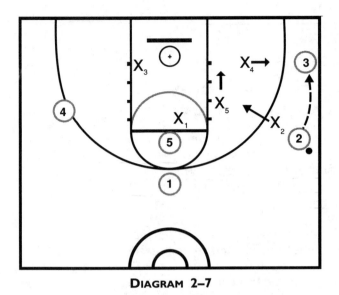

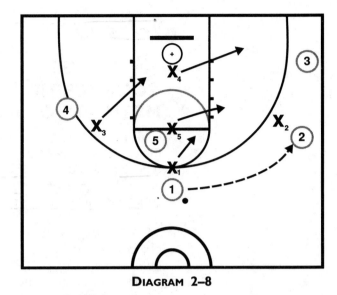

DIAGRAM 2–7   DIAGRAM 2–8

Similarly, attacking the 2-1-2 zone by attempting a shot from either wing or near the top of the key is most effective when the zoning players are actually in the 2-1-2 alignment. The defenders can be in such a formation (2-1-2) either (a) by being caught in a transitional shift in response to the ball being moved from one side of the floor to another or (b) when the zone is initially set up (see Diagram 2–1).

TWO PRIMARY METHODS OF ATTACKING ZONES (SUSCEPTIBILITY OF ALL ZONES)

The primary methods of attacking zones revolve around two very effective tactics. First is to beat the defensive players down the floor and take a high percentage shot before the zone can effectively be set up. Second is to use quick and accurate passes against the zone so that the defensive players cannot move fast enough (cannot adequately shift from their current positions in the zone

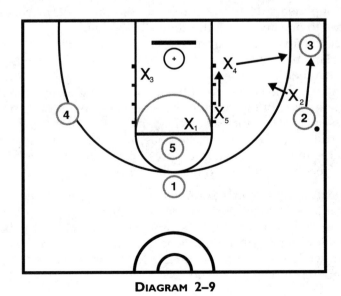

DIAGRAM 2–9

configuration to meet a new offensive threat emerging from a different spot on the floor).

COUNTERING THE TWO PRIMARY METHODS OF ATTACKING ZONES

With this in mind, coaches who employ zones, and the players who execute them, need to be mindful of the importance of (a) getting back on defense quickly, (b) reducing or distorting the passing patterns of the offensive players, and (c) forcing opponents to take poor percentage shots or forcing poorer shooters to attempt the field goals.

1. *Getting back on defense quickly and preventing the fast break:* The objective of getting back on defense quickly and setting up the zone before the offense can score can be accomplished in three ways. Two of the three methods revolve around what the zoning team does while on offense itself. The third centers on what happens during the transition from offense to defense.

First, being successful in scoring forces the opponents to take the ball out of bounds, thus gaining precious seconds for the team that scored to make the transition from offense to the zone defense. Second, the strategic placement of players while on offense—especially guards—can have a significant effect on how these same players play defense.

If offensive players, once their team no longer has possession of the ball, are in a position on the court where they immediately are able to rush down the floor to take up their defensive positions, they can effectively negate or slow down the fast-break efforts of the opposition. Floor position of zone defenders when they are on offense is of paramount importance.

The third factor relating to getting back quickly on defense hinges simply on good, old-fashioned hustle and desire. In order to stop the opponent's fast break, all zoning players must be committed to hustling down court at full speed whenever their team no longer has possession of the ball.

2. *Reducing or distorting the passing patterns of the offensive players:* Another sound tactic that zone defenses should employ to reduce the effectiveness of their opponents relates to preventing the offensive players from easily passing the ball to one another. If the zone allows the players on offense to pass the ball at will, to move the ball from one side of the floor to the other and back again, to move the ball into the middle of the zone, then the defense should not be surprised that their zone is ineffective.

The goal of the zone is to prevent passes from being easily made around the "horn"—from one side of the court to the other. Disruption of the normal passing lanes is essential. When the ball has been moved to the wing, defensive players should not allow the ball to be easily passed back out to the top of the circle. When the ball is moved to the corner, pressure should be exerted against the intended receivers in the wing and near the basket.

3. *Forcing opponents to take poor, low percentage shots:* The third method of countering offensive zone attacks involves exerting extreme pressure on those players most likely to do damage by scoring. The shot clock has been a great help in enabling zones to force opponents to make hurried passes and to take poor shots, all while under extreme pressure. This is especially true in forcing (or inviting) poorer opponents to shoot.

Coaching Hint 30
Offensive floor positioning has a significant impact on players' abilities to get back on defense.

Coaching Hint 31
Insist that players get back on defense immediately when the team no longer has possession of the ball.

Coaching Hint 32
Disrupt the passing patterns of the offense—make it difficult for opponents to pass where they want to pass.

Coaching Hint 33
Do not allow opponents to take uncontested shots—unless there is a specific reason to do so.

Zone defenses do not imply passive defenses. Zone defenses are not played by athletes standing around or lazily moving from one spot to another—quite the contrary. Effective zone defenses are noted for their tenacity, persistence, and assertiveness. Zone defenses are dynamic, quick, vigorous, and aggressive.

Zone defenses attack their opponents. This is done by quick movement of players in response to the movement of the ball and the movement of offensive personnel. With the advent of the shot clock, such pressure tactics have become even more effective since the offense has a limited number of seconds in which to create a high percentage shot.

Thus, if the zoning players can "hunker down" and really work at moving on the court and exerting pressure against the players in possession of the ball (potential shooter), as well as the intended receivers, the advantage lies with the zone. However, if the zoning team is unsuccessful in exerting significant pressure against potential shooters and the pass receivers, the advantage rests with the offense.

A common tactic that some coaches have successfully used is to "invite" certain offensive players—the poorer shooters—to take the field goal attempt. To accomplish this, the zone defenders exert extreme pressure against the best or better shooters while easing or sagging off a little (or a lot) when the opponent's poorest shooter has the ball.

> **Coaching Hint 34**
> "Invite" poor shooters to take shots.

Thus, the defenders are literally inviting this player to take the shot. This tactic also allows the defensive players to cover less territory on the court, since the poorest shooter does not have to be guarded as closely when in possession of the ball.

There is some risk to this tactic, naturally. The so-called poorer shooter might, indeed, have a hot night from the field. However, it is sometimes worth the risk to invite selected offensive players to take more shots. These offensive players are those who, in the past, have demonstrated that they are not exceptionally skilled shooters. When poorer shooters attempt field goals, the opponent's better shooters are not shooting. Of course, if the so-called poorer (poorest) shooter starts to burn the nets, the zone can merely readjust and no longer extend the "invitation."

A STATIONARY 1-2-2 ZONE DEFENSE

The stationary 1-2-2 zone defense, an adaptation of the more common 1-2-2 zone, is designed to significantly increase the potential for defensive rebounds. In the traditional 1-2-2 zone, when the ball is moved into the corner, it is the ball side low post player, X_5 in Diagram 2–10, who must slide out to counter this new potential scoring threat. As X_5 makes the move to the corner, X_4 must slide across the lane to fill the vacancy left by X_5. Simultaneously, X_2 slides down the lane, thereby taking up a position where X_4 was originally stationed. X_1 moves as shown to provide balance.

Two Glaring Weaknesses in the Traditional 1-2-2 Zone

The problem with this traditional shifting is that the guard, X_2, who is usually a shorter player, has become the potential rebounder should a field goal be attempted from the opposite side of the floor. A second major weakness in the traditional 1-2-2 zone involves the two low post players, X_5 and X_4. As X_5 moves out to the corner, and before X_4 can slide across the lane, the zone is especially vulnerable to any offensive player who happens to move into the low post slot, as shown in Diagram 2–10.

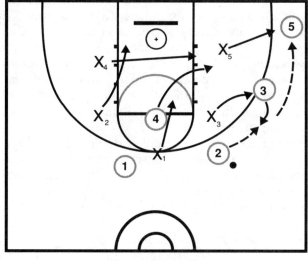

DIAGRAM 2–10

The Uniqueness of the Stationary 1-2-2 Zone

The stationery 1-2-2 zone receives its name from the stationary or relatively fixed positions of the two low post players, X_4 and X_5. These two players take up their respective posts along both sides of the free throw lane, in the two low post slots. *These two players, usually being the best rebounders and taller players on the team, remain in their respective positions even when the ball is moved to the corners.* It remains for the remaining three players (X_1, X_2, and X_3) to make the necessary adjustments in response to the ball being moved around the horn to the wings and to the corners.

Diagram 2–11 illustrates what happens when the ball is moved to the left wing area. When X_2 sees or anticipates the pass to the wing, X_2 immediately slides out to confront the new threat posed by ③. Should the ball be further moved to the corner—to ⑤, who has cut across the baseline—it is still the responsibility of X_2 to slide down to the corner to exert defensive pressure against this new threat.

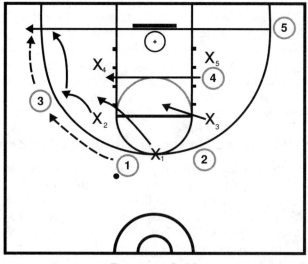

DIAGRAM 2–11

X₄, one of the taller players on the squad and an excellent rebounder, remains in the ball side low post area, preventing any offensive player in the low post from receiving a pass from the wing or from the corner. The other top rebounder, X₅, remains on the opposite side of the lane, in excellent rebounding position should a shot be attempted from the left side of the court. X₁ and X₃ move as shown in reaction to the ball being moved to the left wing and left corner.

Characteristics of the Top Three Defenders

In this zone defense, it is essential that X₁, X₂, and X₃ be physically quick and fast-reacting athletes who are able to move as a coordinated unit. They should also have good anticipation skills because these three players have responsibility for covering—defending—a large area of the court.

X₁ has responsibility for the top of the key and both wings—areas A, B, and C in Diagram 2–12. X₂ must cover areas C, D, and F, while X₃ has responsibility for areas B, E, and F. The movement and eventual destination of these three defenders depends on where the offense moves the ball. Diagrams 2–13 and 2–14 illustrate the adjustments made by all five defensive players in reaction to the ball being moved from one side of the court to the other.

Sometimes, in an attempt to hinder or slow the passing efforts by the offense, X₃ can overplay (stunt) and thereby threaten the pass from ③, stationed in the wing, to the point guard ①. Such a stunting move forces the point guard to move towards the passer in an effort to safely receive the ball. When this happens, X₃ is able to regroup and shift back to the wing (Diagram 2–13).

Again, the strengths of this zone adaptation lie in the exceptionally strong defensive power in the low post area and the tremendous rebounding potential because X₄ and X₅ rarely have to vacate their respective low post positions.

One of the few times when it might become necessary for one of the defensive low post players to leave the low post area is when the offense is consistently successful in getting the ball into the free throw area from an initial 1-3-1 offensive alignment. In this event, the defensive low post player who does not have any opponent in the vicinity (X₅ in Diagram 2–15) moves up to the free throw lane to prevent any direct pass from the point guard to ⑤, who is posi-

> **Coaching Hint 35**
> To deny the ball in the high post, have one of the low post players flash to the free throw line.

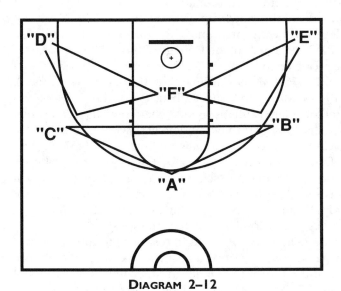

DIAGRAM 2–12

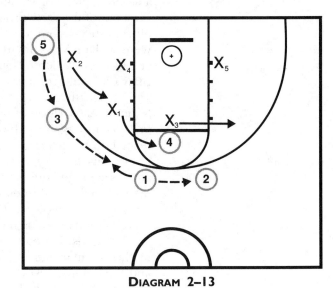

DIAGRAM 2–13

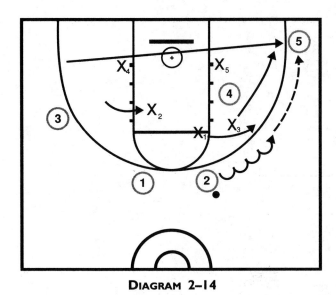

DIAGRAM 2–14

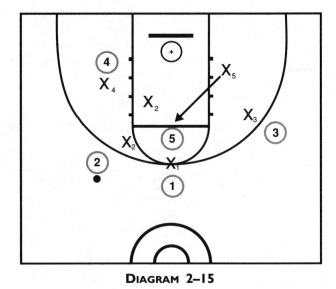

DIAGRAM 2–15

tioned near the free throw line. Of course, assistance in defending the middle is also provided by X_3 and X_2, who shift back and forth into the lane, thereby harassing an offensive pivot player.

Coaches who want to create fast-break situations on a consistent basis and who have two exceptionally tall rebounders might do well to consider the stationary 1-2-2 zone defense. Of course, it does not hurt one bit if the team is also blessed with three additional quick and fast-reacting players assuming the perimeter positions.

THE MATCH-UP ZONE DEFENSE

The match-up zone defense was made popular and came into its own in the late 1960s and early 1970s. The match-up zone is a distinct combination type of defense involving both man-to-man principles and zone principles. This combination-type defense is thought of today as a distinct type of defense rather than a stunting tactic or variation of either a man-to-man or the zone defense.

Four of the early proponents of the match-up zone defense who enjoyed significant success on the college level with variations of the match-up zone defense were William Musselman (1965–1971 at Ashland College, Ohio); William C. Lucas (1960–1974 at Central State University, Ohio); William Stier, Jr. (1968–1971 at Briar Cliff College, Iowa, and 1976-1980 at Cardinal Stritch College, Wisconsin); and Jud Heathcote (1976–1995 at Michigan State). Bill Lucas was the coach of two National Association of Intercollegiate Athletes (NAIA) championship teams, first in 1965 and again in 1968. His 1965 team was undefeated with a perfect 30–0 record. Bill Musselman's NCAA, Division II, teams were known for limiting their opponents to very low offensive outputs. One year, the opponents' offense attacks averaged under 40 points a game. Musselman later was the head coach at the University of Minnesota as well as for the NBA's Cleveland Cavaliers and Minnesota Timberwolves. Jud Heathcote's 1979 Michigan State team, featuring "Magic" Johnson, won the NCAA, Division I, national championship.

The initial impetus for the match-up zone was in response to the traditional method of attacking zones that involved creating a mismatch between the offense and the defense, especially at the top of the circle. In other words, the basis of most zone attacks during this time period relied on the even-odd approach.

The Traditional Even-Odd Strategy of Attacking Zones

The even-odd approach of attacking zones is as follows: If the zone defense consists of two players out front (as in a 2-1-2 or 2-3 zone), the offense players would align themselves with a single player at the top of the key, such as in a 1-3-1 formation. Conversely, if the defense shows a single player front (as in a 1-3-1 zone defense), the offense would counter with a double player front, such as a 2-1-2 formation.

The concept behind the match-up zone involves a shifting of defensive personnel into an alignment or formation that matches the offensive set, player for player. Simultaneously, each of the defensive players continues to operate as a unit, employing very definite zone principles. This shifting requires immediate reaction on behalf of all five defenders and demands split-second timing and expert coordination of all five defensive teammates.

It is almost like forcing the offense to attack a 2-1-2 zone defense with a 2-1-2 offensive alignment and having the offensive personnel not move from the 2-1-2 set—or attempting to attack a 1-3-1 zone with a 1-3-1 stationery offensive set. It is difficult to win by attacking zones in this manner. In either scenario, all offensive players would be guarded by a specific defender, with the ball handler being closely guarded, person to person, by a single defender, while the remaining four defensive players assume their regular zone responsibilities, ready to sag and render help if needed.

INITIATING THE MATCH-UP ZONE DEFENSE

The match-up zone defense can be initiated from either a 2-1-2 or 1-3-1 formation. Typically, offensive teams react to what the defense sets up. If the defense is in an initial 2-1-2 formation, the offense counters with a single guard front, such as a 1-3-1 (see Diagram 2–16) or a 1-2-2 set. However, if the defense is employing a 1-3-1 zone, the offensive players will attempt to create a mismatch at the top of the key (as well as along the baseline) by establishing a double guard front with two wide wing players, such as a 2-1-2 alignment (see Diagram 2–17).

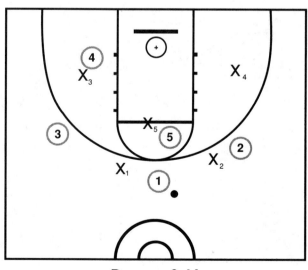

DIAGRAM 2–16

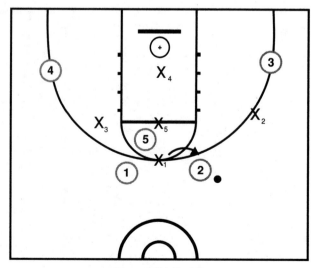

DIAGRAM 2–17

Matching Up from a 2-1-2 Initial Alignment

The defenders, recognizing that the offense is attempting to establish a mismatch against them, must employ quick countermeasures *by rotating the perimeter players, thereby matching up with the offensive personnel*. In the case where the defense is in a 2-1-2 formation (see Diagram 2–18), the defensive player nearest to the offensive point player—in this case X_1—starts to slide out to guard (*in a man-to-man defensive coverage*) the ball handler, as the latter dribbles across the 10-second line.

As X_1 makes this move to match up with ①, the remaining defensive players on the perimeter move (rotate) simultaneously, in relationship to X_1, in an effort to match up with the perimeter offensive players. The defensive player guarding the offensive player with the ball is designated as the *key* and the other defenders must rotate in relation to this defensive player (the key).

These other defenders rotate as follows. X_2 slides to the left and guards the first offensive player to the left of X_1 (the key), in this case ③. X_3 moves out to the wing and guards the first offensive player to the right of X_1 (the key), who is ②, while X_4 seeks out the remaining offensive perimeter player, ④, wherever this player may be. Each of these three players—X_2, X_3, and X_4— must exert defensive pressure against the player in each of their respective areas of the court, just as they would if they were playing a regular zone defense. The only difference is that each of these defensive players will have an opposing athlete in his or her immediate court space.

The remaining defensive player, X_5, the pivot, stays in the middle of the lane (ball side) while exerting man-to-man pressure against any offensive threat emanating from that area. However, if the offensive pivot is not stationed at the ball side of the lane, X_5 assumes a zone position on the ball side of the lane while anticipating that the offensive pivot, ⑤, will be flashing into the lane from behind.

Matching Up from a 1-3-1 Initial Alignment

If the defense starts out in a 1-3-1 set and the opposing team counters with a double guard set, such as a 2-1-2 formation, the now familiar match-up rotation

---

Coaching Hint 36

The defensive player guarding the player with the ball continues to defend that player even on the dribble; the remaining defensive players rotate accordingly.

Coaching Hint 37

In the match-up zone defense, the defensive center assumes a man-to-man posture against the offensive pivot who plays in or near the lane.

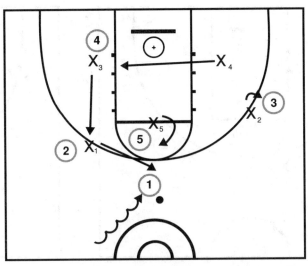

DIAGRAM 2–18

can be accomplished by again keying off the defensive point guard, X_1. In this instance, X_1 (the key) slides out to exert man-to-man pressure against the guard in possession of the ball (see Diagram 2–19). The remaining defensive teammates again immediately react to the key and simultaneously rotate to match up with the other perimeter offensive players. In this example, X_2 slides to the left to cover the first offensive player to the left of the X_1 (the key), who, in this case, is ③, stationed along the sideline. And X_3 moves up to cover the first offensive player to the right of X_1.

All three players exert defensive coverage against the player in their respective areas of the court, just as they would if they were playing a regular zone defense. However, in this situation, each of the perimeter players is now matched up with an offensive player. As before, the defensive pivot assumes a man-to-man posture (ball side) against any offensive player who moves into the lane area.

Countering the "Cut Through" by the Offense

Of course, no offensive attack has players merely standing around. With the typical zone look that the match-up defense presents, offensive teams initially attack from one type of formation (2-1-2, for example) and then rotate into a different set (1-3-1). This shifting is usually accomplished by cutting players through the lane and/or moving others to different areas around the perimeter of the court.

An example of such an offensive thrust is depicted in Diagram 2–20, which shows the defense matched up against the 1-3-1 offensive formation. The offense, in an effort to counter this match-up tactic has the point guard pass to the wing player, whereupon ① cuts through the middle of the lane, as shown, and ends up in the right corner. As a result, the offense is now in a 2-1-2 formation rather than in a 1-3-1 set.

However, the defense adjusts to this cut through in the following manner. When ③ receives the ball, X_2 now assumes the role of the key (since X_2 is now guarding the ball) and immediately begins to exert man-to-man pressure against the player who has possession of the ball. As ① continues the cut through the lane, several defensive adjustments are made simultaneously in reaction to the

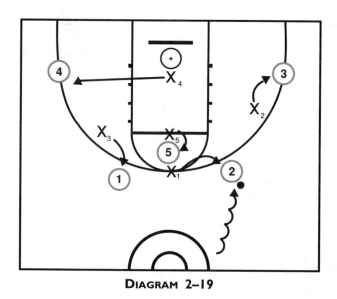

DIAGRAM 2–19

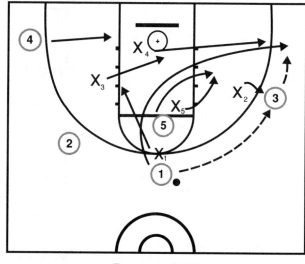

DIAGRAM 2–20

pass to the right wing and in anticipation of an offensive cut or movement of personnel. For example, X_1 starts to fall back into the lane and picks up a new defensive assignment—that is, the first offensive player to the right of the key, ② in this case.

Simultaneously, X_4, who continues to have responsibility for the first offensive player to the left of the key (who is now X_2), must slide across the lane to pick up the new offensive treat, ①. That leaves X_3 to assume responsibility for the remaining perimeter player, who is ④, while sagging toward the ball. And, finally, the defensive pivot plays ball side and exerts man-to-man pressure against any offensive player entering the ball side portion of the lane.

As a result, the defense has again matched up with the offense (see Diagram 2–21). Everywhere the offensive players are stationed, there is a defensive player ready to exert pressure. The offensive player with the ball is being guarded in a man-to-man coverage, as is the offensive pivot who has moved toward the ball. The remaining three match-up players are zoning their respective defensive assignments.

Once the defense has matched up with the offensive personnel, say in a 2-1-2 formation, three possible options are available. First, the defense could continue to match up with the offense, regardless of whether the opponents attempt to move to a different alignment or formation on the court. For example, the defense could stay in the 2-1-2 zone set only as long as the offensive team remained in the 2-1-2 set. When the offense makes a move to a different formation on the floor, perhaps with a single guard front (1-3-1), the defense counters (matches up) by presenting a single guard look (1-3-1) and then executing the 1-3-1 regular zone defense.

Second, the defense could simply stay in the formation they found themselves in after the match up and play a regular zone defense from that alignment. For example, assume that the defense started out in a 1-3-1 alignment and the offense initiated a zone attack from the 2-1-2 set. When the defense adjusts by matching up into a 2-1-2 zone formation, the defense could just continue in that 2-1-2 formation and play the regular 2-1-2 zone defense regardless of subsequent movement of the offensive personnel.

> **Coaching Hint 38**
> Rotating between the match-up defense, a regular zone defense, and a strict man-to-man tends to confuse the offense.

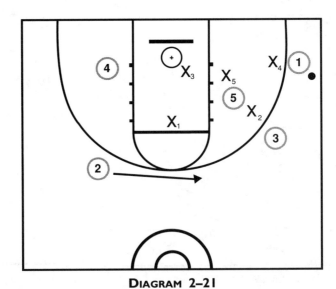

DIAGRAM 2–21

Third, the defense could elect to switch to a strict man-to-man type of defense, upon a predetermined signal or a particular situation. Sometimes, this can be initiated by a verbal command or hand signal by the key player. Such a switch might also take place whenever the offensive passes the ball to the top of the key in an attempt to move the ball from one side of the floor to the other side. When the ball is moved to the top of the key area, the defensive players switch from the match-up defense to a regular man-to-man attack. Finally, a switch could be initiated whenever the ball is passed into a corner.

One of the tactics in effectively running this type of match-up zone defense in game situations is to periodically change back and forth between the match-up zone, a regular zone defense, and man-to-man coverage. This adjustment presents a great challenge for the offense to overcome. It frequently becomes very difficult for the offense even to recognize exactly what type of defense is being thrown at them. Additionally, it is very challenging for offenses to attack the match-up zone, the regular zone, and man-to-man coverage with a single offensive series. Thus, the change, the rotation, is doubly disconcerting for the offense. As a result, the defense has a definite edge.

CONCLUDING COMMENTS ABOUT QUARTER-COURT ZONE DEFENSES

The key to selecting, teaching, and executing any quarter-court zone is to recognize the strengths and weaknesses of one's own players. Additionally, one must have a realistic understanding of the strengths and weaknesses of one's opponents as well. Taking advantage of one's own strengths in light of an opponent's weakness(es) is a critical factor in employing any type of defense. It is especially critical when deciding to utilize a zone defense.

It is imperative that the players executing the zone realize that the zone defense is, indeed, an attacking defense. Furthermore, it takes great skill and determination to execute any zone defense properly. Playing a zone, any type of zone, is not easy, nor is it for the faint of heart. It is not a laid-back, relaxing, take-it-easy type of a defense. If it is implemented that way, one is playing right into the hands of the opponent.

> **Coaching Hint 39**
> No one ever said that playing a zone was easy—it isn't if the zone is played properly.

3 Man-to-Man Defense

ARRIVING AT AN APPROPRIATE MAN-TO-MAN DEFENSIVE STRATEGY

Selecting an appropriate man-to-man defensive stratagem is essential for any successful mentor. However, the implementation of an appropriate strategy depends on many factors or variables, including the skill levels and experiences of both teams.

Not all man-to-man defenses are executed in a similar fashion, nor are they equally effective. There can be many versions or variations of what is typically referred to as man-to-man defense. In fact, there are three factors that help distinguish different variations of this defense from one another: These include:

1. The *extent or amount of pressure* placed on the ball as well as the intended receiver(s)
2. *Where on the floor* (the location) the defense begins to apply severe pressure against the offense
3. The use of some type of *trapping or double-teaming action* against the offense

EXTENT OF THE DEFENSIVE PRESSURE

Just *how much defensive pressure* should be exerted against the offense is a major decision. Many factors such as the skills, abilities, physical conditioning, and experiences of the defenders as well as the offensive players, the score, how the officials are calling the game, the time remaining in the contest, and so on, must be considered in arriving at such a decision.

Pressuring the Ball Handler and the Intended Receivers

Defensive pressure to be applied against the offense can be thought of as pressure against the ball handler as well as against potential receivers. This pressure might consist of all-out, nose-to-nose coverage or may merely involve token presence of defensive coverage. It would be foolhardy for a team to attempt to play aggressive, "in-your-face" defense when the offensive players are decidedly quicker than the defenders and possess superior dribbling and passing skills.

As stated earlier, man-to-man defense can be played where the ball handler is always closely guarded, or the defensive player having responsibility for covering the ball may elect to back off and exert only token defensive pressure. The type of pressure (extreme or token, or in between) against the ball can also be varied at different times of the game. At one point, there may be extreme man-to-man pressure against the ball. At other times, only token pressure will be present. This changing of defensive pressure can sometimes play havoc with the offense by keeping the opposing players off balance.

Additionally, some defensive teams elect to exert extreme defensive pressure against only some of the offensive players, such as those athletes who the coaches have deemed to be susceptible to such pressure tactics. Other offensive players, those extremely skilled in ball handling, might not be attacked to the same degree or as frequently. In other situations, defenders might exert such extreme pressure against those opposing players who are real offensive threats in an effort to reduce their effectiveness.

Rationale for Using Pressure Man-to-Man Tactics

Those teams employing true pressure tactics attempt to make it extremely difficult for the offensive team to pass as well as dribble the ball. The rationale, in the form of questions, goes something like this: Why allow the offensive team to work (via a pass or the dribble) for a high percentage shot in an uncontested environment? Why allow opponents an opportunity to complete easy passes that might well result in excellent scoring opportunities? Why allow the offensive team to dribble the ball where it wants to? Why allow the offense to dictate the tempo and strategy of the game?

Defenders need to take the initiative and make the offensive players work very hard (against intense man-to-man pressure) just to protect the ball. Defenders must make it extremely difficult (a real challenge) for the opponents to actually move the ball with any kind of ease by means of either the pass or the dribble. The end result of such aggravated defensive harassment is that the offensive players find it extremely difficult to protect and move the ball, much less to get off consistent high percentage shots.

When pressure defense is executed properly, defenders are literally able to force the opponents to be so concerned with protecting the ball that scoring actually becomes a matter of secondary importance. The defense can force the offense to spend time, effort, and energy just protecting the ball. For the offense, the effort to move the ball into scoring position becomes just that much more difficult. And, finally, pressure defense also increases the possibility of turnovers by the opponents—miscues that can result in easy scoring opportunities created by the defense.

LOCATION OF DEFENSIVE PRESSURE

One very important factor to take into account when considering applying defensive pressure is *where* on the court such pressure will be applied against the offense. Will the defenders dig deep and start to play tough defense when their opponents reach the top of the key (i.e., at the quarter-court mark)? Or will the defensive players pick up their individual assignments at half court, when the opponents cross the 10-second line?

Coaching Hint 41
There is a time and a place to play aggressive defense and a time and a place to play token defense.

Coaching Hint 42
Take the initiative on defense and strive to prevent the offense from doing what it wants to do.

**Extending the Defensive Pressure
Beyond the Half-Court Area**

Should the man-to-man defense be extended into a three-quarter court alignment, thereby making the offense work even harder to protect and move the ball into scoring position? Or would a full-court, man-to-man defensive attack be more appropriate in terms of creating more opportunities for turnovers and other miscues by the opponents?

Extending full-court man-to-man defense, contesting even the in-bounds pass, creates a great deal of pressure for the offense to overcome. However, such a move similarly places a great deal of stress and strain on the defenders as well. The risks are significant if the defensive players are not adequately prepared—physically, mentally, and psychologically—to implement such extended defensive coverage. For example, if the defensive personnel are not in tip-top physical condition, it would be counterproductive to attempt to press, for any length of time, especially in a three-quarter or full-court, man-to-man configuration.

TRAPPING OR DOUBLE TEAMING FROM THE MAN-TO-MAN DEFENSE

Another variable associated with different types of man-to-man defenses involves the use of *double teaming*. Just because a team deploys a man-to-man defense does not mean that there can be no trapping or double teaming of the offensive personnel or that such trapping is exceptionally difficult or rare—quite the contrary. Man-to-man defenses can switch into a double team or trapping mode quite easily, at any spot on the court. This can be done while still retaining some type of adequate coverage against the remaining offensive players.

Of course, any time the ball handler is double teamed, the defense assumes a risk because there are four remaining offensive players to be guarded by only three defenders. But that is one of the risks assumed by the defense whenever defenders initiate a double-team situation.

Double Teaming When the Offensive
Players Are Close Together

One excellent opportunity to double team the ball while playing man-to-man defense is when a second offensive player moves into close proximity to the ball handler, as seen in Diagram 3–1. In this particular instance, two offensive players, ① and ②, are very close together. This invites X_1 to leave ① and attempt to double team the ball handler, with help from X_2. Once the double team or trap is initiated, there are several options now open to the defense.

The first option is for the remaining defenders to do nothing out of the ordinary. They merely continue to guard their respective offensive opponents, man to man. If ② is able to complete the pass to ① through the double-team trap, X_1 must hustle back to contain any offensive threat provided by the new ball handler.

The Fake Double-Team Situation The second option calls for X_1, as soon as the movement toward the ball handler results in the dribble being stopped, to immediately return back to guard the original offensive player, ①. Many times, this feint toward creating the double team will force the ball handler to stop the dribble and pick up the ball, thereby rendering that offensive player much less a threat. With ② unable to dribble, there is no need for X_1 to continue on to create the double-team situation.

The third option involves anticipation by both X_5 and X_3. Obviously, once the two-player trap has been established, the primary pass receiver is ①. Thus, X_5 and X_3 simultaneously move to pick up new defensive assignments (see Diagram 3–2). X_5 moves out to cover ①, man to man, in anticipation of the pass. At the same time, X_3 slides into the lane in an effort to defend against any pass into the high post. Or X_5 may elect to remain in man-to-man coverage with the offensive pivot while X_3 moves out toward the intended receiver in an effort to thwart the potential pass by ②.

A fourth option calls for the remaining defensive players—X_5, X_3, and X_4—once the trap has been sprung on ②, to zone the floor. Thus, X_5 vacillates between ⑤ and ① while X_3 and X_4 zone the lane area.

Double Teaming When the Offensive Players Are Spread Apart

Diagram 3–3 shows how a double-team attack can be initiated, even when the offensive personnel are some distance from each other. With X_2 pressuring the ball handler toward the right sideline, X_1 leaves his or her defensive assignment and streaks across the floor to set up a double team on the blind side of ②.

Anticipation is the key, since X_3 vacates the normal defensive position in an effort to intercept any possible pass from ② to ①. With such a shift by X_1 and X_3, the only uncontested pass for ② to make is a pass all the way across court to ③—a very dangerous pass, indeed.

ESSENTIAL INGREDIENTS OF MAN-TO-MAN DEFENSE

When teaching and coaching man-to-man defense, coaches must think in terms of two perspectives: *individual* defense and *team* defense. In order to be effective in executing an effective man-to-man defense, each athlete needs to develop a sound defensive philosophy, which, in turn, requires one to possess a well-

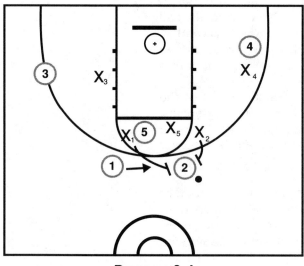

Diagram 3–1

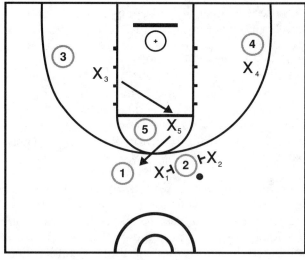

Diagram 3–2

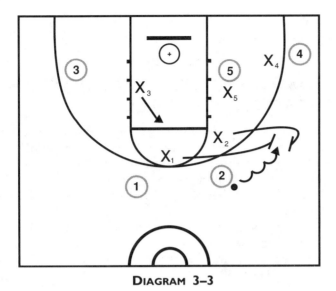

DIAGRAM 3–3

grounded understanding of the principles supporting both individual and team man-to-man defense. The information that follows provides insight into both individual and team defense, in the man-to-man mode.

INDIVIDUAL DEFENSE: MAN-TO-MAN PRINCIPLES

Defense involves an attack mode. Athletes must not assume a passive role when playing defense, especially man-to-man defense. In fact, just the opposite must occur. Athletes on defense must take the initiative and "take it to" the offense. Defense—good man-to-man defense—involves an aggressive, assertive, and dynamic attitude and action on behalf of the participants.

> **Coaching Hint 43:**
> Good defense involves an attack mentality.

Defenders Must Be Wary of the Triple Threat Offensive Player

An athlete's defensive stance is an all-important consideration in being able to successfully confront and control an opponent—with or without the ball. When a defensive player is covering an opponent without the ball, the advantage rests with the defense. However, once the opponent has received the ball and is able to pass, dribble, or shoot (that is, being a triple threat), the advantage shifts from the defense to the offense.

> **Coaching Hint 44**
> An offensive player has an advantage over the defense when in possession of the ball, in scoring position, and/or when able to dribble the ball.

That is why so much emphasis is placed on preventing an opponent from receiving a pass, especially when the opponent is in a critical spot on the floor. A critical spot on the floor can be an area from which a high percentage field goal might be taken or a scoring pass might be relayed.

When the ball handler has stopped the dribble, the advantage again shifts to the defense. This is why it is so important to *exert severe pressure against any ball handler who has relinquished the ability to dribble the ball*. Once a ball handler has stopped the dribble, the advantage immediately shifts to the defense because the ball handler's mobility is severely restricted. The ball handler who has "picked up the dribble" can only pass or shoot—period. Aggressive defen-

> **Coaching Hint 45**
> When the ball handler has stopped dribbling, the defense should exert severe pressure against the ball.

sive pressure applied against such a player makes it even more difficult to pass or get off a high percentage shot.

THE DEFENSIVE STANCE AND POSITION WHEN GUARDING THE BALL

Once an offensive player (stationed away from the basket) has received the ball, the defender should back off a step or two and give the new ball handler some respect—*unless* one of two situations exists: the defender deliberately elects to put extreme pressure on the ball in an effort to force the ball handler to dribble or to pass the ball, or the ball handler has already stopped the dribble and can now only pass or shoot.

In the first instance, the defender must watch out for the penetrating dribble toward the basket. In the second scenario, the defender is able, almost with impunity, to exert extreme, blanket defense against the ball, all the time anticipating and guarding against the quick pass and the resulting give-and-go move by the offense.

Body Position and Center of Gravity

Defending the ball away from the basket is never played standing up. Have you ever seen someone attempt to jump or quickly move while standing straight up, with knees locked while bending only at the waist? It is simply not possible, at least not very well.

Defenders should confront the ball handler with theirs knees bent, buttocks closer to the floor, and bending slightly at the waist. In fact, one indication or sign that an athlete is tired or should be substituted out of the game is when an individual is attempting to play defense while being in an erect position. When a defender starts to play defense while standing straight up, without bending the knees, the athlete cannot be effective or efficient. Either the player in question is tired (and thus should be substituted and allowed to rest) or the individual does not know how to play effective defense (and should surely be sitting on the bench or even in the bleachers).

Defensive Stance and Position When Guarding the Ball in the Low Post Slot

One of the few times when the defender is allowed to stand *almost* straight is when an offensive player has received the ball in close proximity to the basket, in a low post position. In this case, the defender straightens up to provide a larger and more visible threat against a possible shot. Nevertheless, even in this position, the defender's knees are still slightly bent in order to be able to jump in the air in an attempt to provide interference against a short jump shot attempt. To do otherwise would be to give the crib shot to the opponent.

Use of the Eyes When Guarding the Ball Handler Away from the Basket

While crouching on defense, the defender's eyes should be focused at the belly button of the ball handler. The defender should not be watching the shoulders, the head, the ball, or the upper chest. These can easily be manipulated by means of a fake or feint. The result is that the defender is too often left in the dust, standing still, watching as the opponent is heading for the basket. On the other

---

Coaching Hint 46
Do not allow (with few exceptions) an athlete to play defense while standing flat footed or merely bending at the waist.

Coaching Hint 47
When defending the ball handler in the low post area, the defender should stand "tall," with arms extended to impede and obstruct or otherwise hinder any offensive effort.

hand, wherever the opponent's belly button goes, so too will the ball when the opponent starts to dribble.

Use of Peripheral Vision

When guarding a player, especially one who does not have the ball, defenders must always take advantage of peripheral vision. Being able to watch one's defensive assignment as well as other players on the court—especially the ball handler or potential screeners—is a great skill and it should be practiced routinely. Conversely, having tunnel vision, being able only to focus on one's own defensive player, makes one vulnerable to screens, passes, and cutting movements. In fact, lack of peripheral vision can make one an ineffectual defender soon to become a bench warmer.

Use of the Feet When Guarding the Ball Handler

As stated earlier, good defense is played while in a crouching position, with the center of gravity kept low. The body is balanced so that the weight is shifted slightly forward toward the balls of the feet (see Figure 3–1). In this way, the athlete is able to move quickly to either side as well as forward or backward, without losing one's balance.

When moving the feet, the defender should usually slide the feet rather than cross one foot over another. The only time a defender guarding the ball should cross one foot over the other is when the offensive player has already beaten the defender and it becomes necessary to recover and catch up.

There are two different views on how the defensive player guarding the ball should position the feet. One school of thought has the feet positioned in a par-

FIGURE 3–1 PROPER DEFENSIVE STANCE AND POSITION

allel position in front of the offensive threat, as in Diagram 3–4. In this event, the defender is able to move equally well either to the right or to the left should the offensive player put the ball on the floor.

Another perspective suggests the feet be staggered, one slightly in front of the other. Thus, if the dribbler attacks the front foot (the defender's right foot in Diagram 3–5), the defender is able to pivot and push off on the back foot (left) while moving the front (right) foot toward the direction of the dribble. As a result, the defender is able to keep even with the offensive player while also obtaining sagging defensive help from teammates. If the dribbler advances to the other side, the defender merely slides to the left with the back foot being moved first.

The reason the author recommends the staggered defensive stance while guarding the ball is that many offensive players are taught to attack the forward foot of the defender—that is, to dribble to the side of the defender's front foot, as in Diagram 3–5. Thus, the defender can literally encourage (invite) the dribble to be made in a certain direction by assuming the staggered feet position. This can be especially helpful when the defense wants to pressure the dribbler to an area of the court where other defensive players can provide additional assistance.

Positioning of the Hands

Hands are extended shoulder width or slightly wider apart, relaxed, and with the palms up. This is to facilitate the *upward* movement of the defender's hands against the ball. Officials have a tendency to call fouls against defenders who slap downward at the ball. By slapping in an upward motion, with the palms up, the defender is less likely to be called for a foul. If only one hand is extended, it should be the hand on the same side of the body as the front foot. Another advantage of holding the hands palms up is that this discourages constant reaching in by the defender. Reaching in by a defender should be discouraged, since such a move often results in the defender being off balance and thus susceptible to any number of countermoves by the offensive player.

Coaching Hint 48
Defenders should not always try to steal the ball.

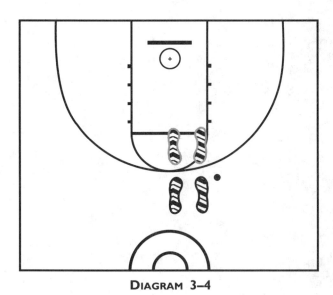

DIAGRAM 3–4

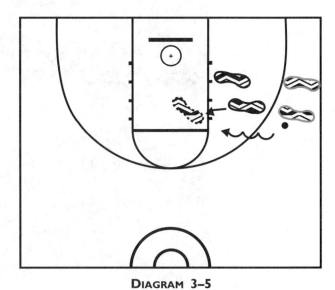

DIAGRAM 3–5

A common mistake made by inexperienced as well as experienced players is to attempt to "reach in" and steal the ball every time their opponent has the ball. Lunging for the ball in an attempt to steal it only places the defensive player at a decided disadvantage. Instead of trying to steal the ball every time, defenders should concentrate on making it difficult for the offensive player to protect the ball and to pass it.

If the opponent moves the ball overhead in an attempt to pass the ball, the defender can counter by raising one or both hands high in the air. Such a defensive reaction serves to interfere with and discourage such a pass. If the opponent brings the ball below the waist, the defender can react by moving a hand (palm up) in a threatening gesture against the ball, thereby discouraging a pass.

Of course, if the opponent with the ball picks up the dribble, the defender can close in and play nose-to-nose, blanket defense in an effort to stop a pass or a field goal attempt. Also, whenever an opponent who is a poor offensive threat or who lacks ball-handling skills receives the ball, it is possible to exert even greater pressure against the ball. In general, defensive players must take stock of the ball-handling skills and offensive potential of the players they are assigned to guard. They then must make the necessary adjustments in exerting individual, man-to-man defensive coverage.

> **Coaching Hint 49**
> Assess the opponent's ball-handling skill and actual offensive threat, and play defense accordingly.

Another use of the hands is to provide interference against a shot by an opponent. When a jump shot (or a hook shot or set shot) is taken from the floor, it is essential that the defender attempt to provide as much interference as possible. This is done by the defender raising the arm and hand (with fingers slightly spread) in front of the shooter's face, thus presenting a "picket fence" through which the opponent must see and shoot through. One must be careful not to shake one's hands too vigorously directly in front of the shooter's eyes, lest the officials call a violation (face guarding).

No one wants the shooter to have an uncontested field goal attempt. Defenders need to make it difficult for a shooter to get a shot off or to become an offensive rebounder of a missed shot. On the other hand, defenders should not attempt to block each and every field goal attempt. This is just not possible, nor is it prudent to attempt to do so.

> **Coaching Hint 50**
> Players should not attempt to block every single field goal attempt—or even every other attempt.

Defenders must exercise good judgment in terms of attempting to actually block an opponent's shot. Far too often, especially at lower skill levels, an attempt to block a field goal is not only unsuccessful but results in a foul being called against the defender. In too many instances, the attempted field goal is successful in spite of the foul. Players should not make stupid mistakes. They should not beat themselves.

The better course of action is to take a middle-of-the-road approach. That is, an attempt to block a shot should be made only when there is a high probability of being successful, without committing a foul. At other times, a defender may put up the "picket fence" against the shooter and then block out the shooter, thus preventing him or her from becoming an effective offensive rebounder.

> **Coaching Hint 51**
> Don't make stupid mistakes—make opponents beat you, don't beat yourself.

Many offensive players are spot shooters—that is, they prefer to shoot from particular spots on the court. Additionally, many teams, especially those that use formal offensive patterns, end up with their players shooting a good number of field goals from predesignated spots on the floor. When facing such teams and individual players, defenders can actually have an advantage in that they can anticipate from where a good number of field goal attempts will be made. Thus, experienced defenders are frequently able to disrupt the rhythm and pattern of such shooters to the benefit of the defense.

> **Coaching Hint 52**
> Determine the favorite spot of spot shooters and deny them access to it.

TEAM DEFENSE: MAN-TO-MAN PRINCIPLES

Coaching Hint 53
Good team defense is dependent on mutual help.

Excellent team defense is dependent on the *help concept*. That is, defenders help one another in their efforts to contain the offensive threats posed by opponents passing and dribbling the ball. This "help" philosophy can be best understood if each defender is thought to be part of a triangle (see Diagrams 3–6 and 3–7). A triangle may be drawn from the ball handler to each defender and to that defender's offensive assignment. Thus, in Diagram 3–6, the ball handler, ②, forms one corner of one mythical triangle while the apex of that triangle is the defender, X_1. Player ① becomes the third corner.

The Triangle Concept Explained

Using the triangle concept, each defensive player has responsibility for guarding a specific offensive threat while also keeping an eye on the ball. The farther away a defender is from the ball, the more the defender is able to sag to help a teammate. Conversely, the closer the defender is to the ball, the closer the defender must be to one's assigned offensive player. The key concept to remember is that each defender has primary responsibility for guarding an assigned opponent. Nevertheless, a defender can sag into the middle of the court to provide help to teammates when such action does not jeopardize one's primary defensive responsibility.

Guarding Potential Pass Receivers

Another essential element to sound man-to-man defense involves the *overplaying* or *denying* of potential pass receivers. This is especially important for those offensive players who are most likely to be passed the ball—that is, those who are one pass away from the ball handler. Those offensive players who are more than one pass away from the ball can be defended or guarded differently.

Specifically, there is no need to closely guard an offensive player who is so far removed from the ball as to pose little threat of receiving a direct pass. Rather, the defender can simply sag toward the middle of the court and render defensive assistance to teammates when guarding an opponent who is two or more passes away from the ball.

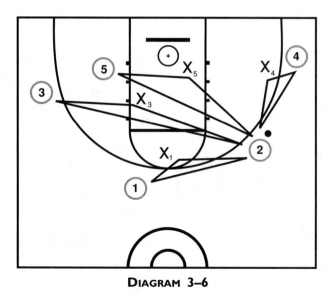

DIAGRAM 3–6

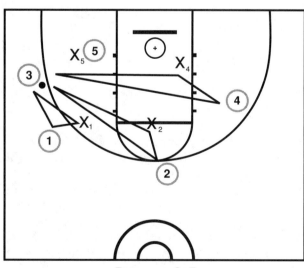

DIAGRAM 3–7

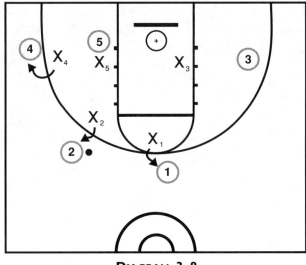

DIAGRAM 3–8

Diagram 3–8 illustrates such "prevent" or overplay defensive tactics against potential receivers. With ② in possession of the ball, the prime receivers are ①, ⑤, and ④. The post player, ⑤, situated in the middle of the court, is obviously the greatest threat. The remaining offensive player, ③, poses the least danger or threat in terms of a direct pass from ②.

In this situation, assuming that ② can no longer dribble, the defenders exert extreme "prevent" type of pressure against ①, ⑤, and ④ by overplaying each of these offensive players. It is X_3, however, who must sag off ③, since the latter is two passes away from ②. It does seem ridiculous as well as a waste of time and effort for X_3 to play ③ nose to nose when this offensive player is so far away from the ball. Besides, this sagging movement is done in an effort to provide back-side or blind-side help in the middle of the court, should a lob pass be attempted from ② to ⑤. Defensive coverage against ① can vary depending on the objective of the defensive team. In Diagram 3–8, the defense is in a true "prevent" or overplay type of man-to-man coverage with the result being that ① is also being overplayed.

Positioning Oneself to Overplay an Intended Receiver

How does one go about overplaying an offensive player and preventing a pass? Figure 3–2 illustrates the correct defensive position in preventing such a pass—in this case, into the wing area. The defender's ball-side arm (the right arm in this example) is extended straight out (palm facing the ball) in front of the offensive player, ready to swat the pass away. The other arm is extended to the left side of the potential pass receiver in order to remain balanced and to enable the defender to feel the offensive player if the latter darts toward the basket.

The defensive player's body should face the potential receiver. However, the head is turned so that the defender can see both the receiver and (through peripheral vision) the passer, if possible. The feet are positioned shoulder width apart with the knees slightly bent, with the center of gravity low, again for adequate body position.

The defender should be like a lion, ready to spring into immediate action, ready for any movement on behalf of the potential pass receiver. It is essential that the defender anticipate the actions of the pass receiver. Obviously, the pass receiver has several options to choose from in an attempt to get open. For exam-

Coaching Hint 54
Overplay the offensive players who are one pass from the ball in a very, very tight ("prevent") defense; sag off those who are two passes away from the ball.

Coaching Hint 55
The key elements in a press are *anticipation*, *desire*, and *hustle*.

FIGURE 3–2 DEFENSIVE POSITONING TO PREVENT A PASS IN THE WING

ple, this player could dart toward the basket, or move toward the wing or side-line areas, or even run directly toward the ball. The task of the defender is to react immediately to any offensive movement in an attempt to maintain constant defensive pressure in spite of the maneuvering by the potential receiver.

The defender playing "prevent" defense must exert intense pressure in order to interfere with a pass to the wing area. In addition to anticipation, defenders playing man to man must possess the desire, willingness, and ability to hustle if they are to be successful in either preventing such a pass or at least making it extremely difficult and time consuming to do so.

Defending against the Backdoor Cut

When a potential receiver, stationed in the wing area, experiences severe defensive pressure, the natural response is to jockey back and forth between the basket area and the wing area in an effort to break free for the pass. If the defender continues to apply "stickum"-type defense, there is always the danger of being victimized by the backdoor cut.

Diagram 3–9 illustrates a typical backdoor attempt. In response to extreme defensive pressure, ④ makes a move toward the sideline. As the defender also moves toward the sideline, ④ abruptly changes direction and quickly cuts toward the basket. This is done in an attempt to blow past the defender and be open to receive a (bounce) pass from ②, resulting in an easy two points.

To counteract this tactic, the defender should usually react by "opening up." This simply means turning the body toward the passer while pivoting on the left foot. The right foot moves, as shown, toward the basket. With this split-second movement, the defender is now moving with and in close proximity to the intended receiver while facing the passer. The would-be receiver is *behind* the defender. The defender should keep both hands extended wide in anticipation of batting down the pass, or even better, intercepting it (see Figures 3–3, 3–4 and 3–5).

Weak-Side Help against the Backdoor Cut

Of course, defending against the backdoor cut in the wing area is not a one-person job. It takes teamwork and requires assistance from teammates. In this

> **Coaching Hint 56**
> Stop the backdoor cut by "opening up."

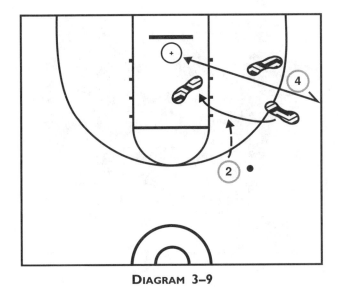

DIAGRAM 3–9

instance, the defensive help is in the form of the weak-side player X_3 who, while sagging off ③, is in an ideal position to render effective assistance against the backdoor cut (see Diagram 3–10). Such weak-side help—in this instance, from the defensive player who is two passes away from the ball—is an essential ingredient in the success of any man-to-man pressure defense. This is true regardless of where the man-to-man defense initially aligns itself, quarter court, half court, three-quarter court, or even full court.

FIGURE 3–3 DEFENDING THE BACK-DOOR CUT

FIGURE 3–4 DEFENDING THE BACK-DOOR CUT

FIGURE 3–5 DEFENDING THE BACK-DOOR CUT

Coaching Hint 57
Exert extreme defensive pressure against players who are playing in the wing or in the middle while allowing (inviting) passes across court (guard to guard).

Sometimes, defenses will elect to exert tremendous pressure against any pass into the wing areas and into the free throw area while allowing (even inviting) passes across court, from one side to another. This is because passes across court from one guard to another are not as much a threat as a pass into the free throw area, into the wing, or, heaven forbid, into the low post slot. Most offenses against the man-to-man type defense are initiated by a pass into the wing or into the middle (high or low) of the lane area. Thus, many coaches attempt to make it as difficult as possible for the offense to initiate their attack by contesting such passes with extreme vigor.

Exerting defensive pressure against the wing player as well as the high or low post is made easier by the sagging efforts of other players. In Diagram 3–10, both X_1 and X_3 are able to sag off their respective defensive responsibilities in an effort to discourage passes to ④ and ⑤. And, of course, X_2 is harassing the would-be passer, ②. As a result, the easiest pass for ② to make is to ①, who is stationed in the other guard slot.

At this point, the defense shifts in reaction to this pass (see Diagram 3–11). Extreme pressure is now placed by X_1 on the ball. X_3 plays "prevent" defense against ③ in the wing area, as does X_5 against ⑤ near the free throw line area. It is important that X_5 attempt to move in front of the offensive high post rather than move behind ⑤ in an effort to exert continuous "prevent"-type defensive pressure against any pass to the high post. Since ④ is now two passes away from the ball, X_4 is able to sag into the middle of the lane to render potential weakside help. And X_2 is now in a position to sag off the other offensive guard while providing meaningful defensive help in the lane area.

Coaching Hint 58
Vary the type of defensive pressure exerted against opponents—don't allow the offensive personnel to anticipate every defensive move or tactic.

Again, defensive teams that are able to vary the type of pressure exerted against opponents and/or against individual opposing players possess a decided advantage. This is because defenders are thus able to dictate the flow and tempo of the game, all the while keeping the offense off balance. Defenders should never become so limited or predictable in their attacking efforts so as to allow the offensive players to anticipate their every move. Variety, indeed, is the spice of life when it comes to defensive tactics.

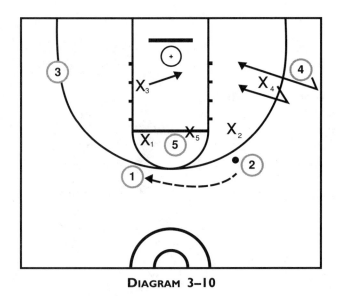

DIAGRAM 3–10

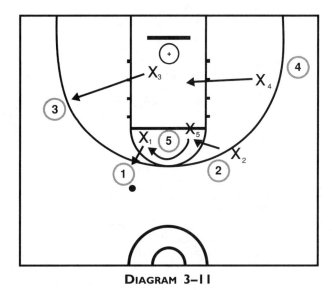

DIAGRAM 3–11

Of course, this does not imply that the defenders should alter their overall strategy or tactics if such efforts are successful in harassing and disturbing the offensive attack. There is no need to reinvent the wheel when one's current efforts are successful. Changing for the sake of change is foolish. If a team's defensive strategy or tactic is effective, keep pouring it on until the opponents are able to solve the riddle, if ever. However, part of a team's strategy may be to implement a variety of defensive tactics, such as switching from a zone defense to a man-to-man defense or alternating from a man-to-man quarter-court defense to a full-court zone press following their own made baskets.

Sometimes, offensive players become so accustomed to solving a problem in a certain way—such as getting the ball into play or moving the ball into the wing or into the post—that they experience great difficulty when forced to solve the problem in another way. Thus, when defenders allow opponents easily to pass the ball into a wing or the high post area, and then suddenly exert extreme pressure against such passes, the result can be catastrophic for the offense.

Consequently, some teams allow their opponents, for a limited period of time, to move the ball to specific areas of the floor. In essence, the offensive players are being lulled into a false sense of security in solving a specific problem—that is, moving the ball via the dribble or the pass. When the defenders change their tactics and no longer permit such ease of ball movement, the likelihood for miscues and turnovers on behalf of the offense is greatly enhanced. The result is an advantage accruing to the defenders.

POSITION DEFENSE: MAN-TO-MAN PRINCIPLES

There are many principles or guidelines that players must remain cognizant of if they are going to be effective in exerting a powerful, man-to-man, defensive attack. The application of these guidelines vary in light of ① the location of each defensive player, ② the location of the offensive personnel, and, most important, ③ the location of the basketball. The following suggestions and guidelines are presented in terms of the position assumed by the defensive players: guard, post play, and the wing area.

> **Coaching Hint 59**
> There is no urgent need to change defensive tactics or strategies when they are working extremely well.

> **Coaching Hint 60**
> Lull the offensive players into a false sense of security by allowing them to temporarily solve the defensive riddle—then deny the opponents the easy solution.

> **Coaching Hint 61**
> Just as the key to real estate is location, location, location, the key to excellent defense is prevention, prevention, prevention.

Defensive Guard Play

The foundation of excellent man-to-man defense rests with good guard play, especially defensive guard coverage *against the ball.* It is absolutely essential that the offensive player in possession of the ball be under severe defensive pressure by the defense. To do otherwise—that is, to simply lay off and attempt to assume a defensive posture some 2 to 4 feet away, when the passer is close enough to complete scoring passes—is to invite disaster. It does not take a highly skilled offensive player to pick out excellent potential receivers if the passer, as well as the intended receivers, have all the time in the world and are not harassed by the defense.

It cannot be emphasized enough that protecting the ball and/or completing a scoring pass successfully becomes even more difficult, and sometimes impossible, if there is sufficient defensive pressure against *both* the passer and the potential receivers. Any potential pass receiver must be pressured. The ball handler must not be allowed to have the luxury of time to think and decide what to do. He or she must not be allowed to look, at a leisurely pace, for a place to move the ball either via a pass or the dribble. Rather, the ball handler must be the primary target of any defensive attack—so much so, that this opponent becomes preoccupied with protecting the ball and is only secondarily concerned with seeking a possible scoring pass to a teammate. In fact, if the defensive pressure is applied correctly, the passer will usually take the first available (invited) pass option open, just to get rid of the ball and the accompanying blanket defensive pressure.

When defending against the ball handler in the guard position, it is prudent to overplay this opponent, thereby forcing the ball to be dribbled where the defense wants the ball to go. This is accomplished by providing a path of least resistance for the ball handler. For example, the defense might desire to force the ball to be dribbled into the middle of the court where there will be defensive help in the form of X_1 in Diagram 3–12.

This is made possible by X_2 overplaying the ball handler to the latter's right side, thereby inviting or forcing the dribbler to move to the left, toward the top of the key. Or X_2 might want to force ② to the sideline, as seen in Diagram 3–13.

> **Coaching Hint 62**
> Guard ball handlers with extreme pressure when they are capable of completing scoring passes.

> **Coaching Hint 63**
> Guard potential pass receivers with extreme pressure when they are capable of receiving scoring passes.

> **Coaching Hint 64**
> Create a path of least resistance for the ball handler to move the ball.

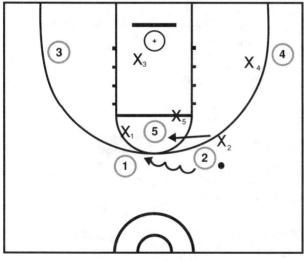

DIAGRAM 3–12

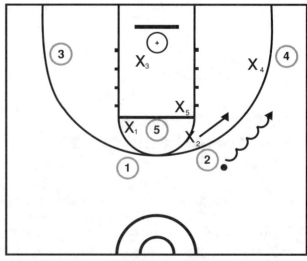

DIAGRAM 3–13

In this case, the defensive pressure would be placed on the left side of ② so that the path of least resistance is toward the sideline.

Defensive Post Play (High, Medium, and Low)

The greatest weakness for any defense, whether it involves a zone defense or a man-to-man defense, is the middle or lane area. Successful passes into the medium or low post slots can just devastate the defense. Even passes into the high post (free throw line area) can create very real difficulties for the defense because of the possible passes that can then be made from that position. Defending a post player can be extremely difficult. Perhaps that is why so many lazy defenders simply play behind their opponents when in this area of the court.

A defensive post player has the responsibility of always challenging any potential pass into the general post area. In a man-to-man defense, just as in a zone defense, allowing the pass into the post area (especially the low and middle post slots) is asking for trouble. Keeping between one's defensive assignment and the ball is a critical rule for any defensive post player.

Playing behind an opponent in the lane, either in the low or medium post positions, is simply inviting disaster. Even offensive players in the high post should be challenged, although it is less of a disaster, although still a matter of concern, when the ball is passed to the high post.

Sometimes, the defensive post player can elect to completely front the offensive player. Other times, a half-front defensive posture is sufficient with the defensive player's arm extended in front of the offensive post player. However, rarely (if ever) should defensive post players, while attempting to prevent a pass, position themselves directly behind their opponents. The lone exception is at the very high post—stationed beyond the free throw line.

Defending the High Post Since the objective of the defense is to prevent or to make difficult a direct pass from a guard or a forward into the high post area, it is necessary to position oneself to the ball side of the offensive player setting up in the high post. Diagram 3–14 provides one scenario in which the offense is set up in a 2-1-2 formation with a single high post, a double guard set, and

> **Coaching Hint 65**
> A pass to an offensive post player *must* be contested at all times.

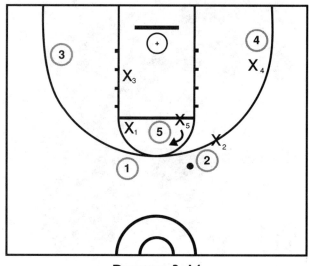

DIAGRAM 3–14

two wide wing players. X_5 must assume a defensive position to the ball side of ⑤. The left hand and left foot of the defensive high post player is extended across and in front of ⑤ in an effort to prevent a direct pass from ② to ⑤ (see Figure 3–6).

Additional Weak-Side Help Any attempt by ② to lob a pass into the high post should be contested by X_1, who sags off the other guard and drops back into the key area. This move can provide very effective defensive assistance. Additionally, X_3 should simultaneously sag off ③ on the weak side of the court to complete the weak-side backup.

Reacting to the Cross-Court Pass A common tactic by offenses seeking to pass into the high post is to move the ball from one guard to the other and then to relay the ball into the post (see Diagram 3–15). To defend this maneuver, it is necessary that the defensive post player attempt to slide in front (over) the high post, while weak-side help comes from X_4, who sags into the lane, as shown, to prevent a lob pass from ① to ⑤.

If X_5 is unable to slide in front of ⑤, it will be necessary to move behind the offensive post. However, in so doing, the defense is vulnerable to a direct pass from the guard slot, ①, to the high post. The only assistance comes from the defensive guard, X_1, who can exert some pressure against the ball handler in an attempt to hinder such a pass. Once such a pass is made from the guard to the high post situated on the free throw line, both defensive guards should sag into the key area to contest any significant offensive movement on behalf of ⑤ and to invite a release pass into the back court area.

Defending the Medium Post A pass into the medium post (side of the lane) can have greater negative consequences for the defense than a pass to the high

FIGURE 3–6 DEFENDING THE HIGH POST

post. This is because of the closer proximity of a potential scorer and passer to the basket. To help negate this potentially dangerous situation, the defender must be positioned to the side of the offensive pivot with an arm in front of the offensive player so as to discourage any pass.

In Diagram 3–16, with the ball in the wing in possession of ②, the defensive pivot, X_5, plays on the *high side* of ⑤. Defensive help is received from X_4, who sags slightly off of the corner player. Should a pass be made from the wing to the corner, X_4 must immediately move out to challenge this new threat. *Simultaneously*, the defensive post slides in front of X_5 by extending the front leg forward and stepping across and in front of X_5. This enables the defender to stay between the new ball handler and potential passer, ④, and the potential receiver, ⑤. Once on the *low* side of the offensive post player, X_5 now half-fronts the post player while extending the right arm in front of this offensive threat. Weak-side defensive help, in this situation, comes from X_3, who sags off of ③ and slides into the lane.

Defending the Low Post The same principles involved in defending against the medium post are applicable in guarding the low post player. To combat (guard) the low post threat, the defender has three options: Two are acceptable; the other should never be done. First, the defender may attempt to completely front the low post player. Second, the defender may overplay one side of the offensive low post threat. And third, the defender—if foolish enough or lazy enough—may elect to attempt to play defense from behind the low post opponent.

When completely fronting the offensive low post threat, ball side, the defender must anticipate that the opponent will probably not just stand there, at least not for very long. One option always open to such an offensive player is to vacate the low post position and cut across the lane. Another option involves maneuvering around the defensive player to once again take up a position in front of the defender.

Playing Defense on Top of or Below the Low Post Opponent If the defender elects not to completely front the low post player, there is always the question of whether one should take up a position on the "bottom" or on "top"

> **Coaching Hint 66**
> Always front or half-front the offensive low post player.

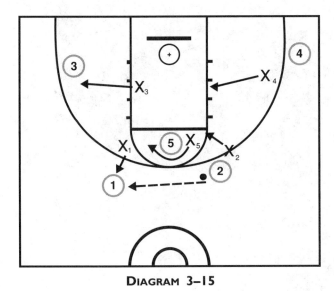

DIAGRAM 3–15

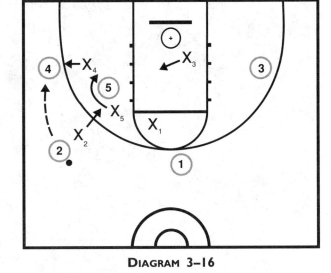

DIAGRAM 3–16

of the offensive low post player (see Figures 3–7 and 3–8). When the ball handler is stationed in the wing, it is best for the defensive post player to be positioned on the high side (see Diagram 3–17). The reason for this is that the passing angle is more difficult from the wing. Also, if there is a teammate in the corner, there is the possibility of receiving sagging assistance from X₄.

On the other hand, when the ball is moved to the corner, the defensive post player should preferably be half-fronting ⑤ from the low or baseline side (see Diagram 3–18). Again, this is because of the poor passing angle that exists for the corner ball handler coupled with the availability of weak-side help from one's teammates. And, as stated earlier, when such a pass is made from ② to ④, the low post defender should slide in front of ⑤. This is done in an effort to provide continuous defensive coverage against ⑤ as the defender shifts from the "top" to the "bottom" defensive position against the low post threat.

Preventing the Lob Pass into the Low Post Slot Whenever a defender plays in front of or to the side of an opponent in the post area, there is always the danger of a lob pass being attempted. To help counteract this constant threat, two things are necessary. First, it is necessary that intense pressure be applied against the ball handler (the potential passer), to prevent just such a pass. Second, weak-side help must be available.

Defending the "Flash Pivot" Cut Typically, an offensive post (pivot) player, located on the opposite side of the free throw lane from the ball handler, will execute what is called a "flash" cut or pivot in an effort to become free for a pass. This "flash" pivot maneuver involves a quick move across from one side of the free throw lane to the other (ball) side, as in Diagram 3–19. When this happens, it is essential that the defensive post player lead the offensive player who is

FIGURE 3–7 DEFENDING THE LOW POST

FIGURE 3–8 DEFENDING THE LOW POST

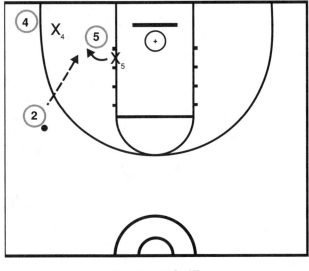

DIAGRAM 3–17

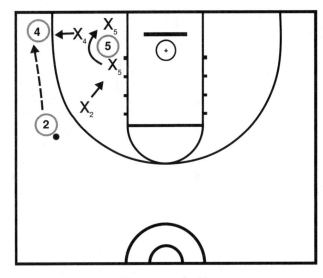

DIAGRAM 3–18

"flashing" across the lane, keeping between the ball and the intended receiver. The concept is simple: The defensive player must stay between the ball and the assigned offensive player.

In Diagram 3–20, there were originally two post players, both situated on either side of the lane, in low post positions. With the ball on the right side of the floor, ④ "flashes" across the lane toward the ball side of the lane. This move across the lane must be vigorously contested and defended by X_4, so that ② will not be able to complete the pass. Remember, a pass into the pivot or lane area places the defensive team in a decided disadvantage. This is because the receiver is then in a position to turn and face the basket, where this new offensive threat may now attempt to score or complete any one of numerous passing options, some directly in front of the basket.

> **Coaching Hint 67**
> Defenders should position themselves between the ball and their defensive assignments.

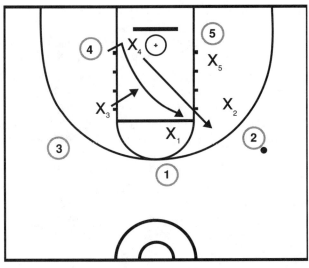

DIAGRAM 3–19

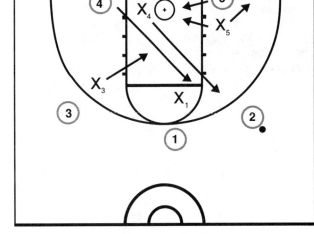

DIAGRAM 3–20

Thus, it is essential that X_4 move as shown, stepping in front of ④ and keeping between the passer and the intended receiver. The defender's left arm is extended in front of ④ in an effort to discourage the pass or to swat away the ball. The defender's head is slightly turned to be able to watch both the passer and the intended receiver. Of course, it is also necessary that X_4 be alert for a possible lob pass from ②. However, if X_2 is doing a good job in exerting blanket defensive coverage against the passer *and* if X_3 (being two passes away from the ball) is properly sagging into the side of the lane, such a successful lob pass becomes highly unlikely.

In this same diagram, a second post player, ⑤, is situated in the ball side low post slot. To prevent a pass to this player, X_5 must half-front, ball side, ⑤. A common offensive maneuver in this situation is what is referred to as a "vacate" move. This tactic has ⑤, realizing that the defensive player is half-fronting, vacating this low post area and sliding across the lane in an effort to either receive a scoring pass or to be in position for a potential rebound should a shot be taken on the right side of the floor.

To counteract this move, X_5 must "open up" toward the ball, as described earlier in this chapter (Diagram 3–9). By pivoting on the left foot and extending the right foot, X_5 is able to keep in close proximity of the low post player. Such a move puts X_5 in an excellent position to intercept an intended lob pass from ②.

Defending the Wing Area

Most offenses start with a pass to the wing area. In fact, if such passes could be prevented, there would be few teams that could run their offense to any great extent. However, it is really not possible to prevent passes into the two wing areas.

What is possible, what is practical, however, is to make these passes so difficult that the offense expends an inordinate amount of time, energy, and effort just to get the ball into play. Such defensive pressure plays havoc with the frustration and patience levels of the offensive players. Even when such a pass is completed into the wing, the receiver should be forced farther away from the basket than would be normal had such pressure defense not be present.

As stated earlier, the greatest danger of exerting pressure against the wing player is the fake to the sidelines followed by the backdoor cut toward the basket. However, if the offense is merely successful in completing the pass to the wing player, in spite of defensive pressure, what has the defense lost? Nothing. Absolutely nothing.

Defenders need to realize that they lose nothing by exerting defensive pressure against their opponents as long as the offense is unable to gain easy baskets as a result of defensive mistakes or poor choices. If the offense is able to overcome defensive pressure and is able to complete the pass into the wing area, the defense has not really lost anything.

To the contrary, even with the pass being completed by the opponents, the defense has made the offensive players really work for it. The defense has pushed the offense, has challenged the offense, has attacked the offense, and all that has happened to the defense is that the ball ends up in the wing slot.

On the other side of the coin, however, the offensive players have been exposed to severe and constant pressure (punishment) and have had to work very hard just to get the ball close to where they wanted it. In many instances, the pressure tactics have prevented even this from taking place, since the receiver should have been pushed farther from the basket because of the defen-

Coaching Hint 68
Make the offense work really hard to complete the pass to either wing areas.

Coaching Hint 69
Defenders have nothing to lose and everything to gain by applying pressure defensive tactics—as long as the defense does not give up an easy basket.

sive pressure. Should the defensive pressure periodically cause a turnover or a hurried shot, the effort would have been rewarded twice over.

Coaches should instill in their players the reality that excellent defense will not cause turnovers on a consistent basis. Defenders should get used to the fact that they will sometimes have to work very hard for a long period of time in a game before realizing the benefits of a turnover or a major miscue by the opponents. However, that does not mean that defensive pressure should be abandoned when the offense fails to immediately give up the ball as a direct result of the defenders' efforts.

It may take 5, 10, 15 minutes or longer before the fruits of one's defensive labors may be realized. However, usually the teams that stay with sound defensive strategies will experience much success. The key is to stay with sound defense and place the burden and the pressure on the offense.

When mistakes do take place by the offense as a result of excellent defensive pressure, they tend to occur in bunches, several at a time, sometimes one right after another. This may be because of the ever-increasing pressure that builds up against the offense. Or it may be the result of the defense's mastery of the pressure tactics and adjustment to the countermeasures and tactics of the opponents.

Regardless of why, one mistake typically follows another—and another. Uncannily, mistakes run in streaks. Frustration of the players mounts. Offensive countertactics quickly deteriorate, resulting in another miscue or another poor decision made. And, if the opposition is poised to take advantage of such miscues and lapses in judgment, defensive tactics can become significant offensive weapons.

Defending the Baseline

The key to playing defense along the baseline is usually to prevent the ball handler from driving baseline. Allowing an opponent to drive to the basket via the baseline is typically a cardinal sin by the defense. Defenders should use the baseline as a "teammate"—to trap the dribbler along the baseline and turn him or her back away from the baseline, where one is likely to receive defensive help.

Competent defenders force dribblers away from the baseline, into the wing or even into the middle of the lane where there will be additional defensive assistance. Generally speaking, allowing a dribbler to beat a defense player to the baseline is inexcusable—period. Such a defensive lapse is a sign of poor execution or poor judgment—or poor coaching.

There is one exception to this rule. Specifically, when the defenders "invite" or trap the dribbler along the baseline, it is permissible—even imperative—to encourage the dribbler to advance in that direction. However, in this event, the dribbler soon finds that the defenders have shifted their positions in an effort to double team the would-be offensive threat down "deep" along the baseline. This tactic, although not recommended for continual use, can prove effective in isolated situations.

DEFENDING AGAINST SCREENS

A critical decision for any team employing man-to-man defense is what to do when offensive players screen for one another in an attempt to create a high percentage scoring opportunity. An even more crucial situation is when the screening action involves the ball handler or when the screening action takes place in

> **Coaching Hint 70**
> Pressing teams should not expect to force turnovers every time they apply pressure—turnovers do not occur on schedule.

> **Coaching Hint 71**
> Turnovers and miscues caused by defensive pressure tend to occur in bunches—sometimes after long dry spells.

> **Coaching Hint 72**
> With one exception, never, never, ever allow the dribbler to drive baseline—deny the baseline.

close proximity to the basket. This is because any miscue by the defense could result in an immediate scoring opportunity.

Thus, how a team defends against screens is of paramount importance. For example, coaches need to decide how they want their players to defend against a screen involving a guard and a forward, and between a forward and a post player, and, heaven forbid, between a guard and a post player.

Five Options in Defending against Screens

The most common offensive tactic at all levels of competition is to employ screens against defensive personnel. Screens can be used in many different ways. There are single screens, double screens, and even triple screens. There are screens involving the ball handler and screens involving offensive personnel away from the ball. There are face screens and blind screens. Screens can be erected to create a scoring opportunity for the ball handler who dribbles off of the screen. Screens can also be used to free a player for a scoring pass following a cut around the screen. Screens can be used against man-to-man, zone, and match-up defenses.

In countering all screens, there are two essential elements that must exist. First, it is absolutely essential that the defender guarding the player setting the screen yell out to and otherwise alert the teammate being screened. Second, all defensive personnel should be alert to and anticipate that screens will be created by the offense. Forewarned is forearmed.

Regardless of who sets the screen, the location of the screen(s), or where the ball is located, the defense has five possible options in responding to such tactics. The first four (of the five) tactics are acceptable; the fifth is to be used only rarely, and then in only selected situations. If Option 5 is consistently used by the defense, the ball handlers will have a field day in shooting uncontested jumpers. These five possible options call for the defensive player being screened to:

1. Switch with the defensive player who is guarding the screener (Diagram 3–21).
2. Slide (fight) through (behind) the screen (Diagram 3–22).

> **Coaching Hint 73**
> In countering all screens, the back defensive player has responsibility for warning one's teammate of the impending screen.

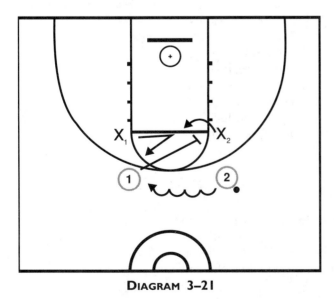

Diagram 3–21

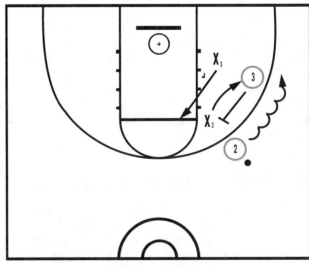

Diagram 3–22

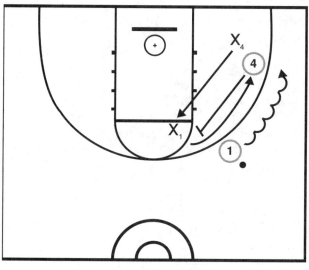

DIAGRAM 3–23

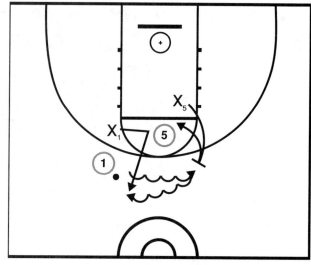

DIAGRAM 3–24

3. Fight over the screen (Diagram 3–23).
4. Have the back player step out and prevent the dribbler from moving around the screen (Diagram 3–24).
5. Move behind both the screener and the defensive teammate guarding the screener (Diagram 3–25).

> **Coaching Hint 74**
> Keep defensive switches to a bare minimum.

Switching in Reaction to a Screen The general rule of thumb regarding defending against screens is to keep defensive switches to a bare minimum, if at all. In reality, the only time when defensive switching might be appropriate is when the screening action involves two offensive guards and the screen takes place well away from the basket (see Diagram 3–21).

For a very important reason, defenders should never allow a screen to force a switch. Such a switch usually creates a mismatch in terms of height or ability between the offensive players and their new defenders, with the advantage

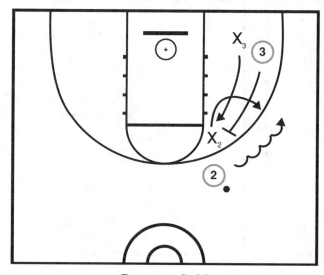

DIAGRAM 3–25

invariably resting with the offense. All too frequently, following a screen, one of the offensive players streaks for the basket in hopes of receiving a scoring pass, being guarded by a smaller opponent.

Another reason why a defensive switch should be discouraged is shown in Diagram 3–26. This illustrates the famous "screen and roll" play—in which the defensive player being screened, X_2, is now positioned behind the screener, ③, who then breaks for the basket in anticipation of the pass from ②. It is very difficult to stop ③ from behind. The reason X_2 is behind is because of the defensive switch. Thus, switching defensive assignments in response to a screen is generally discouraged, except when the switch involves two defensive guards who are well away from the basket.

Another critical defensive mistake is to allow a defensive post player to switch with a teammate in response to a screen and end up attempting to cover an offensive guard. Such a switch usually results in an immediate disaster for the defense by creating a mismatch—a significant mismatch—that almost always favors the offense. Either the offensive post player is defended by a smaller guard as a consequence of the switch or the defensive post is forced to cover a smaller, but quicker guard. Sometimes both situations result. Nothing good for the defense can come from a defensive switch involving a guard and a pivot. On the contrary, the defensive consequences of such a switch are usually catastrophic.

> **Coaching Hint 75**
> Don't accept a defensive switch between a post player and a guard.

A guard-post exchange can be created by the post setting a screen for a guard. However, the defense could also find itself in a situation in which the offensive guard has set the screen against the defensive post player, thus allowing the offensive pivot to break for the basket (see Diagram 3–27). In this example, the defensive guard must now attempt to guard the offensive post player from behind or from the side.

Sliding through the Screen   A generally acceptable option available to the defense in countering a screen is to have the defensive player guarding the opponent setting the screen step back and allow the teammate who is being screened to slide behind the screener (see Diagram 3–22). In this way, the

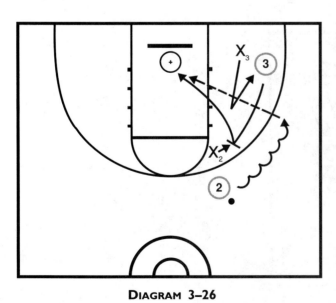

DIAGRAM 3–26   **DIAGRAM 3–27**

defender who is being screened is able to slide between the teammate and the screener while still maintaining some resemblance of defensive coverage against the opponent (see Figure 3–9).

Attempting to slide behind the screener has some very definite drawbacks, however. The primary problem is that this sliding move by X_2 (Diagram 3–22) prevents X_2 from continuing tough defense against the ball handler, ②. In fact, it is entirely possible that ② could just sit behind the screener and take a high percentage field goal attempt, if close enough to the basket.

Fighting over the Top of the Screen Many times, especially when the screening action takes place within close field goal range, the defender who is being screened simply must fight "over" the screen, as shown in Diagram 3–23. That is, X_1 squeezes between the screener, ④, and the offensive player for whom the screen is being set. This requires much practice, but it can be mastered. It takes more desire, hustle, and determination than skill. It is imperative that X_1 be able to place one leg between the screener and the player being screened before squeezing one's body between these players. This is where anticipation, determination, and perseverance place the defensive player in good stead (see Figure 3–10).

Stepping Out to Stop the Dribbler An even more effective defensive response to an attempted screen for the ball handler is illustrated in Diagram 3–24. In this situation, the defender who is guarding the screener simply steps out into the path of the ball handler who is attempting to dribble off of the screen. By stepping or "jumping" into the intended path of the dribbler, it is hoped that the ball handler will be forced to stop and change direction, or to pick up the dribble, or to possibly be called for a charge. If the defender could be successful in forcing ① to turn and dribble back in the opposite direction where X_1 can once again provide defensive coverage, the tactic is successful (see Figure 3–11).

When teaching this "step-in" technique, it is important that the player who steps in be prepared to hustle back to continue coverage against the screener. If not, ⑤ is in a perfect situation to head toward the basket in anticipation of a lob or bounce pass from the ball handler.

FIGURE 3–9 SLIDING THROUGH THE SCREEN

FIGURE 3–10 FIGHTING OVER THE SCREEN

FIGURE 3–11 COMBATTING THE SCREEN BY STEPPING INTO
THE PATH OF THE DRIBBLER

Moving behind both the Screener and the Screener's Defender The worse reaction possible for the defense in response to a screen set by the offense is to have the defender who is being screened move behind *both* the screener and the other defender assigned to guard the screener (see Diagram 3–25). This is because in doing so, the defender being screened is so far removed from that person's offensive responsibility that it is almost impossible to prevent a shot from being taken. Going "behind" two people in an effort to maintain defensive coverage against one's assigned defensive player is suicide, plain and simple.

CONCLUDING COMMENTS REGARDING MAN-TO-MAN DEFENSE

The key to an effective and efficient man-to-man defense rests in the proper execution of those *individual* and *team* skills so necessary in this type of defense. Of course, plain old hustle and hard work are also necessary. Man-to-man defense has been called the "working person's" defense. This is because it demands real work, real dedication, real commitment—almost a devotion—to the art and science of playing man-to-man defense, in a nose-to-nose confrontation. Man-to-man defense is not for the feint of heart.

Aggressive, confrontational, man-to-man defense involves attacking the opponents, individually and collectively. It requires teamwork and cooperation. It involves two-timing or trapping. It involves anticipation and quick reaction. It involves jumping into passing lanes and avoiding and/or fighting over or through screens. It involves denying to the offense what the offense desires.

Good man-to-man pressure defense means making the offensive players work for everything they get, whether it is mere protection of the ball, completion of a pass, executing a dribble, launching a shot, or snaring a rebound. It means making the offense thankful for little things, like getting the ball across the 10-second line, completing a pass, protecting the ball, and preventing numerous turnovers. It means that the offense is thankful in getting off a shot—even if it is not a high percentage shot or is taken in haste against extreme pressure. It means controlling the opponents and taking charge of the tempo of the game. In the end, good defense means success. It also can mean victory for those who are willing to pay the price for mastering the skills and being willing to work in the trenches where man-to-man pressure defense is played.

> **Coaching Hint 76**
> Good man-to-man defense is the "working person's" defense.

4 Zone Presses

A zone press can be a truly effective and devastating tactic when executed properly. It can be effectively implemented as a half-court attack, a three-quarter court pressure attack, or an entire full-court attack. Such an attack can, indeed, play havoc with the very best of opponents.

There are many reasons to utilize zone presses. One of the primary reasons to throw up a zone press is to attempt to force the opponents to turn the ball over either by means of a bad pass or because of a violation. Other reasons are equally as valid. For example, the defense might want to distort the opponent's offensive patterns and force the opponents to shoot outside of their normal patterns or away from their favorite spots. Additionally, zone presses are used to create a defensive rebounding edge and to initiate a fast-break situation from the opponent's missed field goal.

> **Coaching Hint 77**
> Zone presses disrupt opponents' normal tempo.

HALF-COURT ZONE PRESSES

The initial alignment of the half-court version of the "invitational" zone press is shown in Diagram 4–1. The point defensive player, X_1, is positioned just beyond the midcourt line and attempts to force the ball to one side of the court. The objective is to invite the ball to be dribbled or passed across the 10-second line, along the sideline, where two defensive players will attempt to effect a pincher's maneuver or double team the player in possession of the ball.

It is imperative that the double-team action not occur until the ball has been brought across the midcourt line. This is because, once it is across the 10-second line, the ball cannot be moved back across without turning the ball over. Once the double teaming effort has been executed by X_1 and X_2, forcing the offensive player to stop dribbling, there are only four general directions for the ball to be passed (see Diagram 4–2): along the sideline, parallel to the 10-second line, into the middle of the floor, and diagonally across the floor toward the opposite corner area.

The greatest danger area, insofar as the defense is concerned, is for a pass to be made into the middle of the half-court area, near the top of the key. Defensive teams that allow such passes on a consistent basis are not executing the

> **Coaching Hint 78**
> Never allow the ball to be advanced up the middle of the court against the zone press.

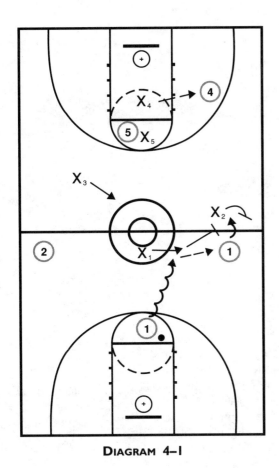

DIAGRAM 4–1

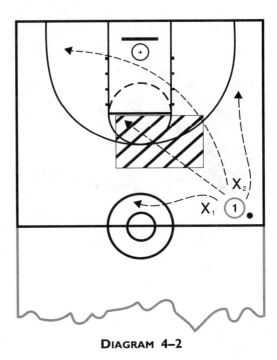

DIAGRAM 4–2

zone press adequately and certainly will not win many games. This deadly pass into the middle of the half court is called the "backbreaker pass" because that is exactly what it does to the team attempting to zone press. It breaks the back of the zone and frequently results in an excellent field goal attempt, if not an actual crib shot.

As a result, it is imperative that no pass be allowed into this critical area. To counteract such an attempt, the middle defensive player, X_5 (see Diagram 4–3), must exert blanket coverage against any offensive threat moving into this middle area. The remaining two defensive players, X_3 and X_4, guard against any potential passes along the 10-second line and along the side line, respectively. This leaves, of course, a part of the court not covered by any defensive pressure—the corner or baseline area diagonally across from where the ball is located.

However, a pass to an offensive player in these areas can be extremely difficult if not downright hazardous for the potential passer, ③. This is because there are two aggressive defensive players, X_1 and X_2, with their hands extended high in the air attempting to deflect or prevent any pass diagonally across the court (see Figure 4–1). The defense is also gambling that if a long lob pass is initiated from ③ to ②, diagonally across the court, the defensive players will be able to react and adjust quickly enough to prevent a high percentage shot from being taken.

In this situation, the defense has, in effect, invited the defense to move the ball across the midcourt line (where it was double teamed). The zone press has

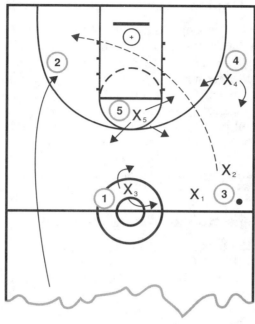

DIAGRAM 4–3

also invited the long lob pass to be made diagonally across the half court. In light of such a zone press, the offense finds itself harassed, double teamed, and denied easy, short passes into the middle, along the sideline or across court parallel with the 10-second line. Also, there is a very definite prospect of having the ball being stolen if a poor pass or violation is made.

FIGURE 4–1 DOUBLE TEAMING THE POTENTIAL PASSER

Use of the Fake Double-Team or Pincher's Attack

Once the ball handler has stopped the dribble, both the defensive pinchers, X_1 and X_2, do not necessarily have to remain and continue to exert pressure on the ball. Rather, the point defensive player, X_1, may simply release from the double-team trap and sag into the middle of the court (see Diagram 4–4). This frees up X_5 to vacate the key area and to concentrate on defending against either the long pass to ② or against a short pass near the top of the key area.

Of course, X_2 still pressures the ball. But ③ is now relegated to being only a passer, having lost the dribble, and is no longer as great an offensive threat. At this point, the five defenders can elect either to stay in a half-court zone set or switch into a man-to-man defense and provide blanket coverage against all four potential receivers as well as against the ball handler.

Inviting the Offense to Pass Along the Sideline

This "invitational" zone press presents the defenders with several additional options to use against the offense. Instead of "inviting" the ball to be passed to the opposite corner (or baseline), as in Diagram 4–3, the defense can adjust the coverage of its personnel and invite the offense to pass along the sideline (see Diagram 4–5). This is done by having X_4 sag more into the middle of the court, thereby helping guard against a potential pass (the backbreaker pass) into this danger area. Such a move invites the pass to be made from ③ to ④, who is roaming along the sideline as shown.

Should such a pass be made, it is the responsibility of X_4 to move out immediately to challenge this new threat while the remaining defenders move as illustrated in Diagram 4–6. If X_2 elects to slide down the sideline and attempts to double team the receiver, the defense can continue in its zone-trapping efforts with X_4 and X_2 being the pinchers, X_5 protecting the baseline and low post, X_3 covering the always dangerous middle area, and X_1 vacillating between helping out the middle area and cutting off any release pass back out along the sideline.

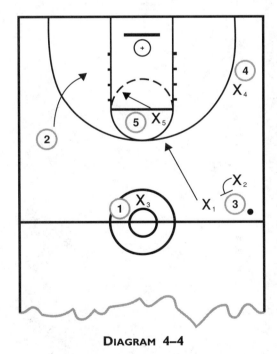

Diagram 4–4

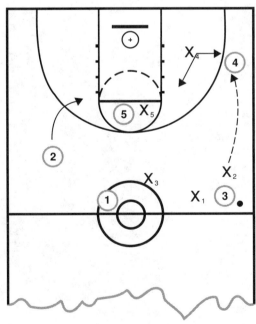

Diagram 4–5

However, if X_2 elects not to attempt to double team the player in the corner, but rather moves into a regular zone defensive position, this is a signal for the other defenders to take up their normal zone posts, as shown in Diagram 4–7. This ability on behalf of the defense to make critical adjustments in the heat of battle can create chaos with an offensive team's pattern or rhythm of play. It also places great pressure on the offense by forcing the offense to interpret what the defense is doing and react accordingly and appropriately in a minimum amount of time.

Inviting the Offense to Pass Along the Ten-Second Line

While ③ is being double teamed in the corner (see Diagram 4–8), another option to open to the defense is to invite a pass along the midcourt line, from ③ to ①. In reaction to this pass, the defense can simply fall back into a regular zone set. the players can attempt to slide across the court in an effort to reestablish another double-team situation against the offensive player who has received the pass.

Yet another variation to this zone press is to allow the offense to advance the ball across midcourt without being double teamed or trapped (see Diagram 4–9). Rather, X_2 stops the forward progress of the ball and X_1 sags into the middle of the court, near the top of the key, thereby inviting a pass along the 10-second line. As the ball is passed from ③ to ①, who relays the ball to ②, the defenders shift their positions to the new ball (left) side of court. It is ② who becomes the victim of the trap or double-teaming action by X_3 and X_1.

The defensive post player, X_5, remains in the middle area to prevent the backbreaker pass. It is the responsibility of X_4 to hustle across the lane to cover any potential pass along the left sideline while X_2 assumes a defensive position between the midcourt line and the top of the key.

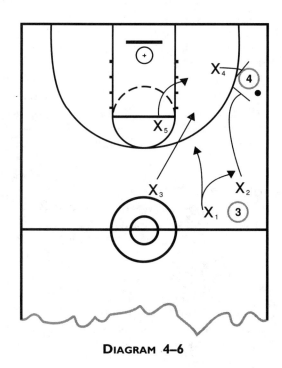

DIAGRAM 4–6

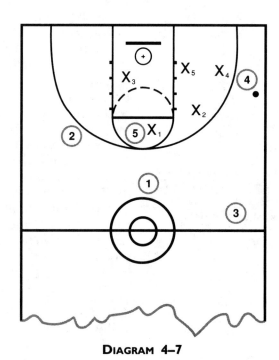

DIAGRAM 4–7

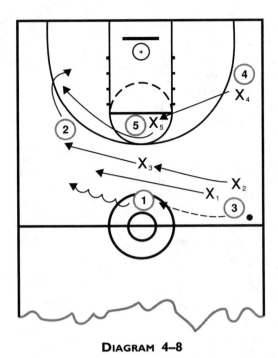

DIAGRAM 4–8

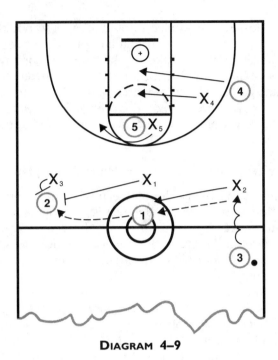

DIAGRAM 4–9

Presenting Different "Fronts" to the Offense

One of the advantages of the half-court zone "invitational" press is that the defense can present a variety of different pressures against the offense in an effort to steal the ball or force a turnover. This is done by inviting the offense to use very specific passing lanes that are deliberately not closed off.

However, at any time during the game, this situation might change, and the passing lane that the offensive team has been successfully using in advancing the ball toward the basket might suddenly disappear and be no longer available to the offense. In this situation, the offense has been lulled into a false sense of security by having been able to "break" the press during one stretch of the game only to find, at a later time in the contest, that this method is no longer available. The end result can be catastrophic for the offense.

Even if the offensive team is able to get off a shot (see Diagrams 4–3 and 4–5), such a shot is usually taken on the run and is hurried. It is hurried because the shooter realizes that a defender is quickly closing in to exert pressure. As a result, not only is there a hurried shot, or a shot taken out of the normal set pattern of the offensive team, but if the shot be missed, the defense is in excellent position to garner the rebound.

This is because the offense, in an effort to attack the zone press, is usually spread over the entire area of the half court, while the defense is more strategically positioned to hit the boards and grab the missed shot. As a consequence, the zoning (pressing) team is also at an advantage in terms of initiating its own fast break down the floor against players who are in less than an ideal defensive posture to prevent a fast break.

> **Coaching Hint 81**
> A zone press can facilitate the defenders' efforts to initiate their own fast break.

Three-Quarter Zone Presses

Zone presses can be extended from the half-court area to cover three-quarters of the court. They can also be extended to cover the entire length of the floor, in which case they are referred to as full-court presses (discussed later). The major distinction between a three-quarter and a full-court zone press is the location on the court where the defense begins to apply extreme pressure against the ball. In the three-quarter zone press, the in-bounds pass is not severely contested. Rather, the defense begins to attack the ball only after the ball has been put into play.

The popular versions of the three-quarter zone press include the 1-3-1, the 1-2-1-1, and the 2-2-1. The major difference between the 1-3-1 and the 1-2-1-1 zone presses, both three-quarter court and full-court presses, is the initial position of the middle defensive player. In the 1-3-1 alignment, the middle defender is aligned even or almost even with the two wide wing players. In the 1-2-1-1 alignment, the middle player is initially stationed closer to the midcourt line. Once the ball has been moved into the back court, the defenders in both the 1-2-1-1 press and the 1-3-1 press move essentially in an identical fashion. The less popular 3-2 zone press usually reverts into a 1-2-1-1 or 1-3-1 defensive alignment once the offensive team positions a player in the middle of the floor.

Trapping in the 1-3-1 or 1-2-1-1 Three-Quarter Zone Presses

The typical three-quarter zone press allows the offensive team to pass the ball into the offensive team's back court without a great deal of pressure. This type of zone press usually allows the player who has been passed the ball to dribble a few steps before the double-team situation is established. This is because once an offensive player stops the dribble, the only option remaining is to pass. Ideally, the defenders will attempt to erect the double screen either in the corners or along the sideline (see Diagram 4–10).

In this instance, ② has received the ball from ① and dribbles along the sideline a few steps before being attacked by two defensive players. Once the double-team trap has been sprung, it is up to X_4 and X_3 to attempt to provide defensive coverage against any passes into the middle, along the sideline, or back to ①, who has now stepped into the playing court. X_5 serves as the safety valve against a successful long court pass up the floor to ⑤.

It is not necessary to attempt to steal the ball every time the ball is put into play. Sometimes, the defense elects not to immediately establish a double-team situation on the initial in-bounds pass. Instead of trapping all of the time, or even at all, the defense exerts light or token pressure against the offense while essentially remaining in the initial formation, whether that alignment is a 1-3-1, a 1-2-1-1, or a 2-2-1 set. The defense is thus able to exert pressure without committing itself. The defensive players must remain vigilant and ready, poised to react to what the offense does, ready to take advantage of any miscue or hesitancy on behalf of the opponents, ready to spring the double-team trap should the opportunity present itself.

A variation of the trapping action involves the defending team *allowing* the ball to be passed back across court (not toward the basket) from ② to ① and on over to ③ before attempting to double team the ball (see Diagram 4–11). In this situation, X_3 and X_1 shift over and act as the pinchers against the ball while X_4 and X_2 attempt to cover two of the remaining passing lanes (along the sideline, along the end line, and in the middle). The long pass is again discouraged by X_5.

Defending against the Easy Basket

One of the greatest dangers for the team employing the zone press is that the ball will be passed beyond the double-team action into the middle area. Less dangerous, but still threatening, is a pass along the sideline toward the offensive

Coaching Hint 82
Defensive players don't have to double team every time the ball is in the corner or along the sideline.

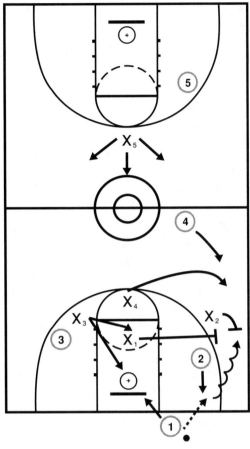

DIAGRAM 4–10

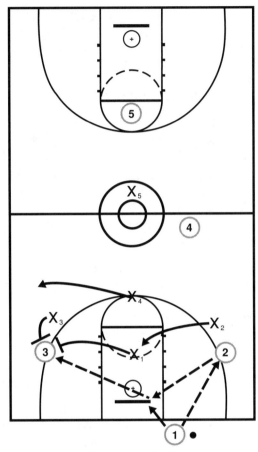

DIAGRAM 4–11

team's basket. In reality, any pass that moves the ball beyond the pinching action toward the opponent's basket is hazardous to the defense's health and well-being. If the defense is not careful, the result will be a easy score by the opponents.

The response to any such offensive tactic must be both immediate and full out—that is, the defenders must turn and hustle down court in an effort to prevent the offense from gaining a numerical advantage in the scoring area down at the opposite end of the court. If defensive players truly hustle down the floor when the offense is successful in advancing the ball (avoiding the double-team action), many, if not most, of the so-called easy shots can be prevented.

A Gambling Three-Quarter Court Zone Press

There will be times when the defense finds itself in a situation in which it may be possible or advantageous to be more of a gambler in terms of executing the zone press. That is, in some game situations, the defense is willing to take greater risks in anticipation of greater rewards (poor shots, turnovers, disruption of the offensive team's tempo). At other times, the defense might find itself in a position in which it desperately must attempt to gain possession of the ball in order to stay in the game, and thus must assume even greater risks.

In either situation, the defensive players must go all out for the steal or turnover. In this gambling three-quarter zone press, the three defensive players not involved in the trapping or pinching maneuvers—X_3, X_4, and X_5—find themselves aligned in a slightly different formation once the double-team trap has been sprung (see Diagram 4–12).

One of the big differences in this version of the zone press is the role that X_5 assumes in this attack. Rather than roaming at the opposite end of the court, attempting to discourage any full-court pass, X_5 must now move toward the ball and assume responsibility for preventing a pass into the back court key area as soon as the trap has been established against ②. With the middle area thus staunchly defended by X_5, it is imperative that X_4 move toward the sideline, ball side, to prevent any escape pass along the sideline from ② to ④. Similarly, it is the responsibility of X_3 to prevent any end line pass along the endline, from ② to ③. The defense, at least at first glance, has put itself in an almost untenable position, by bringing X_5 up the floor to assume a more active defensive posture in the middle of the offensive back court. However, even if the offense has stationed a player, in this case it is ⑤, at the opposite end of the court, it may be extremely difficult for the offense to get the ball to ⑤ from ②.

This is because ② is being aggressively double teamed, trapped, by two defensive players. Both pinchers realize that the greatest potential weakness in this current version of the zone press is the long pass—way down the floor. As a consequence, their hands are up in the air and they concentrate their defensive pressure against any potential full-court pass.

It is exceptionally difficult to make this pass from ② to ⑤ under such severe defensive pressure. Additionally, most offensive players have been taught to

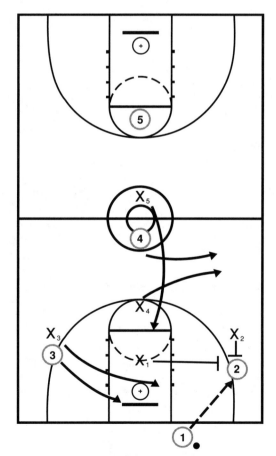

DIAGRAM 4–12

make short passes when facing a zone press. They have been indoctrinated with the expectation that when a zone has effected a two-player trap on the ball, there has to be a nearby mismatch, in terms of players, with the advantage being with the offense. This is not so in this particular situation. Other than ⑤, all of the potential receivers are being covered—almost in a man-to-man type coverage.

Once the trap has been established on the ball, there are two options open to the three remaining defensive players who have taken up their positions zoning the pass lanes. First, X_3, X_4, and X_5 can play any offensive player that comes into their respective areas in an actual man-to-man mode. This makes it extremely difficult for ② to complete a pass. Second, these three defensive players can elect merely to zone their respective areas while assuming their defensive postures.

If executed correctly, either option results in X_3, X_4, and X_5 providing intense defensive pressure against all three nearby offensive players, leaving only ⑤ totally unguarded. But, as stated earlier, ⑤ is a long way from the potential passer who is being harassed by two determined defenders (pinchers).

Yet another option for the defense, and one that can be executed any time there is a double-teaming effort in a zone press, involves one of the pinchers leaving the trap. Specifically, one of the two defensive pinchers, usually the point player on the initial zone formation, releases from the trap and immediately falls back into the middle of the court. This tactic provides much needed, additional pass protection in this vital area.

Naturally, this stunting move does not take place all the time. But, for a variation or as a novelty, this maneuver can be quite effective. The ball handler, not being able to dribble, can just as easily be guarded by *one* defensive player as well as by *two*. And the defensive player who releases can provide additional coverage in the middle of the court.

It is important to realize that this releasing movement by one of the pinchers can be executed at any time a double team situation is established. This is true, whether the initial zone press was initiated as a half-court press, a three-quarter press, or a full-court zone press. In fact, this maneuver can also be initiated from a man-to-man alignment.

For example, there may be times when defensive players elect to double team the ball while being in a man-to-man defense. From this double-team formation, once the dribbler has picked up the ball and is no longer able to move via the dribble, one of the two pinchers can release and fall back so that the defense can once again provide man-to-man coverage against all offensive players. (Refer to Chapter 3, which deals with man-to-man defense, for additional information about double teaming the ball while playing man-to-man defense.)

The 2-2-1 Three-Quarter Zone Press

This particular version of the zone press became extremely popular throughout the country during 1964 to 1975. During these 12 years, the mighty Bruins of UCLA, under the brilliant coaching of John R. Wooden, won 10 NCAA, Division I, championships. This is a feat that will probably never be duplicated again in the sport of basketball.

The particular adaptation of the 2-2-1 zone press is referred to as the "inviting press" because the defense invites the opponents to pass the ball or dribble the ball into specific areas of the floor. Diagram 4–13 illustrates the initial alignment of the players. A imaginary line of 5 to 7 feet is drawn parallel to the end line. It is into this general area that the defense invites the in-bounds pass to be thrown.

Coaching Hint 83

Pass defenders in the zone press can exert either man-to-man coverage or the typical zone-type coverage.

Coaching Hint 84

Once the double-team trap has been established, and the defensive player has ceased dribbling, one of the pinchers may "release" and provide defensive coverage elsewhere.

Coaching Hint 85

The release by one of the two pinchers from the double-team trap can be effected any time and from a half-court, a three-quarter court, or a full-court zone press.

While the initial in-bounds pass is vigorously contested to the ball side corner area by X_1, the pass is invited by X_2 to be made to the weak side of the court, to ③. This is because as the distance of any pass increases, so too does the likelihood for an interception. However, it is not the end of the world if the in-bounds pass is completed to the ball-side corner, to ②. The same zone pressing and trapping principals can be executed on either side of the floor. Later in this chapter, other defensive options are suggested.

The next two defenders, X_3 and X_4, take up positions just beyond the top of the key, as shown. The lone defensive safety player, X_5, may roam side to side just beyond the midcourt line, depending on the position of ⑤, and has responsibility for preventing the full-court pass. X_4, stationed on the weak side of the floor near the midcourt line, has responsibility for defending against any player cutting into the middle of the back court. And X_3 discourages any pass along the sideline area.

Reacting to the In-Bounds Pass

When the ball is passed to ③, the defensive coverage and position of X_2 will vary, depending on what the defense is attempting to accomplish. Assuming that the defense wishes to double team the initial pass receiver, ③ is forced to dribble toward the right sideline, as shown in Diagram 4–14. It is important that the defensive players begin to shift their position as ③ begins to dribble up the court, along the sideline.

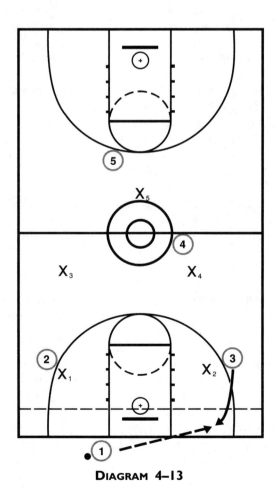

DIAGRAM 4–13   **DIAGRAM 4–14**

It becomes the responsibility for X_4 to move toward ③ to apply the pincher action in conjunction with X_2. Immediately seeing this pass to the weak side, X_3 must move to the middle of the floor while X_5 continues to guard against the long bomb. In reality, X_3 and X_5 can assume almost man-to-man coverage on ④ and ⑤. This is possible since X_1 is in a position—for a few seconds—to guard successfully both ① and ② by merely moving into the middle of the free throw lane. As Diagram 4–14 illustrates, X_1 is directly in line of the flight of any potential pass to either ① or ②.

However, the ability of X_1 to cover two offensive players lasts for only a few seconds, at best. As soon as either ① or ② cuts down court, thereby effectively splitting X_1, the defensive advantage ends. Nevertheless, in many instances, this is all the time that the defense needs to force a turnover. If either ② or ① continue toward the offensive basket, both X_3 and X_1 must, between the two of them, be able to exert defensive coverage on ①, ②, and ④. It now becomes the responsibility of X_3 to protect against the sideline pass while helping to defend, along with X_1, against a pass to the middle. X_1 must guard against the baseline pass as well as pass into the middle area.

Many times, a press that uses a double-team pinching action can be defeated by a quick outlet pass through or over the trap either into the middle or in the direction of the offensive team's basket. If such a pass is completed, the defense is left at a decided disadvantage, since a mismatch is thus created with four offensive players against only three defenders. However, if the pinching action is executed correctly, there is no reason for such a situation to occur consistently.

Far too often the two defensive players acting as pinchers merely stop the dribbler and then act as if their job is finished. In reality, it has only begun. In order for the pincher's movement, and thus the zone press itself, to be successful, it is essential that the trappers exert vigorous pressure to discourage, delay, or prevent the escape pass.

Since the trapped ball handler has four general passing lanes to exploit (baseline, sideline, middle, and long bomb), the pinchers must exert all their efforts, energies, and skill against the passing lanes that are most vulnerable in the particular situation in question. This most vulnerable passing lane will vary as the offense seeks to split the defensive personnel, but generally speaking, the middle of the court is always the most dangerous pass to defend against.

Diagram 4–15 shows the now familiar release tactic in which one of the pinchers falls away or releases from the trap once the dribbler has lost mobility by stopping the dribble. In this scenario, X_4 collapses back to protect the sideline passing lane. Although this move diminishes the pressure and the interference against the passer, it has nevertheless gained man-to-man coverage against all the offensive players.

Reacting to the Successful In-Bounds Pass into the Middle

Should the offense successfully in-bounds the ball directly into the middle of the court, the defenders execute what is called the "flip-flop" maneuver. This tactic has the two midcourt players, X_3 and X_4, immediately exchange positions with X_2 and X_1 (see Diagram 4–16). X_4 and X_3 must immediately trap the receiver, thereby depriving the ball handler of the use of the dribble as well as an outlet pass down the floor.

As soon as X_1 and X_2 realize that the in-bounds pass is being thrown down court, they must scramble toward midcourt, where they will take up their new positions as the back line of the 2-2-1 press. Meanwhile, X_3 and X_4 are constantly harassing the ball carrier as the front two players on the 2-2-1 zone. And X_5 retreats to the basket area, preventing any direct scoring pass from being completed.

Coaching Hint 86
When double teaming, don't just stand there with arms aimlessly waving in the air—be aggressive and purposeful in throwing up the "picket fence."

Coaching Hint 87
If the in-bounds pass goes into the middle against the zone press, retreat and press another time.

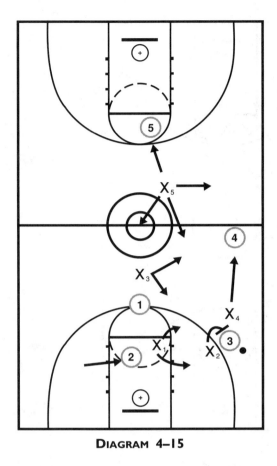

DIAGRAM 4–15

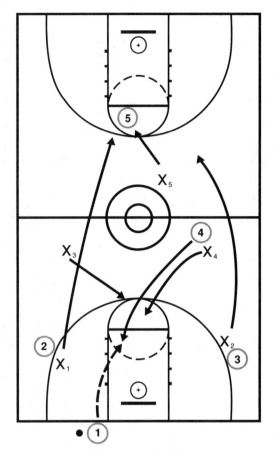

DIAGRAM 4–16

Reacting to the In-bounds Pass to the Ball-Side Corner   If the in-bounds pass is made to the ball-side corner player, the defense is able to initiate two different attacks. The first option open to the defense is to continue the 2-2-1 zone press. This is done by X_1 forcing the dribbler, ②, along the sideline where X_3 can help trap. In this case, X_4 would slide across the court, as shown, with X_2 taking position along the baseline (see Diagram 4–17). As usual, X_5 serves as the safety valve, protecting against the long pass. However, there is another option that can be successfully used and involves changing from a zone press into a man-to-man defensive posture.

This second option open to the defense in reaction to a pass to the ball-side corner involves having each of the defenders pick up an offensive player in a man-to-man defense. For example, X_1 naturally would cover ②. X_2 would have responsibility for guarding ③. X_4 would have responsibility for ④, and X_3 would pick up ①. Naturally, X_5 would have defensive responsibility for ⑤.

There are decided advantages in being able to switch from a zone press to a man-to-man defense. The offense is constantly kept off guard when such a switch occurs. The offense must adjust and adapt in reaction to what the defense does. In short, the defense retains the initial advantage of determining the action, the tempo, and the type of defense and offense that will take place. It is this controlling or dictating ability that gives the defense a decided edge.

Coaching Hint 88
There are definite advantages in being able to switch from one type of pressure defense to another.

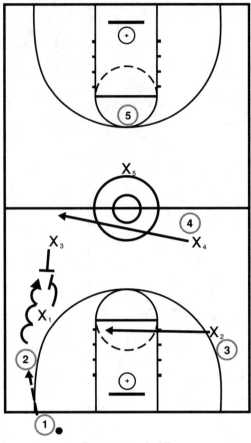

DIAGRAM 4–17

FULL-COURT ZONE PRESSES

The full-court zone press is typically initiated from the familiar 1-3-1 or 1-2-1-1 alignment. This type of formation, with a single point defensive player, enables the defense to cover the floor adequately, places pressure on the in-bounds passer *and on the potential receivers,* and provides for quick trapping action should the ball be successfully passed in-bounds. However, the full-court zone press can also be executed from the 2-2-1 set. The two biggest differences between full-court and three-quarter zone presses center around the initial position of the players making up the press and the amount of pressure placed on the in-bounds passer. In the full-court zone press, the defenders are stationed close to the end line and the in-bounds pass is aggressively contested, making it extremely difficult to successfully complete the in-bounds pass.

Usually, full-court zone presses have one major goal or objective: to steal the ball, *to create a turnover.* This is attempted either by preventing the ball from being successfully passed in-bounds (thereby forcing a turnover) or by establishing an immediate double-team trap as soon as the in-bounds receiver gets the ball. As the pinching action evolves, the remaining three defenders can attempt to cover the various passing lanes (sideline, end line, middle, long bomb), just as in the three-quarter zone presses.

Coaching Hint 89
Utilize the whole-court press to get the ball *now,* to force a turnover or generate an interception.

The point to remember with the full-court press is that the defensive pressure, the defensive attack, is initiated against both the in-bounds passer and against the potential receiver. Thus, the in-bounds pass itself is pressured or threatened. Once the ball is safely passed into play, the double-team trap is immediately created, with a vengeance. The result is that the ball and any subsequent pass is once again placed in jeopardy.

The Pseudo Full-Court Zone Press

Some coaches have found success using a pseudo full-court zone press. This is a press that looks like a full-court press but, in reality, is not. It operates much like the three-quarter zone press or even the half-court zone press in terms of where the double-team trap is established.

Teams running the pseudo full-court zone press create the look of a full-court pressure attack by having the defenders align themselves in an extended formation with the point player aggressively challenging the in-bounds passer. However, the remaining defenders do not pressure the in-bounds pass, nor do they immediately attack the in-bounds receiver. Rather, once the ball has been put into play, the defense retreats back down court, essentially remaining in the 1-3-1 or 1-2-1-1 set.

> **Coaching Hint 90**
> Not all zone presses are what they seem.

The defense is waiting for an opportune time to set an ambush—to create the familiar two-player trap. This trap might be sprung at any time, at the three-quarter mark or even at the half-court area. Thus, this pseudo full-court zone press presents yet another different variation of a press for the offense to recognize and work its way through. Again, the defense has set the tempo, forcing the offense to react to what it, the defense, has initiated.

The 2-2-1 Full-Court Zone Press

Even the 2-2-1 zone press can successfully be used as a full-court attack. Diagram 4–18 shows the initial alignment in which X_3 and X_4 play between the in-bounds passer and their offensive players in their zone areas, all the while harassing the latter. Such an action invites a lob pass *over* their heads. This version of the full-court 2-2-1 zone press is primarily designed to do one thing: gain possession of the ball via a turnover. Meanwhile, both X_1 and X_2 zone their respective areas of the court, preventing a direct in-bounds pass to ④. Both X_2 and X_1 must anticipate cutting up behind and to the blind side of either ③ or ② should the high lob pass be attempted.

CONCLUDING COMMENTS ABOUT ZONE PRESSES

The success of any pressure zone defense is dependent on several variables. First, the players executing the zone press must be confident. They must believe in what they are being asked to do. This does not mean that they should expect to steal the ball or force a turnover every time they run the zone press—far from it, in fact. It does mean, however, that the players must feel comfortable and confident in executing the actual defensive attack. They must know what they are doing and understand the rationale behind the specific zone attack they are being asked to execute.

> **Coaching Hint 91**
> Athletes are more successful in executing that in which they have confidence.

The second factor determining the success or failure of any zone press is the ability of the defenders to react to the offensive tactics in a split-second fashion.

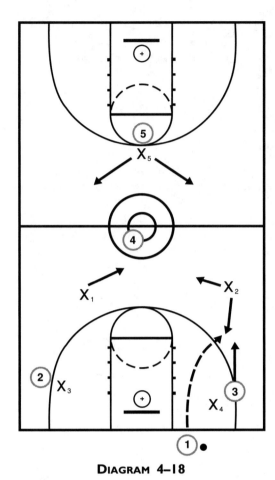

DIAGRAM 4–18

Immediate reaction to the offensive tactics and strategies is absolutely essential if a zone press is to be effective.

The third ingredient in the success or failure of a zone press revolves around the words *dedication* and *hustle*. How hard are the defenders willing to work to get the job done? How dedicated are the athletes to learning, practicing, and perfecting the intricacies of the zone press? How willing are the players to exert maximum effort all the time, in practice and in every minute of every game?

If the athletes being asked to master the zone press have confidence in what they are being asked to learn and execute in actual competition, if they have excellent reaction and anticipation skills, and if they are dedicated and are willing to hustle in executing the zone press, then the likelihood of success is very high. If any of these factors are missing, failure should not be a surprise.

The Offensive Side of Coaching Basketball

ONE HAS TO SCORE TO WIN

To state the obvious, a team has to be able to score if it is to win. This section will deal with ways to do just that—to gain high percentage shots regardless of the type of defensive attack an opponent throws against you. Regardless of how good one's own defense is, a team must still be able to put more points on the board than the opponent if one is to emerge victorious. Thus, individual players, working as a team, must be able consistently to put the ball in the basket. The closer the shot and the less contested, the higher the percentage of the field goal attempt. Usually, the higher percentage shot, the better.

This does not mean, however, that field goal attempts taken at a greater distance from the basket are ill advised and should not be taken; quite the contrary. With the advent of the 3-point shot (in 1986 for college and in 1987 for high schools), there has been a new emphasis on field goal attempts taken from beyond the 19-foot, 9-inch mark. The presence of the 3-point shot has forced both defenses and offenses to reevaluate their thinking and adjust their strategies and tactics. Prior to the 3-point shot, offensive teams usually took such long-distance shots only when they were forced to do so.

Today, by necessity, coaches are deliberately including such field goal attempts in their teams' arsenals because of the greater benefit—that is, 3 points instead of 2. The 3-point shot has had great impact on both man-to-man and zone defenses. Today, zone defenders can no longer just sit back in the pack and invite outside shots to be taken—not when successful field goals result in 3 points. Zone defenses have become more aggressive in defending the perimeter shots, especially those attempted by superior shooters.

> **Coaching Hint 92**
> Coaches should deliberately incorporate the 3-point shot in their team's arsenal not only as a last second, catch-up ploy but also as a regular part of the offense.

ESSENTIAL INGREDIENTS FOR AN EFFECTIVE AND EFFICIENT OFFENSIVE SERIES

There are several essential ingredients for any offensive series to be productive and successful. These include being able consistently to create high percentage shots with the potential for securing offensive rebounds should a field goal be unsuccessful. This ability to garner second, and even third, shots via offensive rebounds is a mark of an excellent team and a well-designed offensive attack. Another essential prerequisite for an effective offense is for the offensive players to maintain good floor balance throughout their attacking maneuvers. This floor balance facilitates offensive rebounding *and* prevents the defensive players from gaining too much of an advantage in the transition from defense to offense.

It has often been said that defense begins while a team is still in the offensive mode. This means that what a team is able to accomplish on offense, in terms of both shot selection and floor position, will have a great impact on that team's ability to play defense following a successful or unsuccessful field goal attempt or after a turnover. For example, two excellent ways to diminish the effectiveness of an opposing team's fast break (also see Chapter 2) is to score *and/or* to have excellent floor balance so that one's players are able to make the transition quickly from offense to defense.

Thus, the offenses cited in Chapter 5 (zone offenses) as well as in Chapter 6 (man-to-man offenses) have been designed to accomplish three major objectives: (a) to create high percentage field goal attempts, (b) to provide offensive rebounding opportunities should a field goal attempt be unsuccessful, and (c) to provide excellent floor balance throughout the specific offensive assault, thus enabling the offensive players to immediately make the transition from offense to defense once the opponents gain possession of the ball.

Coaching Hint 93
Defense begins while still on offense.

RECOGNIZING THE TYPE OF DEFENSE BEING PLAYED

If teams are to be consistently successful, they must be able to attack any type of defense thrown against them. To be caught off guard by the defense, to lack the knowledge and ability to solve the defensive puzzle, is usually a mark of an inferior team and/or inadequate coaching.

Thus, a well-coached team is one that has knowledgeable athletes who are ready, confident, and experienced in attacking the defense, regardless of the type employed. A big part of being effective offensively is being able to recognize the type of defense one's opponents are playing and to understand the rationale behind the defenders' choice of a specific type of defense. Thus armed and prepared, the implementation of appropriate countermeasures is much more likely.

Coaching Hint 94
Successful basketball players understand what their opponents are attempting to accomplish by their defensive tactics.

TYPES OF OFFENSES BASED ON DEFENSIVE ATTACKS

A team's offense, in a very real sense, is somewhat dictated by the type of defense being employed against it. Thus, one must be familiar with various possible defensive attacks that one might face in developing a team's offensive repertoire. Typically, there are two types of defenses that most teams utilize as part of their regular quarter-court defensive attacks: the zone defense and the man-to-man defense. Thus, coaches need to prepare their charges to learn how to attack both.

Since both the zone and man-to-man defenses can be adapted and adjusted to be used as half-court, three-quarter, and full-court presses in addition to the regular quarter-court defense, it is necessary that teams be capable of countering such attacks. And, since combination-type defenses (box and one; triangle and two; match-up defenses) also surface from time to time in different situations, offenses against these types of attacks must be learned.

Additional Offensive Maneuvers, Strategies, and Tactics

Additional offensive strategies and tactics must be mastered in terms of using the fast break against both man-to-man and zone defenses. Offensive strategic decisions must be arrived at in terms of special out-of-bounds plays against both zones and man-to-man defenses. Both are examined in Chapter 8.

Not only can an opponent's defense have an effect on a team's choice of offensive tactics but also the skill level, the experience, and the abilities of one's own players will have a major impact on what a coach will employ in terms of offensive attacks. It seems foolish, indeed, to attempt to implement an offense designed to get the ball inside to low post players when these players are very short and/or lack the skills necessary to score from that position. Similarly, the fast-break attack may be inappropriate when the players are very slow and lack good ball-handling skills.

Experienced coaches attempt to adapt their offensive (and defensive) philosophy in light of the caliber of athletes they have on the team. Asking players to do the impossible just because a coach prefers that a specific style of play, strategy, or tactic be employed is imprudent at best and asinine at worst.

This reality is especially important for those coaches who do not enjoy the luxury of being able to recruit from a large area those candidates who will make up their basketball team. At the youth sport level, as well as at most junior and senior high level, coaches usually must work with those youngsters who are available to try out for and actually make the team. Thus, these coaches must adjust or adapt their preference for specific offensive strategies and tactics in light of the caliber of those athletes available within the local talent pool.

College coaches, on the other hand, usually have the resources to recruit athletes from great distances to their programs. These coaches are able to select athletes, wherever they may be, to fit their predetermined offensive philosophies. Even at this level, however, coaches must still take into account individual differences and abilities among their athletes.

Coaching Hint 95
The choice of offensive strategies, tactics, and plays are determined by the skill level and abilities of one's players.

Coaching Hint 96
Adapt an offensive philosophy to match your players' competencies and experience.

5 Attacking Zones

ATTACKING THE REGULAR ZONE DEFENSE

There are several principles that can be followed in attacking regular zone defenses in quarter court:

1. Beat the defenders down the floor and get off a high percentage shot before the zone defense can be set.
2. Once the zone is established on the quarter court, exhibit team and individual patience in attacking the zone and wearing the defenders down (and out).
3. Overload the defense so that there are more offensive players than defensive players on a specific area of the court.
4. Move the ball from one side of the floor to the other before the defenders can react and move.
5. Pass the ball into the low or high post areas, thereby forcing the defenders to sag into the lane.
6. Cut offensive players through the zone and behind individual defenders in an effort to create a numerical mismatch in favor of the offensive team.
7. Move the ball "around the horn" while looking to pass inside.
8. Be patient when attacking the defense; haste does, indeed, make waste when facing the zone.

THE FOUR CARDINAL SINS IN ATTACKING ZONES

In years past, there were four major sins that offensive teams were warned to avoid in their attacks against zone defenses:

1. Do not dribble *against* (around the perimeter of) the zone.
2. Do not dribble *into* the zone.

3. Do not use the so-called *skip pass* (passing the ball from one side of the floor to the other over the outstretched arms of the defenders).

4. Do not *screen* against the zone defenders.

Today, however, many highly successful zone offenses, including the versions presented in this chapter, utilize the tactics of dribbling, screening, and the "skip pass" against all zones, even combination and match-up zones. The reasons for this are because the game of basketball has evolved, the strategies have become more sophisticated, the abilities of the players have increased significantly, and, most important, *the tactics work*.

The Even-Odd Attack Concept against Regular Zone Defenses

Another common practice that has formed the foundation of attacking zones has revolved around the even-odd attack philosophy (see Chapter 2). Simply stated, the even-odd concept means that if the defensive team is aligned with only a single player out front near the top of the key (such as in a 1-2-2 or 1-3-1 zone defense), the offensive players would set up with two players, splitting the lone defender (such as in a 2-1-2 alignment). Conversely, if the defenders presented a double player front (such as in a 2-1-2 or 2-3 zone alignment), the attackers would set up in a single player attack (such as a 1-3-1, 1-2-2, or 1-4 set).

> ### Coaching Hint 97
> Whatever advantage the traditional even-odd zone attack possesses is lost once the ball is moved away from the top of the key.

However, this traditional even-odd attack fails to take into consideration the fact that all standard zones are virtually identical once the ball has penetrated into either wing or has been moved to the baseline area. In short, there is no longer a mismatch or numerical advantage in favor of the offense once the ball is moved away from the top of the key, unless there are some type of additional offensive initiatives. Thus, all even-odd attacks against zone defenses must rely on other tactics in an effort to consistently create high percentage field goal attempts once the ball is moved away from the top of the key. Many of these efforts and tactics involve cutting players through the zone, quickly moving (shifting) the ball from one side of the floor to the other, and using an offensive post player to pose a passing and scoring threat against the zone.

The Ability of Zones to Deny the Inside or the Outside Game

Zone defenses can usually reduce the offensive effectiveness of either the opponent's inside or outside (around the perimeter) game. However, it is usually very rare for zone defenders to reduce or eliminate both the inside and outside attack of the offensive players. Since most defensive teams are usually more concerned with the inside threat than the perimeter attack posed by the opponents, it is not surprising to find that the majority of zones employing a strong defensive pivot player stationed inside the free throw lane, somewhere between the free throw line and the basket (2-1-2, 1-3-1).

> ### Coaching Hint 98
> It is difficult for zone defenses to deny both the "inside" and the "outside" to opponents.

Even those teams (1-2-2, 2-3, or 3-2 zones, for example) that do not initially place a defender in the lane usually give responsibility for defending this critical scoring area to specific defenders, depending on the position of the ball and the location of the opposing players. Thus, the middle area on any zone is always of prime concern to the defenders. This is not to say that the perimeter area is of no concern, especially in light of the 3-point shot. However, in terms of priority, teams usually are more concerned with preventing the close proximity shot than with stopping the 20-foot (or more) field goal attempt, except in special situations usually associated with the closing seconds of a game.

A Baseline Zone Attack from the 2-3 Alignment

This specific offensive attack is equally effective against all types of regular zone defense (1-2-2, 2-1-2, 1-3-1, 2-3, and 3-2), regardless of whether there is a single guard or a double guard front. It is also equally effective regardless of whether there is a defensive post player situated in the lane. This offensive series against zones is unique because, in contrast to most attacks against zones that utilize a strong high post offensive player, this specific offense does not. Rather, there are two low post offensive players, one on either side of the lane, coupled with a single wing player and two guards stationed on either side of the top of the key (see Diagram 5–1).

Overloading the Zone

Using three rotating pivot players takes advantage of the first rule of attacking zones—that is, flooding or overloading (outnumbering the defenders) the zone in a high percentage scoring area. Although this offense is initiated with no single pivot player located in the high post area, there are actually three post players—④, ⑤, and ③—involved in this attack. These three attackers run a continuous, alternating cutting pattern along the baseline area in an effort to free up one of the players for a high percentage shot. The two guards are paired together at the top of the key, ignoring the conventional wisdom that would dictate mismatching the defense at the key area. Thus, whether the defense was in a 1-3-1 or a 2-1-2 initial alignment, the offensive players would still set up and run the offense from the 2-3 set.

Initiating the Offense

The offense can be initiated with the ball being passed or dribbled to the weak-side position, in this example, to the right side of the court. When the ball is moved to the weak-side guard position, the strong side post player, ⑤, cuts across the lane to the right side of the court, to the corner or the wing area. This cutter, in anticipation of a pass from the guard, maneuvers along the baseline and around the face screen set by the weak-side offensive low post teammate,

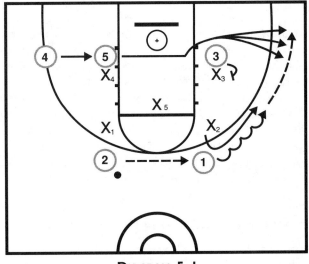

DIAGRAM 5–1

③. Player ④ fills the low post position recently vacated by ⑤, in an effort to gain excellent offensive rebounding position.

In a game situation, the offensive low post player who acts as a screener for the player cutting across the lane is the key in respect to the effectiveness of this initial maneuver. To make this simple screening maneuver effective, it is necessary that ③ merely delay X_3 from exerting continuous coverage against ⑤. Following the face screen, ③ should execute a reverse pivot and open up toward the ball. This simple reverse pivot will position ③ for a possible scoring pass either from the guard or from ⑤ now stationed in the wing area.

It may be necessary for the ball handler to dribble some steps toward the wing to gain a better passing angle to ⑤ or even to ③. This dribbling on behalf of ① also forces X_2 to continue defensive coverage against the ball, so to prevent a high percentage shot to be taken. Thus, this defensive guard cannot sag into the lane and clog up the middle. If ⑤ is not adequately guarded, a pass from ① to ⑤ can result in a high percentage field goal shot. The offensive rebounding chores are assumed by ④, ③, and ②.

The move by ⑤ to the corner or wing area creates several scoring options for the offense. This is because the move forces X_3 to leave the low post in order to defend against this new offensive threat. Once X_3 vacates the low post to extend defensive coverage against ⑤ in the corner, the offensive low post area is vulnerable to a pass from either ⑤ or ①. This vulnerability exists until defensive help arrives in the form of X_5. If a pass can be made to ③, the defense can be attacked by any number of low post power moves in an effort to get off a successful field goal.

Adjustments by the Defense

Once this offensive series is executed a few times, some defenses will attempt to make adjustments, usually in terms of the defensive post play. One of the common adjustments is to remove the single defensive post player and simply align three defensive players along the baseline to match the offensive personnel. However, this adaptation poses no significant challenge for the offense since the same maneuvers can still be executed. In fact, such a move by the defense actually creates some excellent stunting opportunities that can be exploited by the offense, resulting in excellent high percentage field goal attempts.

Use of the Flash Pivot

If the defense matches up along the baseline, the offense is able to counter by moving players to the ball-side high post area. For example, with X_5 situated in the low post (see Diagram 5–2), ④ may elect to cut diagonally across the lane (becoming a flash pivot) toward the high post side of the free throw line. This is done in anticipation of a possible scoring pass from ⑤ or from ①. Should ④ receive the ball while in the high post slot, there are four options available. First, ④ can immediately dribble toward the basket, if not challenged by a defender. Second, a 15-foot shot can be taken (with ③ cutting to the offensive boards). Third, a direct scoring pass may be made to ③, who may attempt to slide in front of the defensive player, X_5. And, fourth, a release pass can be made to either guard or to ⑤ in the corner.

Another Stunting Move Involving the Low Post

Another variation that can be keyed by the offense involves ③, who can elect to move away from the low post slot to the free throw line, ball side. This is done

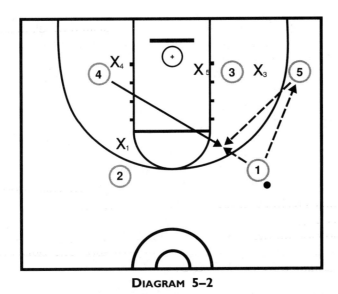

DIAGRAM 5–2

in anticipation of a pass from either ⑤ or ① (see Diagram 5–3). Should ③ vacate the low post area, ④ may slide across the lane, as shown in anticipation of a scoring pass. What the offense has accomplished by such a maneuver is to split the ball-side, low post defensive player, X_5. Should X_5 follow ③ to the high post area, the low post is open for ④ to receive a scoring pass. Should X_5 stay in the low post, a pass to the high post area may be possible.

Continuation of the Offensive Series

If the offense is unable to pass the ball into the lane or elects not to attempt a field goal from the perimeter of the zone, the attack may be continued by moving the ball to the other side of the floor. This is illustrated in Diagram 5–4. Both low post slots are filled by two offensive players, as shown. As the ball is moved from one side of the court to the other, the guards are alert for a possible passing opportunity into the middle.

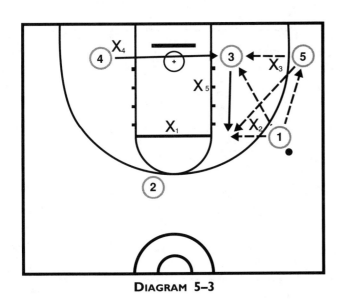

DIAGRAM 5–3

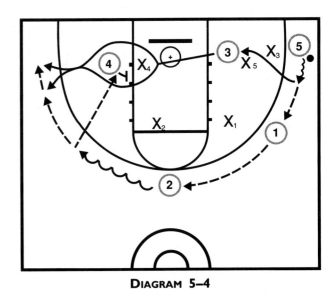

DIAGRAM 5–4

As (or after) the ball is moved to the guard on the opposite side of the court, ③ initiates the now familiar baseline cut out to the corner or the wing area, aided by the face-screening tactics of ④. Once again, the same options described earlier may now be executed but on the left side of the court. A pass may be made directly from ② to ③ or to ④ in the low post. Or ③ can shoot or relay the pass to ④. Of course, ④ may also slide to the high post position at the edge of the free throw line in anticipation of a pass.

Diagram 5–5 shows the continuation of this offensive series with ③ now stationed in the corner or wing area. The now familiar diagonal cut by ⑤ to the ball-side high post creates additional scoring possibilities. The concept behind this zone attack is as simple as the attack itself. The offense attempts to move the ball into the wing or the corner; the defensive player whose responsibility it is to exert defensive pressure against this potential threat is delayed by the screening action of the low post player. The ball is either passed to the wing for the excellent jumper or is passed to the low post player who wheels and deals with a variety of low post power moves.

Lulling the Defense into a False Sense of Security

Many times, the defenders are able to be lulled into a false sense of security by the continuous repetition and execution of this series of alternating cuts and maneuvers by the three baseline players. And, as stated earlier, many defenses leave the 3-second lane area vacant in an effort to exert tight coverage against the two low post threats. When this happens, the offense can exploit the openness of the lane by having either of the low post players fake the familiar cut along the baseline while actually moving into the lane for a quick scoring pass.

THE INSIDE ZONE ATTACK OFFENSE

This inside zone attack gets its name from the fact that the offense seeks to exploit the inside weaknesses of zones by moving the ball inside. The primary scoring opportunities are inside the lane and involve the low post players. An added advantage of this attack is that it is equally effective against a variety of defenses.

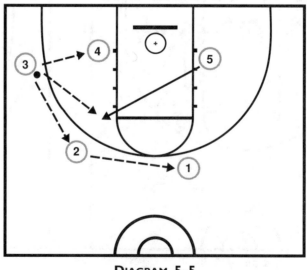

DIAGRAM 5–5

This inside zone attack utilizes a double guard set: two players situated on either side of the lane and a single post player who slides between the high and low post slots. This attack is unique in that the initial offensive alignment is always in the form of a double guard set, whether the defense shows a double guard set or a single defensive player at the point. No effort is made to create an even-odd mismatch in the guard position by the offense.

Since zones essentially have identical defensive alignments in reaction to passes made to the wings or along the baseline, the more effective offensive aspects of this attack do not materialize until the ball is moved to either of the wings or along the baseline. As a result, this inside zone attack is equally effective against all types of zone defenses regardless of their initial formation (1-2-2, 2-3, 3-2, 2-1-2, or 1-3-1).

The Initial Attack

The initial alignment of the offensive zone is a 2-1-2 formation, with a double guard set, a single post player, and two players situated along the baseline, one on each side of the lane. The initial objective is to move the ball to either wing slot, with a teammate either moving toward or already positioned in the corner on the same side of the court. This can be accomplished in one of three ways.

First, the ball handler can merely dribble over to the wing slot. In this event, the nonball guard moves just to the right of the top of the key for floor balance (see Diagram 5–6). In this example, ③ merely slides out to the corner position. Second, the ball handler remains stationary and the nonball guard cuts diagonally through the lane and on out to the wing in anticipation of the pass from the ball handler (see Diagram 5–7). Again, ③ slides out to the corner. Frequently, this cut through the top of the key by ② creates an excellent scoring opportunity for the cutting guard, ②. This is because the defensive player, X_1, who has responsibility for covering ①, cannot drop off to pick up the cutting guard for fear that the ball handler will simply step toward the basket for the high percentage shot. If X_3 attempts to come out to challenge the new wing player, ③, who is along the baseline, is left wide open for a scoring pass from ② or ①.

The third method of getting the ball into the wing involves having a baseline player, ③, cut into the wing area for a possible pass from the guard (see Diagram

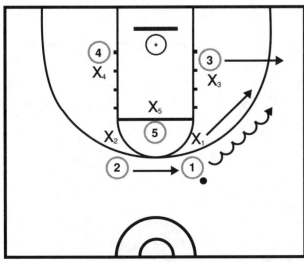

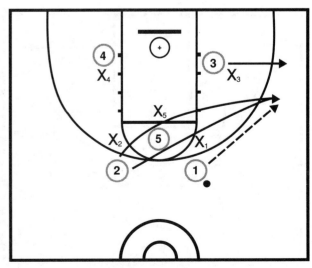

DIAGRAM 5–6   **DIAGRAM 5–7**

5–8). In this event, the opposite offensive baseline player, ④, slides across the lane to fill, momentarily, the vacated baseline slot created by ③, who had moved to the wing. In this scenario, ④ has the option of either taking up position in the ball-side low post slot or moving out to the wing. Simultaneously, ② slides down to fill the baseline slot vacated by ④, thus completing the rotation, culminating in a rough approximation of the initial 2-1-2 formation.

It is important to remember that this offense really begins when the ball is moved to the wing slot. The single offensive post player is free to vacillate between the high and low post, on the ball side. The ultimate objective, however, is to pass the ball to an offensive player who is playing along the baseline area or into the post area, either high or low.

Diagram 5–9 shows a typical example of the resulting alignment of any zone defense once the ball has been advanced into the wing or baseline scoring areas. The goal of the wing player who is in possession of the ball is to relay the ball to the baseline. Once this happens, the offensive players begin a clockwise rotation in which ③ dribbles toward the free throw line extended. At the same time, ④, ②, and ① complete the clockwise rotation cycle. The offensive pivot hovers and jockeys within the lane, near the edge of the free throw line, in an effort, at best, to receive a scoring pass, and at least, to force X_5 and X_2 to be worried about a scoring threat from the high post area.

It is important to note that the entire rotation is keyed by the pass being completed to the corner or baseline area and that the entire rotation is executed *simultaneously*. The success of this offense lies in the movement that is literally forced on the defensive personnel. Specifically, X_3 has responsibility for ③ in the zone. As ③ dribbles away from the baseline toward the wing area, X_3 *must* continue to exert continuous defensive coverage against the ball (until X_1 can assume coverage), so that a high percentage field goal cannot be scored. In so doing, the baseline is vulnerable for a short period of time. Even the ball-side low post slot is of concern to the defense, since the defensive post player must be able to cover the low post slot as well as contest ⑤, who is hovering near the side of the free throw line. Thus, ④ is frequently able to take advantage of this situation by rotating across the lane, along the baseline, to the area previously vacated by ③, in anticipation of a possible scoring pass from ③.

Coaching Hint 99
The offensive rotation is keyed only when the ball is passed into the corner, along the baseline.

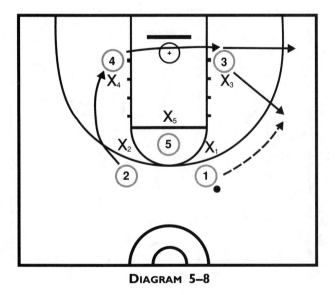

DIAGRAM 5–8

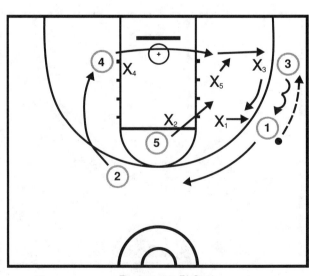

DIAGRAM 5–9

The only defensive player able to exert adequate coverage against ④, who moves across the lane near the baseline, is the defensive pivot who must vacate the defensive position in the lane in order to do so. If X_5 vacates the post position to extend defensive coverage against ④, who has moved toward the corner, the offensive post player merely slides down the lane in anticipation of the potential pass from either ④ or from ③.

One adjustment available to the defense is to send X_4 across the lane to challenge the low post play by ④. However, this reduces, if not eliminates, defensive rebounding strength. Another recourse for the defense is to keep the defensive post player, X_5, near the basket area and require X_3 to leave ③ as soon as the latter passes to the baseline and attempt to stifle any offensive threat by ④. However, from experience, X_3 is just not capable of successfully covering both ③ (who has moved from the corner slot to the wing area) and also ④ (who cuts along the baseline midway between the lane and the corner). Also, if X_3 fails to follow ③ on the dribble to the wing, the offense has an excellent scoring opportunity by splitting the defensive alignment, as X_1 must defend against both ③ and ①.

The continuity of this offense can be seen by having the offensive player who dribbles away from the baseline pass the ball to the player moving along the baseline, across the lane toward the corner slot (see Diagram 5–10). It is this pass from the wing to the corner that keys the entire rotation. The new corner player then begins the familiar dribble away from the baseline and the continuity is in effect.

If the dribbler chooses (elects) not to pass back to the corner area, the ball may be "turned over" to the other side of the court where the rotation is executed counterclockwise. The post player moves to the ball side of the floor and the identical principles are employed on the left side of the court.

THE SPREAD ZONE ATTACK: THE 1-2-2

The spread zone offense has all of the ingredients for an effective and efficient offensive attack against all types of zone defenses. These components include:

1. The use of quick passes
2. Movement of the ball from one side of the court to the other

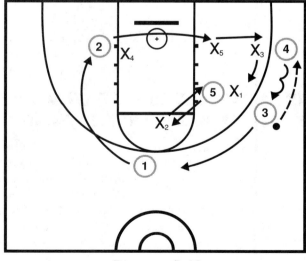

DIAGRAM 5–10

3. The use of the "skip pass"
4. Sliding a post player between the high and low post slots
5. Cutting players through the zone (both toward the ball and away from the ball)
6. Dribbling against the defenders
7. Overloading the zone in the wings
8. Mismatching the defensive personnel at various areas of the court

There are two advantages or unique aspects of the spread zone offense. First, this offense, with very little modification (if any), can also be effective against man-to-man defenses, even those that involve stunting tactics, as well as combination-type defenses. This is because of the positioning of the players, coupled with the simple cutting, dribbling, and screening maneuvers involved in the attack.

The only major adjustment or stunting strategy that may be necessary when facing man-to-man pressure is for the offensive players to more frequently utilize the dribble, in moving the ball and in driving toward the basket, thereby keeping the defenders honest. With patience and repetitive drilling of the fundamentals involved in this attack, players should be able to master the necessary intricacies involved in using this attack against all types of zones as well as man-to-man and even combination-type defenses.

The Value of a Multipurpose Offense

There is an important advantage for a team to be able to attack a variety of defenses with a single offensive series. Such an attack requires less adjustments by the offensive players and thus prevents the opponents from confusing the offense through stunting moves or constant changing of quarter-court defenses.

There is a trend in some coaching circles for teams to employ a variety of different types of defenses throughout a game, continually switching from one type of defense to another. Thus, in some situations, it is far better to stay with only one offensive attack when faced with such switching defenses or combination-type defenses rather than to attempt to read the type of defense being played each and every time players initiate the offense. Also, to totally change one's own offense in reaction to the defense sometimes causes a team to lose momentum, timing, rhythm, and execution, all too often resulting in a lower point production and a loss. This, of course, is exactly what the defense is striving to accomplish.

The second unique feature of this offense is the fact that there is initially no post player in the middle area, near the lane. Instead, the players initially align up in a 1-2-2 spread alignment.

AN OFFENSE EQUALLY EFFECTIVE AGAINST ALL ZONES AND MATCH-UP ATTACKS

Frequently, the defenders attempt to match up with the offensive players. It makes no difference, since all zones, as stated before, react the same once the ball is moved to the wings or to the baseline area. Diagram 5–11 shows the defense set up in an initial 1-3-1 formation to counteract the 1-2-2 offensive set. However, the zone defense could be of any alignment. The zone defense might be executed from a 2-1-2, 2-3, 3-2, or even 1-2-2 formation. It literally makes no difference what type of zone is employed by the defense. *This offense is equally effective against them all.*

> **Coaching Hint 100**
> The best of both worlds is to run an offense that is effective against both zone and man-to-man defenses.

> **Coaching Hint 101**
> A zone attack should be equally effective against all zones.

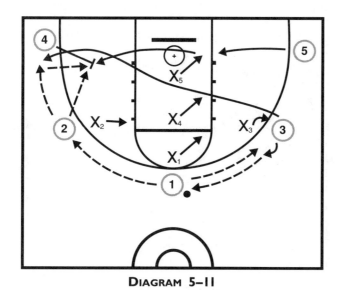

DIAGRAM 5–11

Regardless of the defensive alignment, this spread zone attack is initiated from the 1-2-2 formation. Although there is not a pivot player in the initial alignment, this offense does place different players into the lane to assume temporary positions as post players. This flashing of various post players into the lane, especially when these players come from the so-called blind side (from behind) of the zone defenders, is especially effective. This is because the defenders who are facing their opponents on the perimeter have difficulty in seeing or anticipating when an offensive threat is developing from behind.

The initial offensive thrust involves a pass to either of the two wing areas. Such a pass forces the defenders to react and shift the zone in that direction. This zone shift is very important, as the offensive players will now attempt to utilize a traditional attacking technique of cross-courting the ball from ③ back to the point guard ①. The point guard, in turn, relays the ball to the opposite wing slot, to ②.

The "Skip Pass" or the Cross-Court Pass

There is a very effective alternative to passing the ball to the point guard in an effort to move the ball from one side of the court to the other. This option involves a skip pass or cross-court pass directly from ③ to ②, over the outstretched arms of the defenders. In the past, this skip pass or cross-court pass was considered ineffective for offenses because of the inherent danger of being intercepted by the defense. However, modern thinking has changed the attitude toward this type of pass. Today, players can easily complete such a pass, to the detriment of the defense. This is especially true when defenders sag into the lane in an effort to clog the middle area.

As soon as ③ releases the ball (either to ① or to ②), ③ may immediately cut through the zone, across the free throw lane. As ③ makes this cut out to the opposite corner area, ④ sets up a face-screening action against any defensive player who attempts to shift back to the new ball-side area of the floor. If this delaying (screening) action on behalf of ④ is effective, ③ should be able to receive a pass from ② and may be in a position to take a high percentage shot (see Diagram 5–12).

Coaching Hint 102
The skip pass or cross-court pass, when used judiciously, can be an effective tactic in moving the ball from one side of the floor to the other.

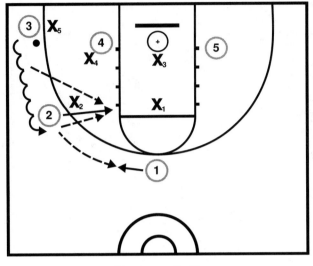

DIAGRAM 5–12

The Face Screen

This baseline screening action by ④ can create several opportunities. If the screener is successful in delaying X_5 from guarding ③, the field goal can be taken by ③. However, if X_5 is able to break through or around the screen successfully, it is only necessary for ④ to execute a reverse pivot and wait for a possible scoring pass, while in the low post area, from either ③ or from ②, who is stationed in the wing.

The off-side offensive rebounding responsibility falls on ⑤, who must crash the board with authority and determination. For the defense, it is X_3 who must retreat from the wing area to compete with ⑤ for the rebound.

If No Field Goal Is Attempted: Continuing the Continuity

If no scoring opportunity presents itself with this initial offensive thrust, the continuity of the offense may be exploited by having ③ dribble away from the baseline while looking to pass to ④ in the low post (see Diagram 5–12). Additionally, the wing player, ②, moves into a temporary high post position and the point guard slides a few steps toward the ball side in order to possibly receive a pass, as shown. These offensive moves create three possible passing options for ③. First, a pass might be made to ④ in the low post. Second, a pass can be made to ②, who has taken up temporary residence as a high post player. And, third, a pass can be made from ③ to ①, who has moved slightly toward the ball side, as illustrated.

The defense is faced with a challenge in that X_5 must continue to provide defensive coverage against the ball so that a high percentage field goal attempt cannot be made. A real dilemma faces X_2. X_2 has to worry about ③ as this offensive threat dribbles from the baseline. However, X_2 must also be concerned with ②, who has cut behind this defender on the way to the ball-side high post. The offensive point guard, by moving to the left, is in perfect position to receive an outlet pass should the ball handler elect to do so.

A Pass into the High Post

Should ② receive a pass while in the high post, the obvious options are either to shoot the 15-foot jumper from the free throw line area or to pass to one of three potential receivers (see Diagram 5–13). A pass can be made from ② to ④, who then jockeys in the low post area. This can be especially effective if X_4 has been fronting ④ in the low post slot. This is because once the ball is passed to the high post area, the defender is behind ④ and a lob pass from ② can result in an easy crib shot. Another passing option involves moving the ball to the opposite side of the floor, to ⑤, who has maneuvered out to the wing for a medium-range shot attempt. Yet another passing option involves a release or outlet pass to the point guard. This pass enables the offense to continue its offensive attack without disruption.

Moving the Attack to the Opposite Side of the Floor

When the outlet pass from either ② or ③ is completed to the point guard, the entire offensive series can be moved to the opposite (right) side of the floor. This can be accomplished in two ways. First, ② may simply slide out to the right wing area while ③ assumes a position in the left wing slot. Thus, the offense is once against set up in a 1-2-2 alignment with the ball in the hands of the single point guard. A second option open to the offense calls for the point guard, ①, who now has the ball, to simply dribble over to the right wing while ② vacates the free throw line area and takes up the position as the new point guard (see Diagram 5–14).

It is important to remember that the entire offensive series can be initiated any time the ball is passed from the point guard to the wing *and* the opposite wing player cuts diagonally through the free throw lane. However, as explained next, the opposite wing player need not cut into the lane every time the ball is moved to the wing slot.

> **Coaching Hint 103**
> In attacking zones, quickly move the ball around the horn, all the while looking *inside*.

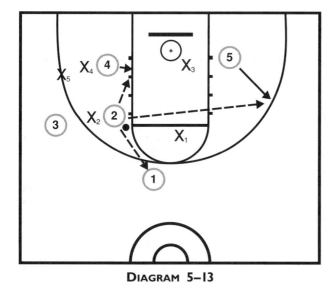

DIAGRAM 5–13

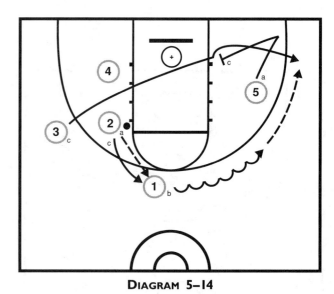

DIAGRAM 5–14

STUNTING MOVES BY THE OFFENSE

Frequently, the ball can be merely moved around the "horn" while the three perimeter players (①, ②, and ③) look inside for a possible scoring pass in the middle. One such stunting opportunity is depicted in Diagram 5–15, which shows ⑤ cutting from behind the defenders as they face the ball handler, ③, who is situated in the left wing. Of course, should ⑤ receive the ball, a turn-around jump shot can be taken. Failing to take a shot, ⑤ could attempt a scoring pass to ④, who should be jockeying for position in the low post. Of course, an outlet pass is always an option to either wing player or to the point guard.

> **Coaching Hint 104**
> Utilize bounce passes and two-handed overhead passes against zones.

OVERHEAD PASSES AGAINST ZONES

To attack zone defenses successfully, players must be competent passers. One should not hesitate to employ the bounce pass as well as the two-handed overhead pass in moving the ball against the zone. The bounce pass enables the passer to take advantage of passing angles that would not otherwise be possible. Regardless of the type of pass employed, athletes must be assertive in their passing. Quick and hard passes (no "balloons" or "floaters") are the order of the day. Soft, floating passes are invitations to disaster.

Another Stunting Maneuver

Yet another stunting move involves the wing player who, following the pass to the corner, cuts not to the high post position (Diagram 5–12), but rather cuts straight toward the basket in anticipation of a return pass from ③ (Diagram 5–16). Failing to get the return pass, ② merely continues through the lane and assumes a position in the opposite wing slot. With ③ dribbling from the corner to the left wing, the original 1-2-2 offensive alignment is once again reestablished and the offense may be continued.

> **Coaching Hint 105**
> Do not hesitate to screen against zone defenses.

It is interesting to note that the screening action in this zone attack is done entirely by either of the two baseline players, ④ and ⑤. When a screen is being set by one of these players, the other baseline player is responsible for the offensive rebound, if any. The remaining three players may rotate to either of the wing slots or can take up a position as a point guard.

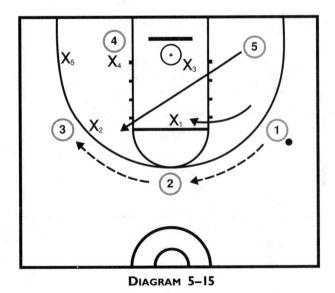

DIAGRAM 5–15

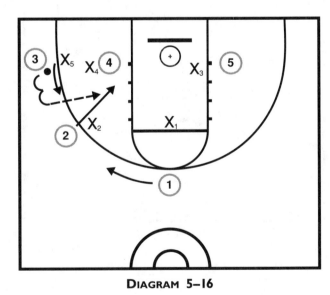

DIAGRAM 5–16

Hiding a Weakness of an Offensive Player

If a team has a specific player who is not suitable for any other position than the point guard, then this offense can be adjusted so that the point guard player *always* remains in position and rarely, if ever, leaves the top of the key to assume a wing position. Of course, this depends on the caliber of athletes the coach has on the team.

Retaining the Threat of Dribbling and Driving to the Basket

This offense creates excellent opportunities for driving to the basket. In fact, ball handlers should take opportunities to dribble into the zone in an effort to force more than one defender to sag and provide defensive pressure. When this happens—that is, when two or more defenders converge to attack the ball handler—a quick outlet pass to an open offensive teammate can result in excellent shot opportunities. As illustrated earlier (Diagram 5–12), once ③ has received the ball following the cut through lane, there are several options open, including taking the shot, passing to the low post player, passing to ② in the high post or to ② should the latter cut directly to the basket, dribbling out to the wing, or passing to ① as an outlet pass.

There is yet another option open to ③, which is illustrated in Diagram 5–17. This option is keyed whenever the ball-side low post player comes out to the corner to set a blind side screen, high or low, against X_5. If ③ elects to drive off of this screen, a give-and-go situation is created, which is just as effective against this zone situation as it would be against any sagging man-to-man type of defense. The fact that ② has vacated the wing position only facilitates the drive off the screen by ③, since X_2 must continue defensive coverage for a split second or two against ②, so that a scoring pass cannot be completed from ③ to ②.

> **Coaching Hint 106**
> Do not hesitate to dribble against zones.

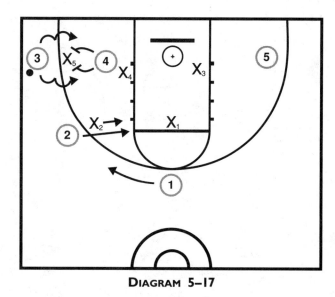

DIAGRAM 5–17

Another Pick-and-Roll Option

Diagram 5–18 shows yet another screening option by one of the wing players that can be utilized to free the point guard for a 15-foot to 17-foot jumper. This option involves a simple screen established by the offensive wing player against the defensive point guard.

If this pick-and-roll maneuver fails to generate a shot, the point guard merely continues to dribble out to the wing and ② rotates out to the top of the key to assume the role of the point guard. The offense then reacts as if the ball was passed to the wing area rather than dribbled there. The offense can continue its attack by moving the ball back around the horn from ① to ② and over to ③, who is stationed in the right wing slot (see Diagram 5–19). As the ball is moved around the horn, ① may elect to cut diagonally through the lane, around the screen set by ⑤, and the attack continues.

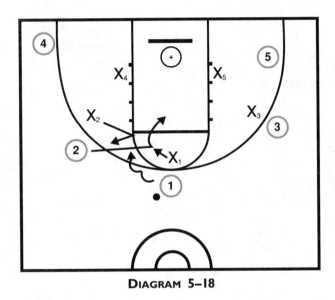

DIAGRAM 5–18

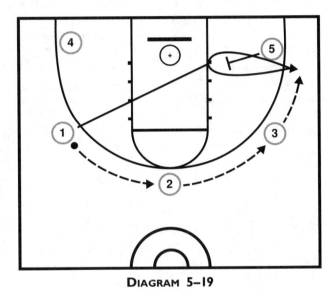

DIAGRAM 5–19

6 Man-to-Man Offense

PRINCIPLES OF MAN-TO-MAN OFFENSE

A man-to-man offense is initiated because the opposing team has chosen to pit one defender against one offensive player in a one-on-one defensive confrontation. This is in contrast to a zone defense in which a defender is assigned a space on the floor and thus defends any offensive player moving into that specific area.

A man-to-man defense can place great pressure against the offensive team. It can also exert significant pressure against individual players because there is usually perpetual defensive pressure against each offensive player, especially the ball handler. Additionally, the presence of other defenders sagging, while playing man-to-man defense, in an effort to render assistance to a teammate can create an even greater challenge for the opponents who are attempting to secure high percentage shots. However, man-to-man defenses, even when executed properly, can be overcome. What is needed is patience and perseverance coupled with a sound offensive attack.

An effective man-to-man offense must be capable of providing protection for the ball itself while simultaneously creating high percentage shots and maintaining proper floor balance. As stated in Chapter 5, offensive floor balance is an absolute necessity if offensive rebounds are to be garnered and if adequate defensive coverage following the transition from offense to defense is to be maintained.

Because man-to-man defenses put such pressure against the offense, especially the ball handler and intended receivers, *it is imperative that players on offense be skilled ball handlers, dribblers, screeners, and passers.* A man-to-man offense must literally attack the defense. This means that each offensive player is literally pitted against the defender in a one-on-one situation (while anticipating that other defenders will attempt to render assistance by sagging). Each offensive player must conquer or overcome or outmaneuver the opponent assigned as that offensive player's defender. Each offensive player must remain a potential scoring threat. This is absolutely critical.

Proper execution of a man-to-man offense implies exactness. Split-second execution and precise timing by the offensive players are required in terms of

Coaching Hint 107
An effective man-to-man offense creates high percentage shots while providing protection for the ball, good offensive rebounding potential, and excellent floor balance.

Coaching Hint 108
An effective offense involves both excellent passing and ball handling.

Coaching Hint 109
Execution and timing are two essential elements in any man-to-man attack.

cuts, feints, drives, screens, fakes, and shots taken. When a screen is set against a defender, it must be set properly, at the appropriate time, and with authority. When a cut to the basket is made, it must be accomplished at the right moment and in an exacting manner if it is to be most effective. When a pass is to be made, it must be executed in the proper manner (perhaps a lob or bounce pass might be required) to the correct receiver and at the appropriate time. And, when a field goal is attempted, it must be the appropriate shot at the proper time by the correct individual from an suitable spot on the court.

SCREENS: AN ESSENTIAL ELEMENT OF ANY MAN-TO-MAN OFFENSE

Every man-to-man offense involves some type of screening action (away from the ball or "on" the ball) in an effort to free a player for an excellent field goal attempt or other offensive move. The three man-to-man offenses presented in this chapter illustrate a wide range of such screening maneuvers. Each of these offenses is also initiated from a different alignment, therefore presenting different "looks" to defenders and thus greater challenges in their efforts to prevent high percentage shots.

In fact, screening is *the* essential ingredient in any successful man-to-man offensive attack or series. It is also one of the most neglected phases of the sport of basketball.

COACHING GUARD PLAY, FORWARD PLAY, AND POST PLAY

When one looks at offensive play, it is natural to look at each of the three major positions on the court—that is, the post position, the forward slots, and the guard area. The following paragraphs speak to some general principles of offensive play in terms of these three major positions on the court.

Players in each of these areas must be able to perform specific skills and assume specific responsibilities usually associated with the type of position played. For example, post play is known for requiring strong rebounding skills, being able to play with one's back to the basket, and possessing excellent low post power moves. Forwards are usually expected to be capable of playing facing the basket, being strong rebounders, fair ball handlers, and capable of shooting off the dribble or from a standing position some distance from the basket. Guards are considered the "generals" of the floor, directing the offense (and defense), being excellent ball handlers and dribblers, and possessing excellent long-range shooting competencies.

> **Coaching Hint 110**
> More and more players are truly multidimensional when it comes to playing different positions on the court.

However, in today's fast-paced game of basketball, more and more players are expected to have abilities and possess skills that, in the not too distant past, would have been normally expected only of players assuming other positions on the court. For example, more and more forwards as well as post players today are excellent ball handlers as well as good perimeter shooters. Guards, too, are assuming more responsibilities for rebounding and posting up in the low post slots. Additionally, in today's modern style of basketball, it is not uncommon to see an individual capable of adequately playing (both on defense and offense) two if not all three positions—that is, being able to successfully compete in the guard slot, the forward position, as well as the post area.

Guard Play

The primary responsibilities for those offensive players in the guard positions are to protect the ball, to remain a scoring threat, to move the ball (via dribbling or passing) into scoring position, and to remain constantly cognizant of offensive floor balance. Some guards even play an important role in offensive rebounding, but this responsibility should never overshadow the need to maintain proper floor balance. After all, it really serves no purpose to score if the opponents are allowed to immediately beat the team down the floor and score in turn.

Guards should be excellent perimeter shooters. This is especially true today with the 3-point shot. Usually, guards attack the defense while facing the basket. If perimeter shooting is lacking, the defensive players are able to sag and clog up the middle of the floor, thereby severely lessening the offensive team's effectiveness. Some offenses even require guards to assume a post position, even the low post. This means that guards must be capable of playing defense while in the low post area.

Typically, it is the guards who become the "floor generals" and who run the offensive show. It is the guards who key and direct the offensive attack. And it is the guards who must be ready to fall back to defend their basket when possession of the ball changes hands.

> **Coaching Hint 111**
> Today, good perimeter shooting is a must on behalf of guards.

Forward Play

Those players assuming the wing or forward position have a primary responsibility of getting into the open while in the wing area in anticipation of a pass from a guard. Most offensive series or attacks are initiated with a pass to the wing. All offensive attacks at least involve a pass from the guard area into one of the two wing slots.

Thus, the forward must be competent in freeing oneself for such a pass. This can be accomplished by using a teammate(s) as a screen or by executing an individual one-on-one move against a defensive player. Once in possession of the ball in the wing area, the forward has very specific responsibilities. However, before the forward can deal with these responsibilities, the player must work to get in the open to receive the ball.

The Backdoor Play   Typically, to free oneself to receive a pass in the wing area, a forward will execute a zig-zag (back and forth) cutting movement toward the basket and back out to the wing area. This is done to shake off the persistent defensive coverage (see Diagram 6–1). This may be repeated several times until the player gets open for a pass. Frequently, especially against very strong defensive ("prevent") pressure, this offensive wing player is able to execute a "backdoor" maneuver. This tactic involves the offensive forward cutting all the way to the basket. In this instance, instead of reversing direction and returning to the wing, the forward continues all the way to the basket in anticipation of the direct scoring pass from the guard.

If successful, this tactic catches the defensive forward in a momentary defensive lapse anticipating either a cut to the wing or literally flat-footed not having anticipated this quick cut to the basket. This is most effective when (a) the defensive player guarding the forward attempts to actually prevent a pass into the wing slot, or (b) when the defender is simply caught napping, or (c) when the defender is watching the ball handler and not paying attention to his or her defensive assignment.

> **Coaching Hint 112**
> A forward must remain a quadruple offensive threat—as a passer, a dribbler, a shooter, and a rebounder.

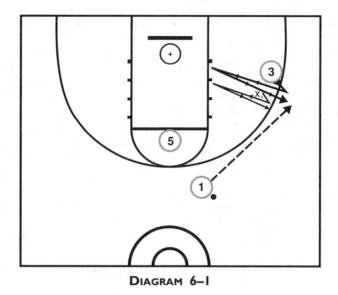

DIAGRAM 6–1

In addition to becoming freed up in order to receive a pass, a forward must be capable of doing something with the ball once the ball is in the wing player's possession. Thus, being able to move the ball by means of the pass or the dribble is absolutely essential. A forward must remain a constant scoring threat to the defense in terms of dribbling, passing, shooting, and offensive rebounding.

In terms of scoring, forwards are frequently expected to be a scoring threat both while away from the basket (facing the basket) as well as when close to the basket (facing away from the basket). The latter situation develops when a forward assumes the role of a pivot player and takes up a position in the low or medium post areas. Thus, forwards are often the so-called Renaissance players who must be able to assume various and different roles while on offense. In some instances, they are called on to play more like guards. In other situations, they assume the responsibilities of pivot players.

Finally, forwards must also assume the role of offensive and defensive rebounders, along with the post player(s). On offense, any time a shot is taken, it is the responsibility for the forward(s) to hit the boards for the potential offensive rebound. Thus, it is very important for any offensive attack to position forwards (as well as the post player) so that they are situated where they can be effective rebounders.

Post Play

Pivot players are primarily responsible for being a scoring threat in close or within 15 feet of the basket. Naturally, they must be strong rebounders and they must be able to handle (protect) the ball while passing to other teammates. More and more teams now involve the post player as an important component of the offensive attack. In modern-day basketball, the pivot player has become an integral part, almost indispensable, of the total offense as a pass receiver, a screener, a shooter, and a passer. In some offensive series, the post player also assumes the role of a dribbler, close to the basket. Of course, rebounding remains a major forte of any post player.

One of the reasons that post players must be good passers is because once a pass has been completed into the post, the typical defensive reaction is for the

Coaching Hint 113
Pivot players must be willing to return passes back to the perimeter if the defense sags.

defenders to sag and render defensive help. This "double-down" reaction by the defenders is to be expected whenever a post player receives the ball in a position on the floor where the post player becomes an immediate scoring threat. When this double-teaming ("double-down") action occurs, the post player must be willing and able to spot the open offensive player(s) and to execute the quick outlet pass, all the while protecting the ball.

Players assuming the pivot position should become comfortable in assuming positions in the low, medium, and high post areas. Far too often, youngsters who are asked to play the post position (especially those tall for their ages) end up playing only with their backs to the basket, while standing around in the low post slot, very close to the basket. Only too infrequently are young pivot players asked to face the basket, either in the high post or the medium post, while in possession of the ball. This is a mistake, because post players today, from the high school level on up, are being asked more and more to assume different responsibilities, including being more mobile and being an offensive threat while facing the bucket some 15 to 17 feet or even further distances from the hoop.

Coaches need to work with their pivot players to teach them how to maneuver in order to free themselves for a potential scoring pass while in the low, medium, and high post positions. Toward this end, offensive post players need to learn how to react in response to a defender who fronts them. These offensive post players must learn how to maneuver in order to get open for a lob pass from a teammate. Once post players have received the ball while in the low to medium post positions, they must be skilled in executing any number of power moves in an effort to score.

> **Coaching Hint 114**
> Post players should be taught to play facing the basket as well as with their backs to the basket.

SPOT SHOOTING

All offensive players must be prepared to shoot the ball in a variety of circumstances, under different situations, and from different positions on the court. Coaches should ensure that players practice taking the types of shots that they will be taking in actual competition. This includes the areas on the court where the players will most likely take shots during actual competition.

Thus, no discussion of offense would be complete without touching on the topic of spot shooting. *Spot shooting* refers to players shooting in practice from specific spots or areas on the court because these same shots will be taken in actual games as a result of the particular type of offensive series or pattern being employed.

For example, an offensive series or attack might call for the guards to be freed for a shot at the top of the key. If this is the case, these guards, during practice, should spend a great deal of time practicing shooting from this spot—the top of the key. If the post player is called on to receive the ball and take a turn-around jumper some 10 feet from the basket, on the left side of the lane, along the baseline, it would behoove this offensive player to practice such shots, at the approximate spots, during practice, with and without defensive pressure. The concept or principle is simple. Players should execute, in practice, the same type of shots that they will take in game situations.

It is important that those players who practice spot shooting do so in a game-like situation. For example, if the offensive series calls for the pivot player to receive the pass after cutting around a screen and then taking one dribble and shooting, then, during practice, this player should practice shooting in a similar

> **Coaching Hint 115**
> Players should practice shooting at those spots where they will usually shoot in games.

> **Coaching Hint 116**
> Simulate actual game conditions when practicing field goal shooting.

fashion. That is, the pivot should practice coming off of a screen, taking one dribble, and then shooting. The coach might even provide minimum defensive pressure (in the form of a defensive player providing token defense—no blocking of the shot) to make the drill even more "realistic."

There are any number of different situations in which offensive players might be called on to attempt a field goal. Some of these include:

1. *Receiving a pass while standing still,* facing the basket, and taking an immediate shot
2. *Receiving a pass while standing still,* facing the basket, then putting the ball on the floor and attempting to drive (with and without the aid of a screen) to the basket against a defender in an effort to get off a shot
3. *Receiving a pass while standing still,* back to the basket, and taking an immediate turn-around shot
4. *Receiving a pass while standing still,* back to the basket, and then dribbling prior to attempting a field goal
5. *Cutting off a screen* in anticipation of a pass and attempting an immediate shot attempt
6. *Cutting off a screen* in anticipation of a pass and then dribbling prior to taking a shot
7. *Dribbling off a screen* for an immediate shot
8. *Dribbling off a screen(s)* and then reversing direction past the screen(s) in an effort to get off a shot
9. *While in possession of the ball and facing a single defensive player,* attacking the defender by attempting either to drive to the basket or to shoot from that spot
10. *Being wide open* (that is, unguarded), then receiving the ball and taking an immediate, uncontested 10- to 15-foot shot

Coaching Hint 117
All practices should emulate game conditions, thus preparing athletes for whatever they might encounter in actual competition.

Each of these situations should be exploited in game situations. In order to do so effectively, players must practice taking shots under these same type of game conditions. One should not practice field goal shooting indiscriminately. Meaningful shooting practice involves shooting field goals under conditions similar to that experienced in games. Practices, in general, should simulate game conditions. The goal is to make practices realistic, especially shooting practice. Thus, players should be placed in situations in practice where they will take the shots that they will take in games.

ATTACKING THE DEFENDER'S FRONT FOOT

When an offensive player has the ball while facing the basket against a single defender, a common tactic is for the ball handler to attack the "front foot" of the defender. This simply means that the ball handler dribbles to the side on which the defender has the front foot extended. Thus, if a defender's left foot is extended forward, the ball handler will dribble off the defender's left side. This is done because it is more difficult, although certainly not impossible, for the defender to maintain proper defensive balance and position while shifting in reaction to the dribbler's move.

QUARTER-COURT OFFENSES

A 1-3-1 Continuity Offense

A 1-3-1 continuity offense has numerous advantages. First, it spreads the offensive players so that there are less opportunities for double teaming by the defense. Second, there is ample movement by the offensive attackers, thus providing a real challenge for the defense to apply and maintain extreme pressure. Third, this attack allows the pivot player to remain in the post, although the pivot player does have ample room in which to maneuver.

A fourth advantage is offensive rebounding is enhanced due to the positioning of the offensive players during and after the various cutting and maneuvering patterns preceding a field goal attempt. Fifth, the offense involves screening and cutting moves, which make it extremely difficult for the defenders to maintain individual one-on-one defensive coverage. As a result, defenders are frequently forced to switch defensive assignments or are placed in the predicament of not being able to apply constant defensive pressure against the ball handler or a potential ball handler. The consequence is that the offensive team is able to create excellent shots with good offensive rebounding possibilities—all the while maintaining good floor balance.

Finally, the offense is a continuity attack. That is, the offense involves a continuous movement of players until a high percentage shot is created. The players do not need to stop attacking the defense in order to reset ("reload") the alignment if the initial option(s) fail to garner a shot. A continuity-type offense has the players constantly attacking the defense. In today's modern game, with the advent of the time clock, a continuity offense can be a decided advantage.

The offense is initiated from the 1-3-1 formation with a single point guard and two wing players. The remaining two players assume positions in the low post and high post slots. Both post players initially position themselves on the same side of the lane (see Diagram 6–2).

Coaching Hint 118
A continuity-type offense can be a significant advantage when considering the time clock.

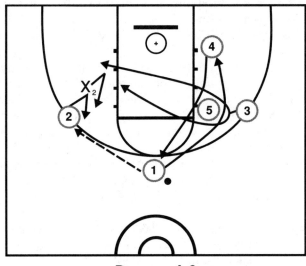

DIAGRAM 6–2

The Weak-Side Attack

A pass to the weak-side wing area keys a shuffle-type cutting action on the opposite side of the floor involving ①, ④ and ③, all three using the high post player, ⑤, as a stationary screen. When the ball is passed to ② in the weak-side wing area, the high post may elect to remain in the high post area or may take a step or two toward the basket and assume a medium post position, on the right side of the lane. This is done in an effort to become an effective stationary screen for three teammates who are now beginning to make their simultaneous cuts.

The point guard and the low post player exchange positions while both attempt to brush their defenders off of the screen set by the medium or high post player, ⑤. Either of the players can cut on either side of the pivot player. At the same time, the strong-side wing player, ③, also uses the post as a stationary screen and maneuvers diagonally across the lane toward the basket, as shown, in anticipation of a possible scoring pass from ②.

This cut by ③ can also be on either side of the screen set by ⑤. Also, this cut by ③ can proceed *or* follow the cutting moves by the other two cutters. If unable to receive a pass on the way across the lane, ③ may elect to vacate the lane area by moving out to the corner. As soon as these three cutters maneuver past the stationary post player, ⑤, the post player moves across the lane, cutting either high, medium, low, in an effort to garner a pass (see Diagram 6–3). There are four passing options available to the ball handler, ②. These include possible scoring passes made to ① in the low post, to ③ cutting across the lane, to ④ at the top of the key, and to the post, ⑤, who subsequently moves across the lane.

Multiple, Simultaneous Cutting Action around a Stationary Pivot The nearly simultaneous cutting movement by these three players around the stationary post is initiated once the successful pass is made to the weak-side wing, ②. Such cutting maneuvers by the three offensive players—all moving at the same time around a single, stationary screen—creates a real challenge for the defenders. There are six players—three offensive players and three defenders—attempting to move around the single post player (and a defensive pivot) who are stationed in either the medium or high post area. All too frequently, a defender will get hung-up on one of the other players or there will be an error involving a defensive switch. The end result will frequently be an offensive player free for a scoring pass.

When these offensive players begin to execute their respective cuts around the stationary post player, it is important that each be able to vary the route they take to reach their eventual destinations. *There are no set rules in terms of which side of the post player the offensive cutters should maneuver as they make their respective moves around the stationary screen.* The three cutters are instructed to vary their routes and to provide as much interference as possible to the defenders. This spontaneity is one of the advantages of this offensive series. Defenders are not able to anticipate the exact cutting avenues and the timing of the offensive players. The advantage rests with the offense.

Stunting Moves Off the Shuffle Cut When defenders do anticipate the cutting avenues of the offensive players, there are various offensive stunting moves that have proven to be successful. For example, Diagram 6–4 shows the point guard apparently making the now familiar move to the low post. However, ① deviates from the expected path and cuts ball side across the lane in hopes of an scoring pass from ②.

| **Coaching Hint 119** |
| Players should not be predictable in their cutting maneuvers or patterns; allow for some spontaneity and individuality. |

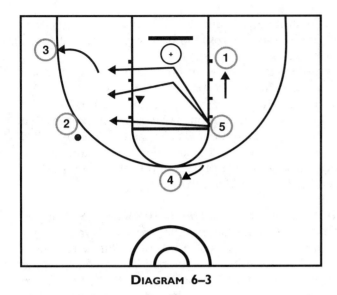

DIAGRAM 6–3

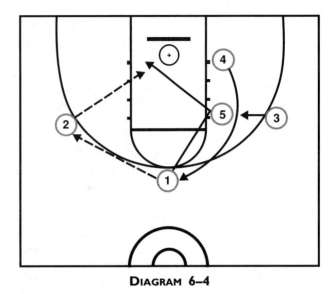

DIAGRAM 6–4

Another very effective stunting move is shown in Diagram 6–5. In this instance, both ① and ⑤ move together to set a double screen for ④, who cuts as shown into the free throw lane for a possible pass from ②. Note that the strong-side wing player, ③, has already made the diagonal cut through the lane by the time the double screen has been set. This stunting move can be keyed by a signal from the point guard or is called by the coach during a time out or during a dead ball situation.

The Continuity Aspect of the Offense Diagram 6–6 illustrates the continuity aspect of this offense with ① darting out to the new weak-side area and the ball being passed to the new point guard, ④. If the ball is moved to the new weak-side wing area, in this case to ①, the familiar shuffle type cutting action is initiated involving ③, ④ and ②, on the left side of the floor. It should be pointed out that ③ can be *stationed either in the corner or in the low post slot* when beginning the shuffle type cut. Regardless of whether ③ is positioned in the corner or in

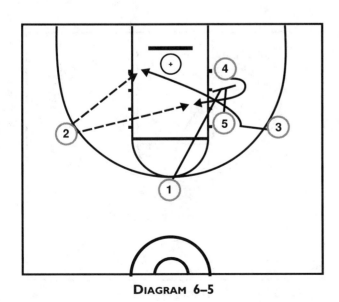

DIAGRAM 6–5

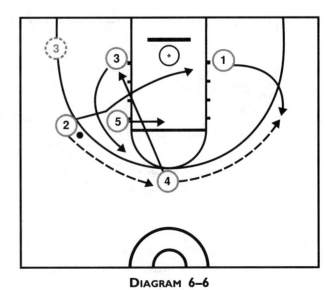

DIAGRAM 6–6

the low post slot, ③ will end up at the top of the key, as shown. The stationary post player, ⑤, makes the cut, high or low, across the lane immediately after the three cutters have made their moves past the post.

This continuity attack from the weak side may be continued until a good shot is taken simply by continuing to move the ball from one side of the floor to the other. With the advent of the shot clock, today's teams do not have the luxury of all the time in the world to get a shot off. Hence, it is important that the offensive players get into the initial alignment (Diagrams 6–2 and 6–6) and start the offense as soon as possible. This weak-side series can usually be run continuously four or five times—from one side of the court to the other—before the players need to be concerned about violating the shot clock.

Beating the Shot Clock: Working One against One in the Wing   Should the players find themselves in danger of running out of time, the 1-3-1 spread alignment of the players (see Diagram 6–7) provides an ideal opportunity to get off a shot in a minimum of time. In this example, once the ball is rotated across the court to the weak-side wing player, the shuffle type cuts by ①, ③, and ② are simply not executed. Thus, the wing player, ④, now has room to work one-on-one against the lone defender without any interference. This tactic should not exceed three to four seconds, at most.

Beating the Shot Clock: Working One against One at the Top of the Circle   Yet another stunting move in response to the shot clock winding down is to have the point guard, ③, attempt to dribble toward the basket, one on one, against X_3, while teammate ④ floats away toward the baseline (see Diagram 6–8). If ③ is unable to drive all the way to the basket because X_4 is sagging into the lane, a simple release pass to ④ will result in a short jumper—all within three to four seconds.

The Pinch Post   An effective scoring option available to the offense whenever the ball is being moved from the strong side of the court to the weak side is called the *pinch post* option (see Diagram 6–9). In this situation, the weak-side wing player, ④, cuts not to the wing but to the edge of the free throw line. This maneuver gives the wing player another place to go in addition to the wing area

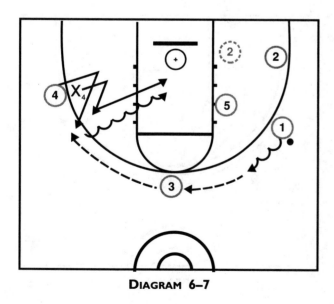

DIAGRAM 6–7

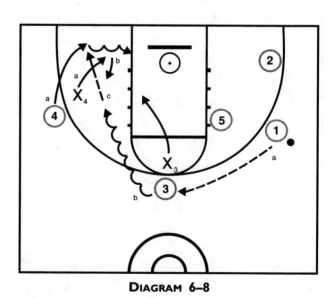

DIAGRAM 6–8

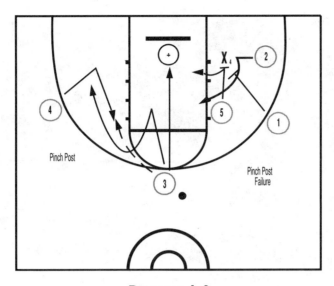

DIAGRAM 6–9

in response to extreme defensive pressure by X_4, while also creating additional scoring options for the offense.

Once ④ has received a pass (while stationed at the edge of the free throw line) from the point guard, action takes place on both sides of the court. Upon passing the ball, the point guard heads directly toward the basket. The guard can continue straight down the middle of the lane to the basket in hope of a return pass. Or, ③ may elect to stop near the free throw line and make a sharp veer cut back out around the ball handler in an attempt to get a hand-off from ④ and take a high percentage shot (see Figures 6–1 through 6–5).

Pinch Post Failure   The action on the right (strong) side of the court involves the pinch post failure option and takes place at the same time that the point guard makes the move toward the basket. The movement on the strong side of the court calls for both ⑤ and ①, once ④ has received the ball from the point

FIGURE 6–1   THE PINCH POST CUT

FIGURE 6–2 THE PINCH POST CUT

guard, to simultaneously move toward teammate ② in an effort to set up a double screen against X₄. Once the double screen has been erected, ② cuts up the lane toward the free throw line extended for a possible pass from ④ and the 15-foot jumper.

Of course, the cross lane pass from ④ to ② will never take place unless the pinch post option fails to garner a high percentage shot, hence, the name *pinch post failure.* A final scoring opportunity involves a direct scoring pass from ④ to ⑤. This pass to the low post slot takes place after ⑤ has pivoted following the screen on behalf of ②. Sometimes, the defenders end up guarding ⑤ from behind, thereby opening the door for this quick scoring pass.

FIGURE 6–3 THE PINCH POST CUT

FIGURE 6–4 THE PINCH POST CUT

The High Post Pass Option

Whenever a pass is completed from the point guard to the high post (see Diagram 6–10), two exchanges take place. First, the strong-side wing player, in this example ③, breaks to the low post to set a face screen against X₄, thus freeing ④ to cut away from the basket and a direct pass from the high post. Following the face screen, ③ pivots clockwise toward the high post with arms outstretched for a possible pass from ⑤. The second exchange takes place between the point guard and the weak-side wing player. This simple maneuver, in which one of the offensive players screens for the other, maintains floor balance while also

FIGURE 6–5 THE PINCH POST CUT

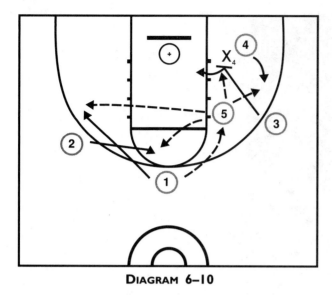

DIAGRAM 6–10

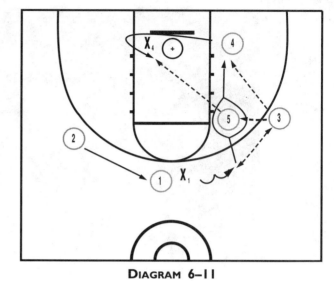

DIAGRAM 6–11

creating an outlet pass for ⑤ if necessary. Of course, ⑤ can also elect to put the ball on the floor and attempt to dribble directly to the basket.

The Strong-Side Attack

The strong-side attack of the 1-3-1 continuity offense is depicted in Diagram 6–11. This is a quick, hard-hitting scoring option that can be concluded in less than 3 seconds. In this instance, the point guard dribbles toward the strong side and passes the ball to the wing player, ③. As soon as the pass is completed, ④, whether stationed in the corner or in the low post slot, slides across the lane, as shown.

At the same time, the point guard heads for the basket using the high post player as a stationary screen to rub off the defensive player ①. If successful, a quick pass from ③ to ① results in a crib shot (see Figures 6–6 through 6–8). Floor balance throughout this attack is maintained by the weak side wing player, ②, moving out to the top of the key.

FIGURE 6–6 SETTING UP THE SCREEN OFF THE HIGH POST

FIGURE 6-7   RUBBING THE DEFENSIVE PLAYER OFF THE HIGH POST

If no pass from ③ to ① is forthcoming, this strong-side series continues with the high post stepping toward the wing in anticipation of a pass, as soon as ① breaks to the basket. Once the pass is made to the high post by ③, the post merely *pivots clockwise* and looks toward the opposite low post slot in an effort to make a direct pass to ④, who has, in the meanwhile, stepped into the lane, in front of X_4, as shown.

Ideally, the attacking options just described would be chosen by the offensive players because that is what they would prefer to execute. However, in actual game situations, offensive teams find that they frequently initiate options because the defense either permits them to do so or because the defense is unsuccessful in stopping the particular option or attack.

For example, if the defender guarding the weak-side wing player (Diagram 6–2) is unable to prevent the ball from being passed to ② in the wing, the offense can initiate the shuffle cut or *weak-side* options. However, if the defender guarding the weak-side wing area in Diagram 6–9 is able to provide such pressure

> **Coaching Hint 120**
> There is nothing wrong with initiating specific offensive options because of the type of defense being played by the opponents.

FIGURE 6-8   RECEIVING THE LEAD PASS FOLLOWING THE HIGH-POST CUT

FIGURE 6–9 SCORING FROM THE LOW POST POSITION

FIGURE 6–10 SCORING FROM THE LOW POST POSITION

Coaching Hint 121

Offensive players can initiate (key) any of the weak-side, strong-side, or high post options whenever the ball is moved to the top of the circle.

against ④ that the pass cannot be safely completed to the wing, it may be necessary for ④ to cut to the edge of the free throw line, thus keying or initiating the pinch post and the pinch post failure options. Or, if the ball cannot be passed to that side (weak side) of the court at all, the point guard may turn to the strong side of the court (Diagram 6–11) and pass the ball to that wing area, thereby keying the *strong-side options*. Or, the ball may be passed to the high post played by the point guard (Diagram 6–10) with the *high post options* therefore being keyed.

The point is that offensive players should not force passes. Doing so results in poorly executed attacks, at best, and in turnovers and failure (defeat), at worst. This offense is designed so that whatever pass is able to be completed (whether to the weak side, to the strong side, or to the high post), an effective, simple, and quick-hitting offensive attack is keyed or initiated. In one sense, the offense keys or initiates those options that the defense allows or that the offense creates (not forces). The key is in knowing the difference between forcing an option and taking advantage of what is available in light of the defensive pressure.

THE 2-3 CONTINUITY OFFENSE

This is a very, very simple offense that is also extremely effective. It can be equally effective at the college level, at the secondary level, and even at the junior high level. The attack is initiated from the 2-3 alignment with two guards, two

FIGURE 6–11 SCORING FROM THE LOW
POST POSITION

FIGURE 6–12 SCORING FROM THE LOW
POST POSITION

wing players, and a single post player situated on either side of the lane, in close proximity of the basket (see Diagram 6–12). The major advantages of this simplistic offense include:

1. The cutting maneuvers required of the players are not difficult to teach or execute.
2. The offensive players are stationed relatively near the basket when they execute their cutting moves.
3. There is almost constant motion of all five offensive players.
4. Excellent, high percentage shots, in close proximity to the basket, are created.
5. All five players rotate to assume all five positions, thus providing a challenge for the defenders who are forced to play unfamiliar areas on the court.
6. Minimal passes are required and the players are close together.

Starting the Offense

The offense can be initiated whenever one of the guards passes the ball to the other guard. Diagram 6–12 shows the initial alignment of the players with the strong-side guard, ①, in possession of the ball. The objective is to pass the ball to the weak-side guard slot, to ②. If there is defensive pressure discouraging such a pass, the weak-side guard and the weak-side forward initiate an exchange, as shown. In this event, the weak-side guard "head hunts" (screens) for the defensive player, X_4. This frees ④ to cut to the now vacant guard slot in anticipation

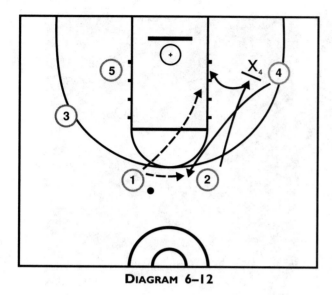

DIAGRAM 6–12

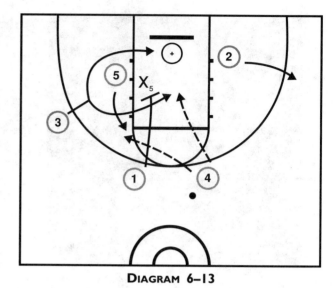

DIAGRAM 6–13

of a pass. If ② is successful in the screening efforts against X₄, it may be possible for ① to make a direct pass to ②, who pivots and breaks for the basket following the screening action.

If the ball is passed to ④ in the guard slot, ② vacates the lane area by sliding out to the right wing. At the same time, both ③ and ① start to initiate cutting moves, as shown in Diagram 6–13. ① cuts down the lane to set a "head hunting" pick for the teammate stationed in the low post (against X₅). Simultaneously, ③ cuts across the lane while using both ① and ⑤, and their respective defensive players, X₅ and X₁, as potential screens.

The Continuity Continues

The weak-side guard, ④, now has several passing options, depending on defensive lapses. The first option involves a pass to ③ as this cutter moves through the lane. The second passing option involves a pass to ⑤, who has moved around the face screen set by ① to the edge of the free throw line. Should this pass result in a 15-foot turn-around jumper by ⑤, offensive rebounding becomes the responsibility of ①, ③, and ②.

It may even be possible for a pass to be made directly to ①, who now assumes the low post position. This third passing option is sometimes feasible because of the confusion created by all of the cutting movements and screening action taking place along the side of the lane. As a result, ① is sometimes not adequately defended and the scoring pass is possible. The only danger involving ① is that this player must not hesitate while standing in the lane, lest the official call the 3-second lane violation.

If none of these scoring passes is made, the initial alignment of the players is as depicted in Diagram 6–14, with ⑤ now assuming a guard position on the weak side and ④ filling the strong-side guard position. The two wing slots are filled by ① and ② and the single post position is taken by ③. As already stated, this offensive series may be continued with a pass from one guard—in this case, the strong-side guard ④— to the weak-side guard, ⑤. Once this pass is completed, the result is the now familiar cutting moves, as illustrated.

It is important to remember that the weak-side guard, ⑤, and the weak-side forward, ①, may interchange positions at any time. This can be done either because they simply desire to do so or because of the extreme defensive pressure being exerted by X_5 against ⑤. Whenever the lateral pass is completed to the offensive player in the weak-side guard slot, the now familiar cutting moves by the strong-side guard, ④, and the strong-side wing player ② are initiated (see Diagram 6–14). In essence, this offense can continue merely with passes between the players who are then stationed in the two guard slots.

A Stunting Move

As stated before, the usual passing option involves a pass from the strong-side guard to the weak-side guard followed by the various cutting moves of the post by the remaining strong-side players. However, the strong-side guard need not always complete this pass to a running mate in the other guard position. Sometimes, the defenders are able to prevent such a pass or the ball handler just elects not to make the pass to the other guard.

Instead, a pass is made to the strong-side wing player, ①, (see Diagram 6–15). This pass is the signal or key for the opposite wing player—①, in this case—to flash across the lane to the high post position, free throw line extended.

This flash pivot cut by ① creates two advantages for the offense. First, the ball might be able to be passed (lobbed) to ③ in the low post position. This is especially true if X_3 is intent on fronting ③, since X_1 is no longer able to provide weak side help. Second, any pass directly to ① following the flash across the lane creates a possibility of a high percentage shot. This is especially true if X_1 fails to follow ① in a "prevent" defensive posture as the latter makes the cross-court cut. If ① does receive the ball following the move across the lane, a turnaround jumper might result or ① might simply dump the ball into the low post player who has meanwhile executed a step into the lane, toward the basket.

The flash pivot by ① can play havoc with the defender guarding the offensive low post player. If X_3 plays behind ③, it is very simple for ② to complete a bounce pass to the low post. However, if X_3 attempts to front the low post player, there is no defensive help on the weak side once ① and X_1 flash across the lane. As a result, a lob pass from ② to ③ can be completed.

Of course, if X_1 is not able to or chooses not to advance across the lane in front of ① as the flash pivot move is completed, the ball will end up in the hands

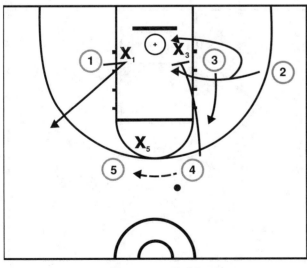

DIAGRAM 6–14

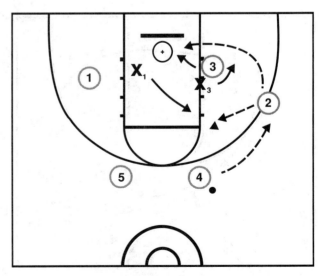

DIAGRAM 6–15

of ① at the high post. In that eventuality, a bounce pass from ① to ③ is extremely successful if X_3 is playing behind ③. If X_3 is in front, a lob pass from ① to ③ is in order. In fact, no matter how the lone defensive low post player is positioned, the offense has several excellent methods to get the ball inside to the low post for a high percentage scoring attempt.

A Second Stunting Move

What happens when the strong-side guard, with the ball, is unable to pass to either the other guard or to the strong-side wing? Well, the simplest maneuver is for this ball handler to simply begin to dribble toward the wing, as shown in Diagram 6–16. In this eventuality, the wing player, ②, vacates the wing area and breaks for the basket as shown, and rotates to the opposite side of the court. Other offensive players also rotate, as illustrated, with ⑤ moving to the strong-side guard slot and ① sliding out to the other guard position. Thus, the initial alignment is again created with a double guard set, two wing players, and a single low post.

A Third Stunting Move

A final stunting move from this offense involves the low post player (see Diagram 6–17). When the ball is moved from the strong-side guard to the weak-side guard and then onto ① stationed in the wing, the offensive player in the low post—in this case, ③—does not wait for the screen to be set by ④. Rather, ③ immediately breaks across the lane with arms outstretched, hoping to receive a scoring pass from ①. This quick-hitting maneuver should not be run too frequently. However, once in a while, this flash cut across the lane will result in a critical easy basket. This option is successful when the defender, X_3, guarding the low post player begins to anticipate the screening action and fails to pay strict attention to the movement of ③.

As a result, this stunting maneuver helps keep the defense honest in exerting pressure against the offensive low post player. Whoever happens to be the defensive low post player must be ever careful and watchful in guarding the post player; he or she cannot always anticipate exactly the cutting and screening tac-

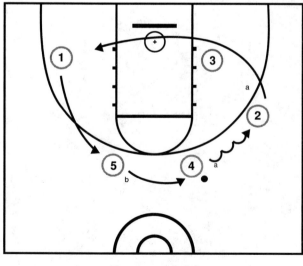

DIAGRAM 6–16

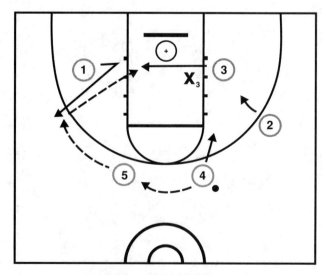

DIAGRAM 6–17

tics of the other offensive players. This uncertainty of movement is a key in keeping the defense off guard and plays a major role in the effectiveness of this man-to-man offense.

THE DOUBLE LOW POST OFFENSE

With the pressure on today's teams—principally because of the shot clock—to be able to get off a good shot in a reasonably short period of time, the double low post offense is receiving renewed attention. This offense, by the mere placement of the personnel, creates very real problems for the defenders (see Diagram 6–18). If the defenders make a mistake while guarding their opponents in such close proximity to the basket, it is quite likely to be a very costly error resulting in a successful field goal attempt by the offense.

Thus, the double low post has four very real and distinct advantages. First, the offense can be set up and initiated within a minimum amount of time, literally within seconds. Second, the offense continuously poses a constant scoring threat to the defense. Third, it creates both inside and outside scoring opportunities as a result of the inside screening maneuvers. And, last, it is very difficult for the defense to double team the ball.

Preventing Double Teaming against the Guard Slot

The presence of the single point guard prevents the defense from exerting too much pressure at the top of the key. The defenders must always be alert, lest the single point guard drives to the basket. In possession of the ball, this single point guard can attack a single defender by dribbling either left or right, since there is so much open space. Generally, double teaming efforts against this point guard only invite disaster. This is because of the placement of the remaining offensive personnel. The reaction of the offensive players to any attempt by the defense to double team the single point guard is simply to move a player to each wing with the remaining two offensive players stationed in the low post, standing on either side of the lane, adjacent to the "block."

> **Coaching Hint 122**
> Spread the offensive alignment in response to double-teaming action against the single point guard.

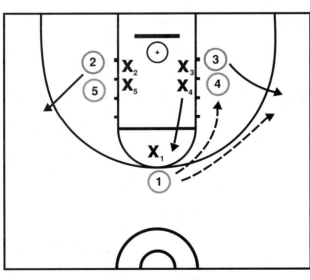

DIAGRAM 6–18

For example, should X_4 elect to attempt to be involved in a pincher's action in concert with X_1 against the point guard, the result will be a scoring pass from ① to either ③, who has moved out into the wing, or to ④, who remains in the low post. In fact, there is no defender stationed anywhere near the point guard, who is in a position to leave one's defensive assignment and attempt to double team the guard, without leaving the defensive team vulnerable to a high percentage scoring attempt.

Of course, the player receiving the pass from ① must be able to make the shot attempt or the defense will constantly attempt to apply pressure via the double team. In reality, few defenders attempt to double team the point guard because of the extreme vulnerability brought about as a result of the floor alignment of the personnel.

Initial Scoring Thrusts

The initial scoring thrust involves moving either one or two players to the wing positions. This can be accomplished in several ways. First, the two baseline players on either side of the lane, ② and ③, may use their respective low post teammates, ⑤ and ④, as stationary screens while cutting out to their respective wing slots (see Diagram 6–19).

Although most of the time the two low post players are stationary, this does not always have to be the case. Instead of standing still and allowing ③ and ② to attempt to run their respective defensive players into the low post players, ⑤ and ④ can assume a more proactive role by actually moving to establish face-to-face screens against the opponents attempting to defend the wing players. Of course, these face-to-face screens must be legal—that is, they must be erected so that the defender can see the screen being set and have time to stop or otherwise avoid contact. Again, a defensive error here, near the basket, can be a catastrophic mistake for the defenders.

A second initial scoring option involves ② and ③, who move across and through the lane on their way to the opposite wing slots (see Diagram 6–20). Of course, this type of movement enables both ② and ③ to use not only the two low post players as stationary screens but they themselves also become legal

> **Coaching Hint 123**
> The low post players can establish a face screen against the defenders guarding the potential wing players.

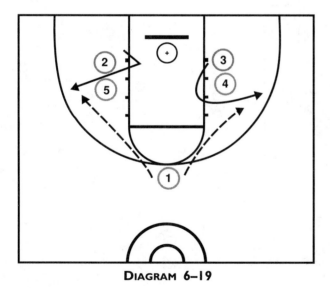

DIAGRAM 6–19

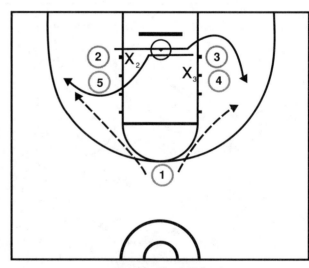

DIAGRAM 6–20

moving hindrances against the two defenders, X_2 and X_3, attempting to guard them.

Offensive Options for the Wing Player

If either of the offensive wing players receive the pass from the point guard, there are four immediate options that may be executed. First, a 12- to 15-foot shot can be taken. Second, the wing player can put the ball on the floor and drive to the basket or may drive off of a screen set by the low post player who has moved away from the basket and established a blind or side screen (see Diagram 6–21). This drive off of the screen can create either a shot or a simple screen-and-roll situation (especially if the defenders switch) in which the screener, ⑤, breaks for the basket in anticipation of a scoring pass.

The third option for the wing man with the ball is to face the basket and attempt to pass the ball into the low post player. If X_5 is attempting to play defense from behind, a simple bounce pass can create excellent scoring opportunities. If X_5 is fronting the low post, it behooves the opposite low post player, ④, to vacate that side of the lane while cutting diagonally across the lane to take up a position, ball side, at the edge of the free throw line (see Diagram 6–22).

This simple move by ④ can accomplish one of two things. It can force X_4 to leave the low post area, thereby depriving any weak-side defensive help against a lob pass from ③ to ⑤. Or it can create a scoring opportunity for ④ as this player makes the diagonal cut across the lane. If X_4 hesitates or remains in the lane in order to provide weak-side help, or is slow in reacting to the diagonal cut by ④, a short pass from ③ to ④ places the defense in an indefensible position. ④ is now in a position to pass directly to ⑤ in the low post slot. If a shot is taken by ④, both ⑤ and ② have primary responsibility for offensive rebounding. Of course, if X_1 attempts to sag into the lane to provide help, a release pass from ③ to ① will result in a high percentage shot.

Another tactic that ⑤ may use in response to extreme defensive pressure is to vacate the ball-side low post area completely by moving across the lane to exchange positions with ④ (see Diagram 6–23). Part of this exchange process can involve screening against X_4, thereby helping to free ④ to safely receive a scoring pass from the wing. Of course, the movement across the lane might not

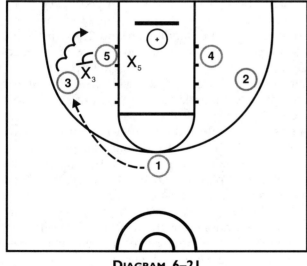

DIAGRAM 6–21

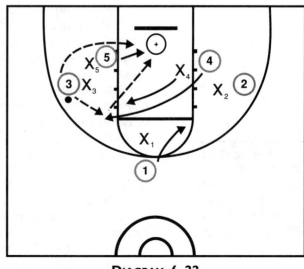

DIAGRAM 6–22

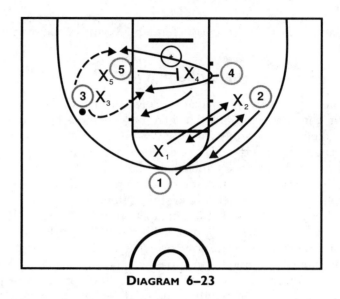

DIAGRAM 6–23

involve any screening action by ⑤ at all. Rather, ⑤ merely leaves one side of the lane while ④ busts across the lane, toward the ball side, completely unaided in an attempt to elude the pressure exerted by the defensive player, X_4.

A key to any offense, but especially to this particular offensive series, is to *be able to complete passes quickly.* This is only possible if the intended receiver is open for the pass *and* if the passer is able to make the pass. Frequently, there is only 1 or 2 seconds (at the maximum, 3 seconds) that any offensive player is actually open to receive a pass. After 1 or 2 seconds, it is useless for the offensive player to stand in the same position because the defender or defenders have already been successful in denying the pass.

As a result, it is imperative that players running an offense not stand still. Standing still is tantamount to committing offensive suicide. One must not stand still if a pass has not been received. In such a situation, a player must always immediately move, fake, make a feint, cut toward the basket, move around the screen, move toward the ball. It is imperative to do something—anything—other than simply standing around, waiting for a pass that will never take place.

In the double low offensive series, the attackers are constantly moving, constantly jockeying for position. No one should be standing around. Even the point guard, following the pass to a wing or to the low post, must move in order to prevent the defender from sagging into the middle and clogging up any inside scoring opportunities. This is illustrated in Diagram 6–23, with the point guard, ①, exchanging positions with the opposite wing player, ②, who moves to the top of the key to assume the new role of point guard.

Naturally, any of these options can be effected on either side of the court. The offensive thrust is dependent on which side of the court the point guard initially passes the ball. All too often, the side of the court the ball is passed to is dependent on how good the offensive player is in breaking free and how effective the defensive player is in preventing such a pass into the wing.

The fourth option available to the wing player with the ball is simply to return the pass to the teammate who is stationed at the top of the key. In this event, the other offensive players merely realign themselves in their initial positions, in a double low post alignment on both sides of the lane. Or, if it is impossible to pass to the point guard, the wing player may simply elect to dribble out to the top of the key, thereby assuming the role of the point guard (see Diagram 6–24). In this eventuality, ② simply vacates the top of the key and heads toward the basket for a possible scoring pass. If a pass is not forthcoming, ② simply takes up a position in the low post and becomes one of the two wing players. The other wing player, ①, takes up position in the opposite low post slot; ③ then becomes the point guard.

Stunting Moves

An excellent stunting move is to have one or both of the low post players, either ⑤ or ④, make the move out to a wing area. These former pivot players then are able to execute any of the options mentioned earlier, while assuming the role of a wing player (see Diagram 6–25). This is especially effective if the offensive pivots are fairly good ball handlers, dribblers, and shooters, and the players assigned to guard them are not.

A final stunting move can involve either one of the two low post players, ⑤ or ④. At any time, either or both of these low post players can simply step in front of their defender, into the middle of the lane, receive a pass, and attempt to score by means of an immediate jump shot or by driving to the basket.

Concluding Comments about the Double Low Post Offense

This hard and quick hitting man-to-man offense is more effective if used as a secondary attack. Although effective and efficient, this attack can become bogged down if a team attempts to utilize it exclusively as the main or exclusive weapon in its offensive arsenal. Better yet, when used as an alternative, as a secondary or change-of-pace attack, the double low offensive series can pay big dividends. It is easy to teach, is easy to learn, and the players are able to execute a number of stunting tactics in response to varying defensive pressure.

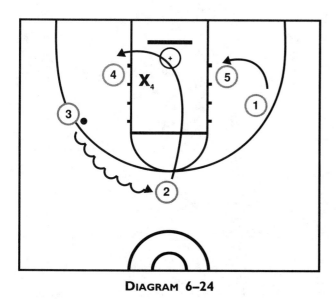

DIAGRAM 6–24

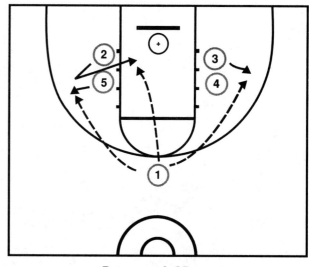

DIAGRAM 6–25

The three biggest weaknesses of this attack rest in the fact that there is only a single point guard. In case of a turnover or a missed basket, the offense is susceptible to the fast break by the opponents. If a field goal is missed close to the basket, the likelihood of an offensive rebound is diminished, This is because the defensive personnel are already close to the basket and there is less physical space for the offensive players to maneuver in an effort to secure an inside position for the offensive rebound.

There is also a danger that the defenders can become used to the simplistic pattern of the offense and can successfully anticipate various cuts and passes involved in the attack. Thus, it is important that field goals taken close to the basket be successful, that there be infrequent forced turnovers, and that effective stunting moves be initiated whenever defenders begin to anticipate the usual offensive tactics.

7 Combatting Presses: Zones and Man to Man

DEVELOPING A SOUND PLAN TO COUNTERACT PRESSES

If all coaches had to do was to prepare their players to attack so-called normal, quarter-court defenses, coaching would sure be a whole lot easier. However, such is not the case. The reality of the situation is such that coaches and athletes must be very proficient in attacking various types of so-called pressure defenses that are extended well beyond the quarter-court area. Specifically, every team should be able to attack the following types of pressure defenses:

1. Half-court zone press
2. Three-quarter zone press
3. Full-court zone press
4. Half-court man-to-man press
5. Three-quarter man-to-man press
6. Full-court man-to-man press

Each of these six presses are designed to accomplish three major objectives: (a) to disrupt the rhythm of the offensive team's attack; (b) to force the offense to take hurried shots, poor shots, or shots that the players would not normally take; and (c) to force a turnover—that is, to get the ball away from the offense.

To counteract these objectives, the offensive players must remember the primary principle in attacking all presses: *Remain calm, cool, and collected in response to any press.* Athletes should not commit the cardinal sin of making poor (hasty) decisions by attempting poor passes and taking poor percentage shots. Instead, the following suggestions should be followed when attacking various types of presses.

1. Be sure to spread the offensive personnel; avoid double-team situations.

> **Coaching Hint 127**
> Be calm, cool, and collected when facing any press; panic results in poor decision making and even worse execution.

2. Attempt to move the ball into the middle of the court—this is especially important against zone presses.
3. Routinely make short and crisp (strong) passes.
4. Be alert for possible long, down-court passing opportunities (and easy scores).
5. Do not get pinned against the sidelines or in the "corners"; avoid potential trapping situations.
6. Always make the defenders pay the price for pressing by attempting to score, especially with lay-ups and short jump shots.
7. Against three-quarter and full-court man-to-man presses, isolate the ball handler and advance the ball up the floor via the dribble, one against one.
8. Do not stop the dribble unless you are going to pass—and then pass.
9. Maintain court balance in the event of a turnover.
10. Potential pass receivers may have to aggressively *advance to meet the ball* in order to retain possession.
11. Anticipate what the defenders are attempting to accomplish by their pressing tactics, then react accordingly.

Coaching Hint 128
Do not make stupid mistakes due to being in a hurry or becoming flustered—don't beat yourself.

As in any competitive setting, no team should ever beat itself. If a team is to lose in competition, it should be due to the superior strength, skill, and execution of the opponents. Therefore, making (repeatedly) really stupid mistakes is not only extremely costly but inexcusable as well. Of course, that is exactly what the pressing team is attempting to do—force the offensive players to commit mental and physical errors in critical situations because of the pressure tactics involved in the pressing attack.

ESSENTIAL PRINCIPLES IN ATTACKING ANY PRESSING DEFENSE

There are two critical principles involved in attacking any type of press. First, the ball has to be protected at all costs. Second, and equally important, an attempt has to be made to score against the defenders who are attempting to press. This is because *if the offense does not make the defense pay the price for pressing (giving up a high percentage score), the defenders have nothing to lose by continuing to press throughout the game.* The objective is to discourage the pressing team from pressing by making it too costly for the defense.

Coaching Hint 129
When facing a press, a team must attempt to score—make the defenders pay dearly for pressing.

When offensive players face the press with confidence and look at the press as an opportunity to get some easy crib shots, or at least some very high percentage field goal attempts as a result of the press, the advantages that would normally accrue to the defenders suddenly vanish. Instead, the advantage shifts to the offense. The best way to attack and discourage the press is to score easy baskets. The concept is clear: Make the defenders pay dearly for attempting to apply the press, regardless of whether the press is a half-court, three-quarter court, or a full-court press.

Coaching Hint 130
Potential pass receivers must advance to meet the ball once the trap has been sprung—don't just stand there and expect to receive the ball.

Against any press, all potential pass receivers must remember to move toward the ball handler in anticipation of a pass. Presses are effective because offensive players stand around and wait for the ball to come to them instead of going to meet the ball. This is doubly important when the ball handler is being two-timed or trapped by the pressing team. The would-be passer needs all the help possible in getting rid of the ball to a teammate who is in the open and can safely catch the ball. The last thing needed is a turnover caused by the press or through negligence of the offensive players.

ATTACKING THE HALF-COURT ZONE PRESS

A half-court zone press involves all five defenders stationed just inside or beyond the 10-second or midcourt line, waiting for the offensive team to attempt to move the ball across midcourt (see Diagram 7–1). When attacking this type of zone press, a critical area of the basketball court is the midcourt line itself. It is this line that will be used by the defenders to aid them in constructing an effective double-team situation when the ball is dribbled or passed across the 10-second line.

Crossing the Ten-Second Line

When attacking the half-court zone press, the ball handler should not automatically and immediately rush over the 10-second line. Instead, he or she should hesitate just in front of the half-court line while surveying (locating and identifying) the defenders and teammates. Perhaps a pass to another teammate might be in order in response to the alignment of the defense. In this type of press, the defenders cannot establish a truly effective trapping or double-teaming situation until the ball is moved across the midcourt line. Thus, before crossing this midcourt line, the ball handler should take time to look over the situation and identify potential pass receivers and defenders, without having to face, at that moment, extreme defensive pressure.

Of course, the offense must always be mindful of the 10-second (midcourt) count, for those teams playing under this rule. That is why the ball should be moved up court to the midcourt line as quickly as possible, providing adequate time to survey the defenders and teammates prior to making an informed decision in terms of where to move the ball.

Once the ball has been moved across the 10-second (midcourt) line, the defenders will likely attempt to stop progress of the ball by pinching or double teaming the ball handler. Once the ball has been moved into the offensive front court, the ball handler cannot (without committing a violation) retreat back across the line to the back court. As a result, the defenders can use the 10-second line as another "teammate" in establishing a trapping situation. It is imperative, then, that the ball handler be able to dish off the ball to any number of teammates immediately after giving up the dribble and prior to being double teamed. It may also be possible, though not likely against skilled defenders, for the ball handler to dribble by or through the two defenders who are attempting to close the trap on the ball.

Using the Post Player in the Middle

Diagram 7–1 illustrates the typical half-court zone press alignment with a 1-3-1 defensive set. Since it is a primary objective of the offense to move the ball into the middle of the front court (and since the defense also knows this), there is no offensive player initially stationed near the top of the key. This is done for a very important reason. Since the defenders also realize that the greatest weakness of the press is in the middle, they will be especially alert to preventing a pass into an opponent who is initially stationed in this vulnerable area of the court.

Thus, the offensive players are spread out on the floor with two guards, two wing players, and a single post vacillating along the baseline, from one side of the free throw lane to the other. When the ball is moved across the midcourt line, the offensive post player, ⑤, in response to the double-team efforts by X_1

Coaching Hint 131
When attacking a press, be constantly aware of the 10-second count.

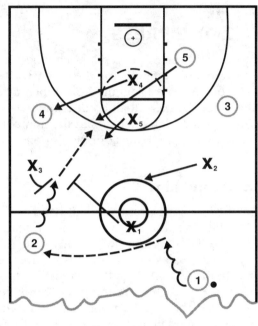

DIAGRAM 7–1

and X_3, can move from *behind* the defensive post player, via the flash pivot cut, into the middle of the offensive front court, in anticipation of a pass.

It is extremely difficult for the defensive player assuming responsibility for the middle of the court to stop a pass to ⑤, who cuts into the middle from behind. This is because ⑤ is coming from the blind side, out of the vision of X_5. This defender cannot see who is cutting into the middle for a pass until it is too late. Also, the mere fact that ⑤ is moving to meet the ball usually prohibits the defender from stepping in front and intercepting the pass from the guard.

If ⑤ is unable to receive the ball while in the middle of the court, it is imperative that this player not merely stand around waiting for a pass that will surely never come. Instead, the post player must move around. A moving target is harder to defend than one who is stationary. There are several obvious options for the post player. First, move even closer toward the ball. Second, slide sideways while in the middle of the court so that the defender who has responsibility for protecting this area is forced also to move. Third, retreat and move toward the basket, thereby vacating the high post area around the top of the key. Fourth, exchange positions with ③ on the opposite side of the court so the wing player might flash, from behind the defenders, into the middle of the court.

Of course, once the ball has been moved into the middle of the front court, all bets for the pressing team are off—the press has essentially been defeated. The new ball handler, in the middle of the floor, can now drive to the basket, take a high percentage shot, or pass off to either teammate in the wings.

A Possible Passing Option: Along the Sideline

Naturally, there are other passing options open to the ball handler who crosses the midcourt line besides the post player. An equally effective pass is one made along the sideline, to ④ (see Diagram 7–2). As soon as the trap is sprung against

②, there are only three defenders left to guard four offensive players. It would seem to be an impossible job. However, defensive presses can be quite effective. Why? Because offensive players make poor choices resulting in stupid mistakes and loss of possessions. In all likelihood, the defenders can make an easy score off such a turnover in this type of situation.

Thus, it is important for the offensive players to remain spread out on the floor, thereby forcing the three defenders to stretch their defensive efforts beyond what is actually feasible. The result is that a pass along the sideline to ④ is frequently possible, especially if this player continues to advance toward the ball. Once in possession of the ball, ④ immediately attempts to advance the ball toward the basket by passing to either ⑤ in the high post or to ③, who has cut across the lane, baseline, in hopes of getting the ball close to the basket. If the pass is made from ④ to the pivot, then it is the responsibility of ⑤ to become a scoring threat or to pass to ③, who is closing to the basket.

A Possible Passing Option:
Diagonally across the Floor toward the Basket

If the defenders make a mistake and fail to adequately guard ③, it may be possible for the ball handler to make a cross-court (skip) or diagonal pass directly to ③, who is on the opposite side of court. Normally, such a pass is of a high-risk nature but the possible consequences—an easy score—is often worth the risk. This pass is more often completed before the ball handler is actually double teamed by the defense, since this type of pass requires great skill and expert execution. But it can be devastating and demoralizing to the defense while at the same time exhilarating and motivating to the offense.

A Possible Passing Option: Along the Ten-Second Line

Another passing option available for the ball handler who has crossed into the front court is to make a pass along the 10-second line to ① who, in turn, has crossed the midcourt line and has moved toward the ball (see Diagram 7–3). This is the escape or release pass that can be made so that the offense can initiate any of the preceding options, but on the opposite side of the court. This pass

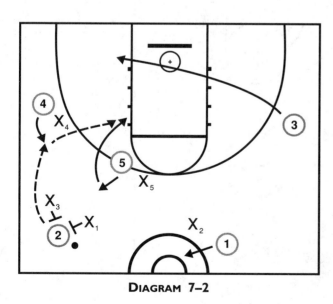

DIAGRAM 7–2

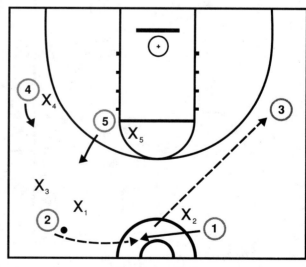

DIAGRAM 7–3

Coaching Hint 135
Moving the ball quickly
from one side of the
court to the other side
can place the defenders
in an awkward, if not
indefensible, position.

also forces the defense to shift in an attempt to cover such a large area of the court, if the defensive press is to remain intact.

Once ① receives the cross-court pass, it may be possible, depending on the placement of the defenders, to pass directly to ③ along the right side wing area (see Diagram 7–3). Such a pass can frequently result in a quick score. However, if a quick scoring pass is not feasible, the offensive team still retains possession of the ball and can begin to attack the defensive press using any of the preceding options, with all five players spread out on the court.

Countering Stunting Moves by the Pressing Team

The same principles just outlined apply if the defenders extend the half-court press just beyond the 10-second line—that is, into the offensive team's back court (see Diagram 7–4). The defenders stunt in this fashion in response to the offensive players hesitating just before they cross the midcourt line, while looking over and through the defense to see to whom to pass the ball. As a result, defenders merely extend the attacking formation across the 10-second line in an effort to put pressure against the guards earlier.

Coaching Hint 136
Be cautious about
attempting lob passes—
those that "hang" in the
air are just waiting to be
intercepted.

From the defenders' perspective, they are attempting either to force a lob pass across the court or to force the ball handler to the sideline where the double team trap can be established, preferably once the ball has been dribbled across the midcourt. Thus, the offensive personnel must attempt to pass the ball using short, direct passes. Similarly, the ball handler would not want to dribble across the midcourt line along the sideline, since doing so would create an ideal double-team situation for the defense.

To counteract the extension of the defensive personnel (and the resulting pressure) beyond the midcourt line, the two offensive guards, ② and ①, should advance toward their own basket, keeping even with each other, thereby maintaining floor balance, while surveying possible pass receivers. It is

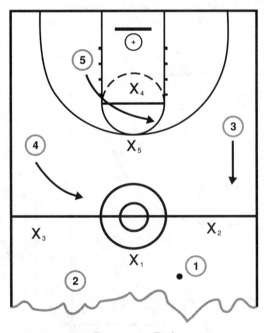

DIAGRAM 7–4

advisable to pass the ball across the 10-second line to the pivot or to one of the players in the wings *before the double team or trap can be sprung by the opposing team.*

Again, the objective is to protect the ball while moving into scoring position. During this time, it is necessary that the offensive players take advantage of the vulnerability of the opponents due to their pressing and double-team antics. Keep the offensive personnel spread, keep passes short (usually), move to receive the ball, and attempt to score off the press, thereby making the defenders pay a steep price for using such a defense. Above all, keep a cool head and do not make any foolish errors, especially those that can result in an easy score by the opponents.

ATTACKING THE THREE-QUARTER AND FULL-COURT ZONE PRESSES

The same general principles utilized in attacking the half-court zone press are also effective against both three-quarter and full-court zone presses. This is true regardless of the initial alignments of the defensive personnel. However, there are some very important variations and deviations that offensive personnel should be cognizant of in reacting to the most popular three-quarter zone presses.

Attacking the 2-2-1 and the 1-3-1 (1-2-1-1) Zone Presses

Typically, three-quarter zone presses take the form of either the 2-2-1 or the 1-3-1, or some variation thereof. A slight modification of the 1-3-1 press is the 1-2-1-1 attack in which the middle post player is positioned a little behind the two wing players. However, for all practical purposes, the 1-3-1 and 1-2-1-1 zone presses are identical. They are indistinguishable, both in terms of how the defensive players react once the ball has been put into play and in how the offensive players begin to advance the ball up the court.

Characteristics of the Three-Quarter Court Zone Press

Three-quarter court zone presses (1-3-1 and 2-2-1) are different from the full-court presses in that the former are set up further away from the end line and there is no contesting of the in-bounds pass (see Diagram 7–5). Also, in a three-quarter attack, the offensive players are frequently allowed to attempt to dribble the ball up the floor a short distance (especially when facing the 2-2-1 press) prior to being vigorously attacked by the defenders seeking to double team the ball handler.

Characteristics of the Full-Court Zone Press

The usual full-court zone press takes the form of the 1-3-1 zone. Used as a full-court press, the defenders are stationed very close to the baseline (see Diagram 7–6). In this defensive alignment, there is frequently direct pressure applied against the in-bounds passer. It is customary for the defenders to attempt to trap the ball *immediately* after the in-bounds pass is completed. In some instances, defenders will even attempt to prevent the in-bounds pass being made in an effort to make an interception. Failing to intercept this in-bounds pass, the defenders can still attempt to establish a double-team situation on the first or subsequent pass receivers.

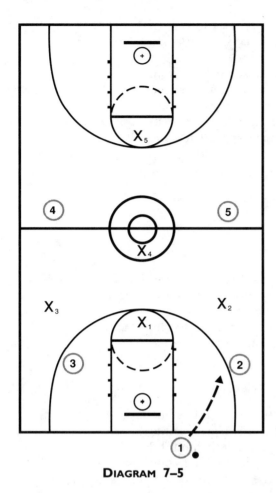

DIAGRAM 7–5

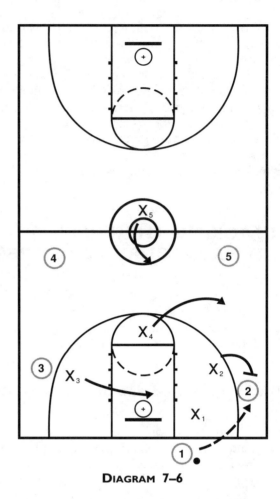

DIAGRAM 7–6

AN ALL-PURPOSE PRESS BREAKER

Coaching Hint 137
Utilizing one offensive attack against all three-quarter and full-court zone presses can be highly effective and efficient—simplicity and proper execution are the keys to success.

An identical offensive alignment may be used to attack both three-quarter and full-court zone presses, regardless of the initial alignment of the defenders. Using a single offensive attack against all full- and three-quarter court zone presses is a great advantage for a team. The players only have to learn one general attacking pattern and can practice it to perfection.

Getting the Ball in Bounds

The four potential in-bounds pass receivers are spread out on the offensive back court, as illustrated in Diagrams 7–7 (against a 1-3-1 press) and 7–8 (against a 2-2-1 press). On the slap of the ball, ② and ③ may elect to execute individual cut and slash moves to free themselves for the in-bounds pass. Or they can exchange positions on the floor while screening for each other to hinder any close defensive pressure. These efforts are especially important should the zone press be established as a full-court attack (usually from a 1-3-1 set) with pressure being exerted against the in-bounds passer and the closest potential receivers (Diagram 7–6).

Of course, if the defenders are not exerting prevent-type pressure defense, either from a 2-2-1 or 1-3-1 set, a simple direct pass to either ② or ③ can be made. The in-bounds passer should also look to see if a direct pass can be made to either ④ or ⑤, stationed along the midcourt line, and who may suddenly break for the ball. If such a pass can be completed, the backbone of the zone press is broken. The result is that the defense is immediately placed at a distinct disadvantage. *It is important to remember that the key to completing passes when attacking presses is for the intended receiver to move toward the ball, rather than standing and waiting for the ball to arrive.*

Advancing the Ball Once the In-Bounds Pass Has Been Completed

If the in-bounds pass is made to either ② or to ③, the passer immediately streaks down court (Diagrams 7–7 and 7–8) in anticipation of an immediate return pass. Simultaneously, the midcourt offensive player diagonally across from the ball—in this case, ④—breaks diagonally across the back court toward the ball for a possible pass from ②. It is very difficult for the defenders to exert pressure against both ① (who is moving through the middle of the court toward the basket) and ④ (who is also in the middle of the floor moving toward the ball).

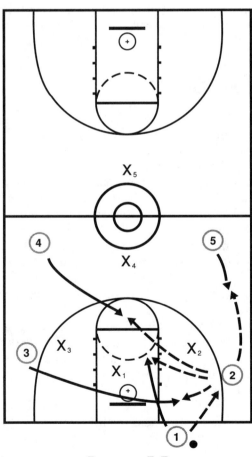

DIAGRAM 7–7

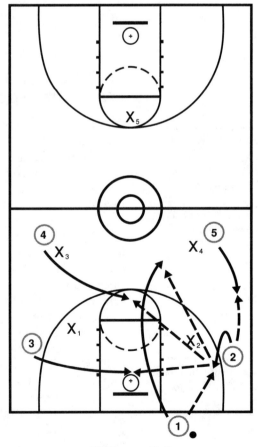

DIAGRAM 7–8

Defensive coverage is even more of a challenge when other offensive players make their near simultaneous moves. For example, ⑤ breaks toward the ball, along the sideline, looking for a pass. ③ breaks along the baseline while serving as the safety outlet pass should ② not be able to pass to ①, ④, or ⑤. Thus, three teammates, in different areas of the court, are moving toward the ball for a pass, in addition to the in-bounds passer cutting up the floor toward the offensive basket.

If the in-bounds passer, streaking up the floor, receives the ball back from ②, the zone press is in deep, deep trouble. This is because the ball is in the middle of the floor, in the hands of an excellent ball handler (dribbler and passer), and being moved up the floor. Whenever the ball has been advanced beyond the potential double-team trap, the offense possesses a distinct numerical advantage. It is imperative that this advantage be exploited to the hilt by actually scoring. *Remember, merely beating the press down the floor is only half the battle. The other half is to score by means of a high percentage shot.*

The offensive players being pressed should take advantage of any numerical superiority in the same way as they would conclude any fast-break situation in which they outnumber the defenders. It is important that the offensive players have a mental set that whenever they are faced with a three-quarter or full-court zone press, they interpret this as just another fast-break opportunity. This is especially true when the defenders attempt to double team or trap the ball. The worse situation for the offensive players to find themselves in is to feel relieved or thankful that they were able just to advance the ball across the 10-second line without losing possession. That kind of mentality is self-destructive. Offensive players need to be assertive and aggressive. They need to score off the press.

Coaching Hint 138 Facing a full- or three-quarter court press is an invitation to execute a fast-break attack.

ATTACKING THE HALF-COURT MAN-TO-MAN PRESS

Man-to-man presses are different from zone presses, although both types of pressure defenses have similar goals. That is, both types of presses attempt to disrupt the offensive rhythm, force poor shots, and create turnovers. However, there are distinct differences between zone and man-to-man presses. The man-to-man presses place more individual and constant pressure against the ball handler as well as potential pass receivers. With the man-to-man press, there is usually—but not always—less efforts to double team or trap the ball.

As a result, the easiest and sometimes the most effective technique to counteract the typical man-to-man half-court press is simply to isolate the defender guarding the ball handler. This can be accomplished by spreading the offensive personnel and allowing the dribbler to advance the ball by dribbling, one against one, all the while looking for potential pass receivers.

It is important that the offensive players be spread out on the half court so that the defenders, even in a man-to-man attack mode, cannot attempt to double team the ball. Since most half-court man-to-man presses involve attempts by the defense to force the ball into a corner where a trap can then be established, it is imperative that the offense is spread out.

Many half-court man-to-man pressure attacks will cease to exist once the ball has been advanced into the offensive front court, near the top of the key. In this situation, many defenders will fall back into a regular quarter-court man-to-man pressure defense.

Coaching Hint 139 When being pressed in a man-to-man situation, don't clog up the middle—give the ball handler room to dribble and to drive to the basket.

Coaching Hint 140 Don't forget to attempt to score when facing a half-court man-to-man press.

COUNTERING THE CONTINUOUS HALF-COURT MAN-TO-MAN PRESS

In some instances, the defenders will continue to exert true half-court man-to-man pressure against the ball handler and all potential receivers, all over the offensive front court. All too often, a team's regular offensive series will not be suitable for attacking such pressure tactics by the defenders. In these instances, it is imperative that the offensive players be able to react appropriately by *setting up an offensive attack specifically designed to meet such constant pressure*. The fact remains, teams must have in their arsenal an attack(s) designed not only to retain possession of the ball but also to secure high percentage shots.

A REGULAR OFFENSE THAT DOUBLES AS A HALF-COURT PRESS BREAKER

The double low post offense, described in detail in Chapter 6, is one offense that effectively counteracts the half-court, man-to-man press while also serving as an effective regular quarter-court offense. This is because the initial alignment of the offensive personnel forces the lone defender against the ball to be isolated and thus unable to secure help from other defenders.

THE SPREAD OFFENSE AGAINST THE HALF-COURT MAN-TO-MAN PRESS

An offense specifically designed to counteract the half-court man-to-man press is the 2-1-2 spread offense. This attack not only affords protection for the ball against the half-court man-to-man press but it also creates excellent scoring opportunities as well. This offense has two guards, a single post player, and two wing players (see Diagram 7–9). The ball handler can simply continue to dribble and back into the front court as long as there is no danger of an additional defender moving to set a two-person trap.

The role of the post is to be in almost constant motion, vacillating on either side of the lane, between the basket area and the top of the key. In this way, the post is always a constant threat as a pass receiver. Once in possession of the ball, the pivot becomes a scoring threat and a passing threat.

While the post player is busy moving to and from the basket, the remaining offensive players are not just standing around. Rather, the guard and wing player on the opposite side of the court from the ball handler are exchanging places with one another. Both ② and ④ move (one screening for the other) so that their defensive players are hindered in their efforts to apply constant defensive coverage. The ball-side wing should zig-zag back and forth between the wing and the basket in an effort to be free to receive a pass.

Vacating the Strong-Side Wing Area

Whenever the ball handler in the guard position is being unduly pressured, the ball-side wing player has the option of simply vacating that side of the court while streaking toward the basket. This simple maneuver enables the ball handler to drive to the basket for the potential score. Or the ball handler might be able to pass the ball directly to the breaking wing player for the crib shot. Since these options always remain a possibility, the defensive players quickly find themselves unable to exert as much pressure against the ball handler and potential receivers as they would like.

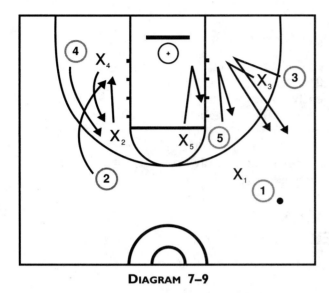

DIAGRAM 7–9

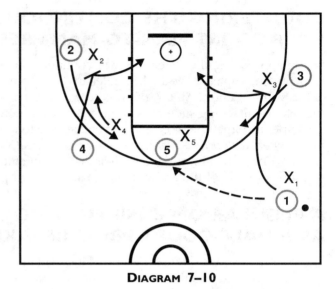

DIAGRAM 7–10

Options Following a Pass to the Post

A pass to the post player who is close to the basket can result in any number of power post moves and possible scoring attempts. Ideally, the offense attempts to get the ball as close to the basket as often as possible. Hence, the ball handler should always be on the lookout for the pivot player who has maneuvered a defender close to the basket. A pass to the low post, especially when the defender is behind the low post player, is the ideal situation. This pass is always a possibility from either of the two guards or either wing player.

When the ball is passed to the post player at the *top of the key*, both guards break along the sidelines to screen for their respective wing players (see Diagram 7–10). After the screens are set, either or both ① and ④ may choose to execute a reverse pivot while breaking for the basket and a possible pass. If a scoring pass is not possible, an outlet pass is completed to either ② or ③, who now assume the roles of the guards.

A Stunting Move: Placing a Guard in the Post Position

Some coaches place a guard in the offensive post position. This tactic presents some interesting and intriguing possibilities. First, a pass to the high post creates an immediate scoring threat because a guard is presumably a very competent dribbler and skilled shooter. A pass to the guard anywhere in the post area poises an immediate scoring threat to the defense. This is because the pass receiver is being guarded by only one player and the other defenders are spread out on the court. The second advantage of this stunting tactic is that the offensive team is able to "hide" a post player who is not a very good dribbler, passer, or outside shooter by moving the player elsewhere on the court.

ATTACKING THE THREE-QUARTER AND FULL-COURT MAN-TO-MAN PRESSES

Man-to-man presses, by their very nature, are susceptible to the offensive players spreading out on the floor and allowing the ball handler to dribble down the floor, one on one. This works fine against the three-quarter court press where pressure against the ball is not exerted until the ball is put into play. However, when the defenders apply extreme man-to-man pressure full court, beginning with the in-bounds pass, coaches need to counter with other options.

Getting the Ball Safely into Play

Getting the ball into play against a well-executed and dedicated man-to-man full-court press can, indeed, be a challenge. This is especially true in the heat of battle; when the pressure is severe, the strain can be relentless and the players can taste the tension. Against a man-to-man press, some type of screening action is especially effective. However, screening action alone is not always sufficient. Breaking toward the passer once the screen has been set is as necessary as the screening action itself.

There are inherent advantages to using the same initial formation in setting up against both zone and man-to-man three-quarter and full-court presses. One benefit lies in the fact that the offensive players do not have to take time to decipher exactly what type of defense is being used by the opponents. A second benefit is that the defenders are not able to anticipate exactly what tactics and maneuvers the offensive players will choose to execute.

Diagram 7–11 illustrates the initial alignment of the offensive players poised to attack either a full-court or three-quarter court man-to-man press. This is the same initial alignment used to attack the three-quarter and full-court zone presses. Of course, once the ball is in the hands of the in-bounds passer, the man-to-man attack is different from the zone press breaker.

On the slap of the ball, ③ moves across the lane to set a screen against X_2, thereby freeing ② to break across the lane for the in-bounds pass. Once the screen is established, ③ merely pivots and takes one or two steps toward the in-bounds passer for a possible pass.

> **Coaching Hint 141**
> When the man-to-man full-court press is used, utilize screening action to get the ball in bounds.

> **Coaching Hint 142**
> Utilize the same initial formation in attacking both zone and man-to-man full-court presses.

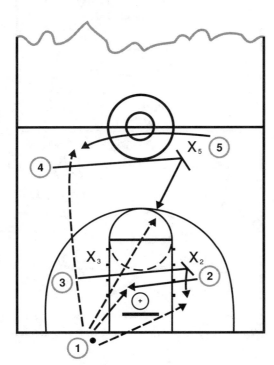

DIAGRAM 7–11

While this screening and cutting action is taking place, ④, being on the same side of the court as the in-bounds passer, moves across court to screen for the defensive player guarding ⑤. As ⑤ cuts around the screen set by ④ and moves across the court, ④ can then pivot and move toward the free throw line, as shown in anticipation of an in-bounds pass. The in-bounds passer literally has four potential moving targets to pass to within the 5 seconds allocated for the in-bounds pass.

As soon as the ball is put into play, ① immediately streaks without hesitation down the middle of the court toward the basket. This cut by the in-bounds passer provides for a moving target for a return pass but also aids in clearing the floor. As a result, the ball handler can work one on one against a single defender while the other offensive players clear out and move toward the basket.

Throwing the Length of the Floor: The Long Bomb Attack

An offensive tactic that can be used, admittedly sparingly and only at the opportune time, involves the long bomb against man-to-man full court pressure. This tactic, when used judiciously can literally destroy a man-to-man press, both in terms of generating a quick score and in terms of demoralizing the defenders.

This strategy is effective when the defenders are strenuously attempting to prevent the in-bounds pass and are adamant about applying pressure against all four potential pass receivers, as well as against the in-bounds passer. Diagram

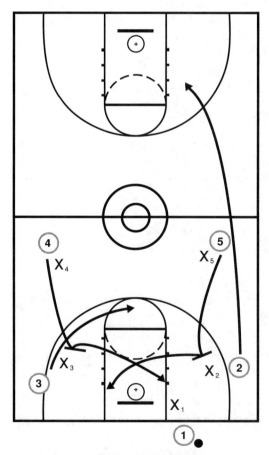

DIAGRAM 7–12

7–12 illustrates the initial alignment of the offensive personnel, with one player in each of the four corners in the offensive backcourt. Again, the familiar positioning of the offensive players prevents the defenders from anticipating exactly what will take place.

On the slap of the ball, both ④ and ⑤ move toward the baseline and erect a blind screen against X_3 and X_2, respectively. Once the screen has been set, ②, being on the same side of the court as the in-bounds passer, streaks around this screen and heads toward the opposite end of the court, at break-neck speed. On the opposite side of the floor, ③ moves around the screen set by ④ and heads to the middle of the free throw line, as shown, for a possible pass.

The first option, naturally, is for the long bomb pass to be completed to ②, who is cutting for the basket. The secondary passing option is to ③ at the free throw line. The third and fourth passing options are to either ④ or ⑤, who criss-crossed across each other's path following their initial screening action.

The reason that the long bomb can be made is that X_2 is at a decided disadvantage in this situation. Not only is X_2 unaware of the back (blind) screen being set, but ② knows exactly what is going to happen and is prepared to streak down court. If the screen by ⑤ is effective, it is literally impossible for X_2 to fight over or around the screen and still maintain adequate defensive coverage on ②. Similarly, if a defensive switch occurs, it is also impossible for X_5 to move initially toward the ball, stop direction, and then begin to move in the opposite direction in an effort to switch defensive coverage and guard the streaking guard, ②. The streaking guard, who is heading for the basket, has too much of a head start.

It is very important that the in-bounds passer is able to throw the long bomb. To be able to do so, it is necessary to have one foot in front of the other for proper balance. However, to stand with both feet parallel and then to shift one foot in front of the other in order to throw the ball the length of the court is foolish. The shifting of one's feet tips off the intention of the in-bounds passer to make the long throw. Thus, on all in-bounds passing situations, the passer should stand with one foot in front of the other so that either a short pass or the long bomb can be completed without giving advance notice to the opponents (see Figures 7–1 and 7–2).

A Second Option Using the Long Bomb: Use of the Fake Screen Option

Another option involving the long bomb is illustrated in Diagram 7–13. In this option, the initial alignment is the same as before. Also, both ④ and ⑤ begin the familiar cut toward the baseline upon the slap of the ball by the in-bounds passer. However, this is where the similarity ends. Instead of continuing all the way toward the baseline to erect the screen against X_2, ⑤ makes a quick stop, some distance away from X_2, and then executes an abrupt turn-around and heads in the opposite direction, toward the basket and the long bomb from ①. The name of this specific option is the fake screen option. This is because the two midcourt players, ④ and ⑤, move as if they were going to erect the screens, as described earlier, but in reality, they do not. Instead, ⑤ stops and heads toward the opposite end of the floor.

This 180-degree change in direction by ⑤ makes it very difficult for the defender to maintain adequate defensive coverage. This is because X_5 cannot anticipate such a quick change of direction. By the time the defender recognizes what is happening and is able to stop and change direction, it is too late. The long bomb has been thrown by ① and ⑤ is dribbling to score the easy lay-up.

Coaching Hint 143
The goal of the long bomb attack is to score off the first or the second pass.

Coaching Hint 144
The in-bounds passer must not give away his or her intention to throw the bomb by the placement of the feet.

FIGURE 7–1   THROWING THE LONG BOMB

While ⑤ is moving on the ball side of the floor, there is simultaneous action on the opposite side of the court. This involves ④, who also moves toward the baseline, only to stop and veer into the middle of the free throw lane to serve as a secondary pass receiver. Of course, ② becomes a potential pass receiver by breaking toward the ball. If the long bomb is not thrown, but rather a pass is thrown into the offensive back court, ① streaks down the middle of the floor looking for a possible return pass.

Several times in the author's career as a coach, players, in the closing seconds of a close game, have executed the long bomb pass to a player streaking for the basket, resulting in an easy lay-up. Immediately thereafter, the so-called fake screen option was also successfully executed, resulting in yet another easy crib shot. Nothing discourages opponents from pressing like breaking their

Coaching Hint 145
Nothing discourages a tough man-to-man press more than an easy, uncontested lay-up.

FIGURE 7–2   THROWING THE LONG BOMB

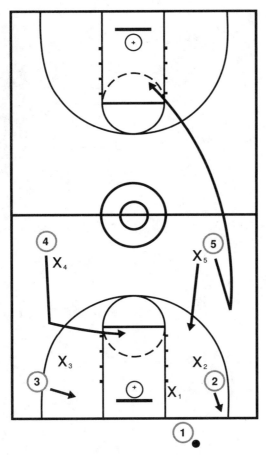

DIAGRAM 7–13

backs with a lay-up or several lay-ups. This is especially true when the defenders have put their hearts and souls, and all of their energies and efforts, into playing nose-to-nose, man-to-man, full-court pressure defense.

One of the inherent advantages of this attack against full-court man-to-man pressure is that even if the long bomb itself is not thrown, the ball can still be safely put into play by passing it to one of the secondary receivers. At best, the long bomb is completed and a lay-up results. Even if the full-court pass is not attempted, the ball should be able to be safely put into play in the back court. And, of course, once the ball is in play, offensive players "clear out," allowing the ball handler to work one on one against a lone defender.

Admittedly, the long bomb attack is not something that can be used a lot. Rather, it is to be used sparingly and judiciously. It is a tactic that can be effectively used only in certain circumstances and under certain conditions. However, when the situation is right, the long bomb attack can be extremely effective in terms of safely getting the ball in bounds as well as in garnering an easy basket or two. This attack is not without risk, but the rewards are great and commensurate with the level of risk involved. In reality, it takes courage for a coach to call for the long pass in a tight game situation. It also requires guts and confidence for the players to actually execute the various options. But, then, fortitude is required to coach and to play the sport of basketball in any pressure-packed situation.

Coaching Hint 146
The long bomb attack should be used sparingly and judiciously.

Special Situations

ANTICIPATING FUTURE SCENARIOS

An important element in successful coaching today is the ability to prepare one's athletes for what might take place in actual competition. Thus, the ability to anticipate or forecast various future scenarios in game situations is very important for the basketball mentor.

PREPARING FOR SPECIAL SITUATIONS

Coaches must be able to prepare their players so that the individual athletes and the team as a whole are able to recognize and adequately react to any number of situations and circumstances on game day—both the expected and the unexpected. The ability to plan, in advance, for any number of possible eventualities or scenarios is critical to the eventual success of any basketball coach, at any level.

In coaching parlance, this planning refers to preparing youngsters for *special situations* and *unusual circumstances* that might occur in actual competition. Of course, no coach is able to anticipate or forecast every single possible scenario that might take place. However, it behooves coaches and teachers of the sport of basketball to attempt to anticipate most of what could happen on game day and to prepare the athletes to meet these challenges, both individually and collectively. Some of these special situations include the following:

1. Initiating fast-break opportunities
2. Out-of-bounds situations
   a. Man to man and zone
   b. From the end lines and the sideline
3. Shooting when time is of the essence
   a. Setting up for the last-second shot

Coaching Hint 147
Coaches need to be able to anticipate the unexpected in terms of game situations.

Coaching Hint 148
Coaches must prepare their athletes to react appropriately to any number of special game situations or unusual circumstances.

    b. Preventing the last-second shot
4. Stalling or freezing the ball
5. Jump ball situations
6. Using special stunting defenses, such as
    a. The triangle and two
    b. The box and one
    c. The diamond and one

All of these special strategies and tactics are examined in detail in Chapter 8. In Chapter 9, the author has provided a wide range of drills to help athletes develop a high level of skills and competencies. Additionally, drills can be instrumental in aiding the players in becoming adjusted to actual game-like situations. And, finally, Chapter 10 deals with the mental and psychological aspects of coaching basketball, including an examination of motivation, psychology of learning, as well as interpersonal relationships between athletes and their mentors.

Since it is the responsibility of coaches to prepare their athletes—both physically as well as mentally—to deal with the challenges and pressures that they might confront in competition, each of these chapters will be of interest to current and future coaches.

8 Strategies and Tactics for Special Situations

THE FAST BREAK: SUCCESS OR FAILURE IN THE TRANSITION GAME

The fast break involves an attempt by defenders to secure possession of the ball, to move down court quickly, and to create a high percentage field goal attempt *before* the opponents are able to make an adequate transition from offense to defense. Thus, there are four essential elements or components to a successful fast break, commonly referred to as the 4Ps: possession, passing, penetration, and points.

The first element of any fast break involves the *possession* of the ball. There can be no fast break without the ball. Players must secure the ball by means of a turnover, a defensive rebound (as a result of excellent positioning), or following a completed basket by the opponents. The second ingredient involves the outlet *pass* to initiate the fast break. The ball must be "released" into one of the passing or dribbling lanes on the floor. The third factor involves the quick but safe movement and *penetration* of the ball (and the players) from one end of the court into the offensive end of the floor. This is the transition phase of the fast break. The fourth component, of course, involves the actual field goal attempt at the conclusion of the fast break, resulting in *points* scored. All four components must be present if the fast break is to be successful.

Preventing the Fast Break

Generally speaking, there are four ways to prevent opponents from successfully initiating and completing a fast break. First, being able to score a field goal or free throw tends to bog down the opponent's efforts to move the ball down floor quickly. Making a basket, either a free throw or a field goal, gives time for the scoring team to readjust and make the transition from an offensive mode to one of defense. However, merely scoring does not preclude the opponents from executing a fast-break attack. Many highly successful fast breaks are initiated with an in-bounds pass following a basket.

> **Coaching Hint 149**
> The transition phase of basketball is an all-important part of the game.

> **Coaching Hint 150**
> It is impossible to initiate the fast break if one does not have possession of the ball.

Coaching Hint 151
Hustling—really hustling—up the floor in reaction to an opponent's fast-breaking efforts can reduce or even completely nullify any initial numerical advantage enjoyed by the offense.

A second technique that is helpful in preventing or at least hindering a fast break is maintaining proper floor balance while on offense. Proper floor balance prevents opponents from gaining a numerical advantage once they have gained possession of the ball. Third, effective offensive rebounding prevents the opponents from grabbing the ball off of the boards and beginning their trek down court. In other words, opponents cannot run the fast break if they do not have the ball.

The fourth technique to foil the opponent's fast-breaking efforts involves pure, unadulterated hustle on behalf of the defenders. Defenders must really want to hustle and be able to move up the floor as fast as humanly possible once the opponents have gained possession of the ball. This hustling effort by the defenders can often completely negate any initial numerical advantage possessed by the fast-breaking team. At the very least, such hustle on behalf of the defenders will make it extremely difficult for the opponents to secure noncontested crib shots or even close-in, high percentage field goal attempts.

If the offensive players know that the defenders are capable of retreating back up the floor with great speed, there is greater likelihood that the offensive attackers will be forced to make physical mistakes or errors in judgment because of the pressure exerted by the defenders. Even if the fast-breaking team has players ahead of and in front of some defenders, the fast-breaking team should nevertheless be under pressure in terms of hearing the "pitter-patter" of the defenders' feet coming up behind them in an effort to put a stop to the break. The defenders against the fast break must never give up in their attempt to hustle to their defensive basket in an effort to hinder, delay, or stop the opponent's fast-break attack.

Effectiveness of the Fast Break

Tradition has the fast-break type of attack being more successful against zone defenses than man-to-man defenses. The rationale given for this position is because the time factor involved for the defense in enabling all five defensive players to have sufficient time to set up in a coordinated zone defense. This is not necessary true, however.

Coaching Hint 152
The fast break can be equally effective against both man-to-man and zone defenses.

Similarly, convention has it that the fast break is more effective when a team plays a zone defense. The rationale is that such a team will be a better rebounding team, thus being in a better position to initiate the outlet pass to start the break. This, too, is a bit of folklore. Yes, rebounding is an essential element in the success of any fast-break attack. However, teams can dominate the defensive boards while playing man to man as well as zone. It is the domination of the defensive boards that is so important in initiating the fast break.

In reality, the success of any fast-break attempt is essentially dependent on the skills of the athletes attempting to initiate the fast break as well as the competency level of the opponents. Effective fast breaks can be initiated by teams playing any type of zone defense as well as man-to-man defense.

Coaching Hint 153
The fast break can be equally effective by teams playing zone or man-to-man defenses.

It is not so much the type of defense being played by the either team that determines whether a team's fast-breaking efforts will be successful. Rather, success is determined by how well the opponents execute their defensive efforts against the fast break. Similarly, the skill level of the fast-breaking team has more to do with the success of the fast break than the tactics themselves. It all boils down to how skillful the fast breaking team is and how adept the opponents are in combating the break.

Initiating the Fast Break

Naturally, the key to initiating the fast break is moving the ball up the floor (penetrating the offensive end of the court) as quickly as possible, hopefully before the opponents are able to make the transition from offense to defense. Whether the fast-breaking team obtains possession of the ball following (a) a defensive rebound, (b) a turnover, or (c) following the made basket, traditional thinking stipulates that the ball be moved to the sideline (or the middle of the court) as quickly as possible.

Thus, as soon as the defensive team has obtained possession of the ball, it is imperative that all of the defenders immediately make the transition (mentally and physically) to the offensive mode. The basketball court should be thought of as having three imaginary lanes in existence from one end of the court to the other—along both sidelines and straight down the middle. Upon gaining possession of the ball, the defensive (now offensive) team should immediately attempt to fill these lanes with players.

Executing the Outlet Pass

The ball is typically moved to the sidelines or to the middle of the floor by means of the outlet pass following a made basket, a defensive rebound, or a turnover. The reason that more passes are made to the sidelines rather than to the middle of the floor is that there are more players (both offensive and defensive) in the middle of the court, and thus it is much more difficult to complete passes into this area.

Diagram 8–1 illustrates such a pass by X_3, who was the defensive rebounder of the shot taken by ④. Upon retrieving the ball off the boards, X_3 becomes an immediate offensive threat by looking toward the sideline for a potential pass receiver. The same type of pass can be effected had the shot been successful. In that instance, X_3 simply grabs the ball as it comes through the net, steps out of bounds, and quickly in-bounds the ball to the sideline area.

This sideline outlet pass to X_2, who has in the meanwhile cut to the sideline, is not the only option X_3 has once the rebound has been garnered. A pass can also be made to the middle of the floor, to X_1 who has begun to streak down court, as shown. There is even a third possible passing option. This involves a cross-court pass to X_4 who is moving along the opposite sideline toward the basket.

The ball can also be moved to the nearest sideline or into the middle of the court by the rebounder merely by dribbling to that area of the floor. Sometimes, especially when the opponents are effectively preventing the sideline or mid-court outlet pass, it is just as effective for the rebounder just to turn and take off dribbling down the floor. *The objective is to move the ball—one way or another—up the floor as quickly as possible.*

The Transition Game

Once the ball has been moved via the outlet pass or the dribble to either a sideline or the middle of the court, the team enters the transition phase of the fast break. Typically, once the outlet pass has been completed, most teams attempt to move the ball into the middle of the court as soon as possible (see Diagram 8–2).

This does not mean that the breaking team will stop or hesitate in terms of moving the ball up the floor—just the opposite, in fact. The ball is continuously dribbled toward the offensive end of the court while the ball handler looks for the opportunity to pass the ball into the middle of the floor. Sometimes, the side-

Coaching Hint 154
When starting the fast break, fill the three lanes and quickly get the ball to the sideine or to the middle.

Coaching Hint 155
Most fast breaks are initiated by a pass to the sideline.

Coaching Hint 156
Don't forget that the ball can be dribbled to the sideline or the middle of the court to initiate the fast break.

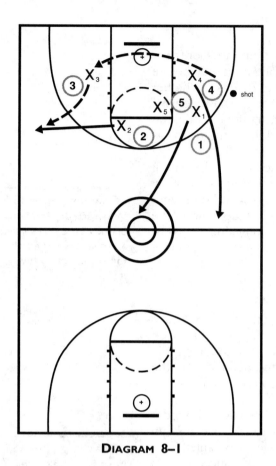

DIAGRAM 8–1

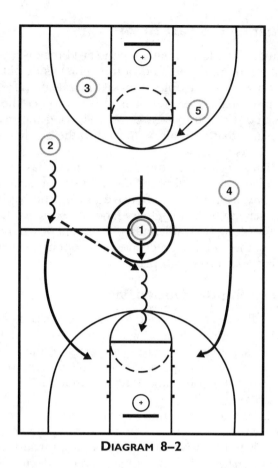

DIAGRAM 8–2

line dribbler can actually dribble into the middle of the floor, although essential seconds are lost in doing so in comparison to passing the ball into the middle lane. It is far more effective to pass the ball to a teammate who is already in the middle lane.

The All-Important Trailer

It is important that the so-called trailer not be neglected in the transition phase of the fast break. The trailer is the fourth offensive player who advances toward the offensive basket, although trailing behind the three teammates who constitute the initial fast-break attack. In this situation (see Diagram 8–2), the trailer is ⑤. This trailer moves to the middle of the floor, as shown. It is the trailer who not infrequently becomes the scorer (or the offensive rebounder) at the conclusion of the fast break. The fifth teammate, ③, the rebounder who had initiated the outlet pass, becomes the defensive safety valve and is the last player to move up the floor.

Concluding the Fast Break

Coaching Hint 157
Don't overlook the importance of the trailer in concluding the fast break.

The ideal concluding formation of the fast break should have offensive players filling all three lanes with the ball in the middle lane. The fourth offensive player, the all-important trailer, follows from behind, also in the middle of the floor. Assuming the ball is in the middle of the floor, the first option is for the dribbler simply to continue to the basket for the close-in shot. This should always be the primary option if the defense is unable to stop such a penetration.

Passing to Either Sideline

In a three against two situation, more likely the defender(s) will be able to put sufficient pressure against the dribbler so that a direct drive to the basket is simply not possible or feasible. In this instance, the dribbler can elect to pull up and stop somewhere between the top of the key and the free throw line (see Diagram 8–3) and pass to one of the two teammates approaching the basket from the wing areas, as shown.

This pass, in all likelihood, will be made on the run rather than completed after ① comes to a complete stop. Once rid of the ball, ① does not continue to the basket but remains near the free throw line or the top of the key ready to receive an outlet pass. The fast break continues with both of the sideline players veering away from their respective sidelines and breaking toward the basket. This is done in anticipation of a pass from ① and a subsequent drive to the bucket.

In this offensive alignment, the fast-breaking team has created a *triangle formation* in which the ball handler, ①, is at the apex of the triangle and the two potential pass receivers on either side. This concluding triangle formation should be the goal any time there is a three against two numerical advantage favoring the offense.

Of course, if the offensive players find themselves in a two against one situation, the obvious stratagem is for the ball handler to split the lone defender

> **Coaching Hint 158**
> Establish the so-called triangle formation when concluding the fast break with a three against two advantage.

> **Coaching Hint 159**
> Split the lone defender by dribbling to the side of the lane when concluding the fast break with a two against one advantage.

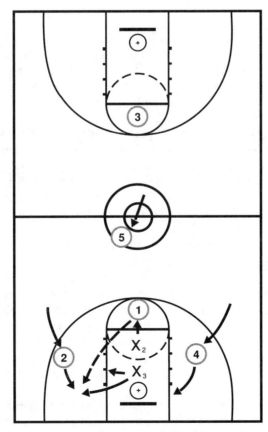

DIAGRAM 8–3

by dribbling to the side of the lane with the other offensive player assuming a position on the opposite side of the lane. This forces the defender to be between the two advancing attackers, at a decided disadvantage.

DEFENSIVE REACTION TO THE SIDELINE PASS

If the defense, in the three against two situation, stops the advance of the ball near the free throw line, the typical defensive reaction is for the back defender, X_3 in Diagram 8–3, to anticipate moving out to the wing where the ball will most assuredly be passed. This move is made to counteract the new offensive threat posed by the sideline offensive player, ②. If ② is not challenged, it is possible that the ball can be dribbled by ② from the sideline or wing directly to the hoop for a score. If ② is prevented from dribbling to the basket, a pass to ④, who has continued moving toward the basket from the other wing slot, should result in a lay-up, or, at worst, a 4- to 8-foot jumper.

Other Passing Options

Of course, there are other passing options open to ②, who has received the ball in the wing. For example, a return pass could be made to ① near the free throw area. This is most likely to occur if X_2 drops off and attempts to protect the basket area. Yet another option is for a pass to be made from the wing area to the trailer, ⑤, who has now moved into the lane on the way to the basket (see Diagram 8–4).

The Fleeting Numerical Advantage

Of course, the reason the fast break is so effective is that the offensive team has a numerical advantage over the defenders, for a limited amount of time. This numerical advantage provides the offensive players with excellent opportunities to get off a high percentage shot as well as securing offensive rebounds should a field goal attempt be unsuccessful.

Since the defenders will not be merely standing around in response to the fast-break attack, however, it is safe to conclude that this "window of opportunity"—the numerical advantage favoring the offense—will not last for very long. In fact, most fast-break opportunities will exist for less than 5 seconds. As a result, it is imperative that the offensive players move the ball up the floor with great dispatch *and* actually score before the defenders regroup and are able to offer some resemblance of defensive resistance. Once the defenders are able to negate the numerical advantage enjoyed by the offense, the advantage of the fast break, in most instances, is quickly nullified.

Typically, two passes are the norm for the fast-breaking team once the ball had been advanced within 15 to 18 feet of the offensive basket. Three or more passes is stretching it in terms of the offensive players having sufficient time to move the ball before the retreating defenders are able to regroup and match up, player against player, with the fast-breaking team. Far too often the players attempting to score off the fast break will end up making too many passes. As a result, the ball is intercepted by a defender coming up from behind in an effort to stop the fast break.

Just because the offense fails to create or maintain a numerical advantage over the defense is no reason not to attempt a high percentage shot. There still may be excellent scoring and offensive rebounding opportunities even when

Coaching Hint 160
When concluding the fast break, be sure to keep passes to a minimum.

Coaching Hint 161
Excellent field goal opportunities can be created in the fast-break situation even without a numerical advantage.

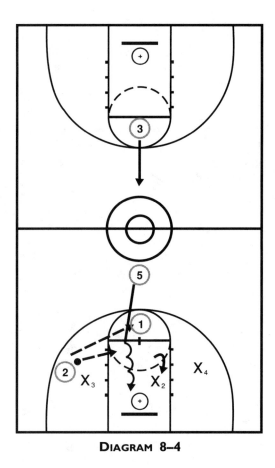

DIAGRAM 8–4

there are the same number of defenders as offensive personnel at the offensive end of the floor. Why should the offensive team pull up and cease their fast-break efforts merely because there are three defenders ready to repel the scoring efforts of three offensive players? Why should the offensive players fail to take a 10- or 15-foot shot merely because there are an equal number of defenders protecting the basket?

There are few reasons to pass up an opportunity to gain a high percentage 10- to 15-foot shot in a three against three or a two against two situation. This is true even if the field goal is not an easy lay-up. This is because the alternative is for the offensive team to bring the ball back out to the perimeter, get reorganized, and then work to create a 15- to 20-foot shot with five defenders guarding the basket. An equally good shot, if not better, can often be taken at the conclusion of the fast break, three against three (or two against two), as can be created in any so-called normal five-against-five situation. The key is to take advantage of and exploit whatever situation is available.

Yet another opportune time for any team to initiate a fast break is when that team has just been victimized by the fast break itself. When one team executes the fast break, regardless of whether a score results, the defenders have an opportunity to initiate a fast break of their own back down the court. This is especially true when the opponents have had a numerical advantage over the defense, because the defenders themselves would have a similar numerical advantage over the offensive players at the opposite end of the court.

Coaching Hint 162
At the conclusion of the fast break, don't hesitate to take the high percentage 10- to 15-foot jumper—that may be as good a shot as can be created even in a five-on-five situation.

Coaching Hint 163
Be wary of players attempting to initiate a fast break following their opponent's successful or unsuccessful fast break.

A STUNTING FAST-BREAK TACTIC

The traditional fast-breaking attack involves moving the ball into the middle of the court as soon as feasible following the outlet pass to the sideline. This is done so as to create a positional advantage for the offense (with the ball in the middle and two potential pass receivers in each sideline) as the ball is advanced closer to the offensive end of the court.

However, the ball does not always have to be moved into the middle of the court for a fast-break effort to be successful. Instead, the ball can remain in possession of the dribbler along the sideline and can be advanced up the court in that area of the floor via the dribble (see Diagram 8–5). One of the advantages of moving the ball the length of the floor by means of the sideline is that there are not many other players in this area to interfere with the dribbler. This is because the opponents are streaking down the middle of the floor in their transition from offense to defense.

Advantages and Perceived Disadvantages of Advancing the Ball along the Sideline

The obvious advantage of keeping the ball along the sideline is that there is less likelihood of a turnover since no dangerous pass must be made into the middle of the floor. The two major perceived disadvantages are that, first, it takes too much time to move the ball to the offensive end of the floor, and second, once there, the offense is not able to create as good a scoring opportunity because the ball is not positioned in the middle of the court.

Neither of these perceived disadvantages should discourage teams from using the sidelines to advance the ball up court. First, often the ball can be dribbled almost as quickly along the sideline as passing the ball to the middle and then dribbling toward the basket. Second, the scoring options that can be created once the ball is moved into the offensive end of the floor along the sideline can be equally effective as those created when the ball is in the middle of the court.

Concluding the Fast Break from the Sideline

Even with the ball being advanced along the sideline, it is still possible for the fast-breaking team to end up with the ball in the so-called middle area between two offensive teammates. The concluding scoring effort can be created in one of two ways. The objective is to have two offensive teammates on either side of the dribbler, who, in turn, is veering away from the sideline and is breaking toward the basket.

In this instance, the player on the right side of the dribbler is ④, who has come from the opposite side of the court. ④ cuts through the lane and takes up a position along the end line and to the right of the dribbler as the latter approaches the basket. The dribbler, ②, stops the dribble some 15 to 18 feet from the basket. ①, who has moved up the floor in the middle of the court, becomes the potential pass receiver to the left of the ball handler.

Thus, it is easy to see that the same triangle formation, with the ball in the middle between two offensive teammates situated on either side of the ball handler, has been established. In this situation, the offense has the traditional three against two numerical advantage. Passes can be made to either ① or to ④ for a quick scoring thrust. Or the trailer, ⑤, can end up with the ball as this player cuts through the middle of the lane.

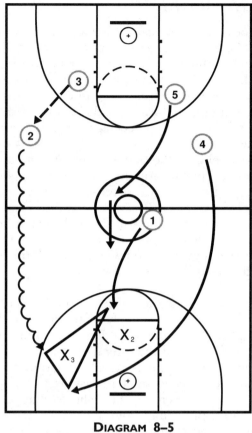

DIAGRAM 8–5

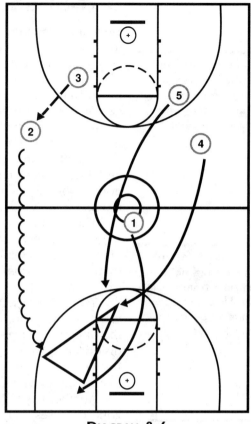

DIAGRAM 8–6

Another way that the concluding triangle formation of the fast break can be established is shown in Diagram 8–6. In this example, it is ① who reaches the offensive end of the floor ahead of ④. Thus, ① immediately cuts through the lane and assumes the position along the end line, some 8 to 10 feet from the basket. And it is the responsibility of ④ to fill in the vacant slot near the free throw line, thus completing the familiar triangle attacking formation. The trailer, ⑤, moves as before, straight toward the basket either for a possible scoring pass or to serve as a potential offensive rebounder.

Success of the Fast Break

Players should be instructed to take advantage of whatever situation is presented or is allowed by the opponents in terms of moving the ball to the offensive end of the court. If the fast-breaking team is able to move the ball into the middle, so be it. The ball is then moved in the middle area of the floor toward the offensive end of the court where the traditional fast-break scoring options may be executed, and the attack is brought to closure with the result being at least two points. However, there can be several reasons why the ball cannot be safely passed or otherwise moved to the middle lane. In this eventuality, the ball will nevertheless still be advanced up the floor, but in this case, along the sideline. The end result, hopefully, will be the same as when the ball is moved into the middle—that is, a numerical advantage by the offense and an excellent scoring opportunity.

OUT-OF-BOUNDS SITUATIONS

Since there are numerous opportunities during any game for a team to in-bound the ball, it only makes sense to be willing and able to attempt to score while in-bounding the ball, if the game situation calls for it. Coaches would do well to plan in advance exactly what their athletes should do in any number of situations in which they are in-bounding the ball. Should the team be satisfied with merely getting the ball safely in bounds? Or should there be an actual attempt to exploit the in-bounds situation by seeking to create a high percentage scoring opportunity as a result of a set, predetermined play?

Out-of-bounds plays may be executed from the offensive team's front court end line, the back court end line, or either sideline. Another variable in the equation is whether the defenders are playing man-to-man defense or are in a zone mode.

The team attempting to score by in-bounding the ball should be careful not to give away its attack by the formation or alignment of the offensive players. It becomes problematic for the defenders if they are faced with a single formation by the offense from which any number of different out-of-bounds plays can be executed.

This is because in the situation just described the defense cannot anticipate exactly which play will be keyed by the opponents merely by the position that the offensive players assume on the court. Thus, the defenders are at a decided disadvantage in not being able to anticipate what the offensive assault will be. Instead, the defenders must wait until their opponents actually begin to move, to cut, and to screen, and then attempt to execute countermeasures.

Another key to any effective out-of-bounds series is the ability to attack both zone defenses and man-to-man defenses, preferably from the same alignment. Some teams will automatically play a zone defense any time the opponents attempt to in bound the ball under the offensive end of the court. Others prefer to attack the offensive team by playing man to man. Still others opt to alternate the type of defense used against the in-bounds play throughout a game. This is done in an attempt to confuse and befuddle the opponent.

The offensive series presented next contains attacking options that can be executed from both the sideline and from under the offensive team's basket. Some of the options are effective against both man-to-man as well as zone defenses. Additionally, some in-bound plays can be used against either zones or man-to-man defenses.

End Line Out-of-Bounds Plays: Offensive Front Court

The most common occurrence for out-of-bounds plays is when the ball is being thrown in under the offensive team's basket. Diagrams 8–7 through 8–10 illustrate four different in-bound attacks that are equally effective against both zones and man-to-man defenses. Additionally, all of these options are initiated from the same box formation.

The Vertical Screen Upon the slap of the ball by the in-bounds passer, ② turns and moves up the lane to set a face screen against X_4, thereby freeing ④ to cut to the wing for the pass and a 10-foot shot (see Diagram 8–7). After the screen has been set, ② pivots and breaks through the lane toward the basket and a short scoring pass. Simultaneously to this action, ③ cuts away from the basket and moves around the top of the key, as shown. This move serves to create an outlet pass. Additionally, ⑤ slides across the lane to the ball side of the court to take up the spot previously vacated by ④. This move by ⑤ provides the

Coaching Hint 164
Offensive teams should always be ready to attempt to score when in-bounding the ball.

Coaching Hint 165
From the same initial alignment, a team should be capable of executing any number of different in-bounds plays.

Coaching Hint 166
A team's arseanal should include out-of-bounds plays that are equally effective against both zones and man-to-man defenses.

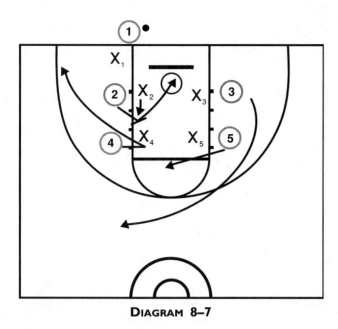

DIAGRAM 8–7

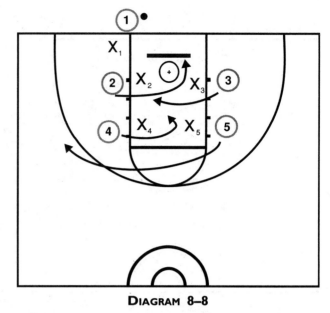

DIAGRAM 8–8

in-bounds passer with a medium-range target, should any of the previously described passes not be made.

The Horizontal Screen   Upon the slap of the ball, ② moves across the lane and erects a face screen against X_3, as shown in Diagram 8–8. As ③ cuts across the lane, the screener, ②, pivots and faces the passer, anticipating a short scoring pass. It is important that ② not stay in the lane too long, lest a 3-second lane violation be called. Nevertheless, if the pick is erected correctly, there is a high probability of getting a very close shot off.

While this baseline screening action is taking place, ④ also moves across the lane to screen for ⑤. As ⑤ moves around this screen and on across the lane looking for the in-bounds pass, either at the edge of the lane or in the left wing, ④ pivots and cuts toward the basket and the possible pass. Again, it is important that ④ not linger in the lane too long, lest a lane violation be called by the officials.

The Diagonal Screen   Upon the slap of the ball, ② moves diagonally across the free throw lane to set a screen against X_5. This momentary screen enables ⑤ to move diagonally through the lane, toward the passer and a possible scoring pass (see Diagram 8–9). After setting the screen, ② pivots and moves down the lane, toward the basket, for a pass. As this action takes place, both ④ and ③ move, as shown, in order to serve as possible outlets or passes of last resort.

The Step Out   Upon the slap of the ball, ② fakes toward the basket but darts back toward the sideline in order to receive the in-bounds pass (see Diagram 8–10). As soon as the ball is passed in bounds, ① steps into the low post slot with arms outstretched facing the new ball handler. A short, quick return pass to ① results in an immediate scoring effort some 5 to 7 feet from the basket.

Although the prime scoring option involves the moves just mentioned, the offensive team must include a secondary attack. This involves the move by ④ across the lane to set a screen against X_5, thus freeing up ⑤ to move either across

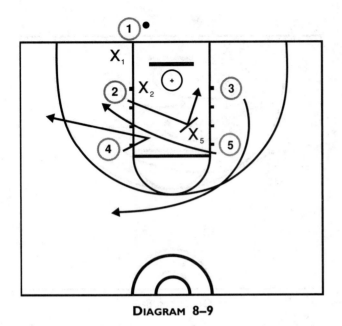

DIAGRAM 8–9

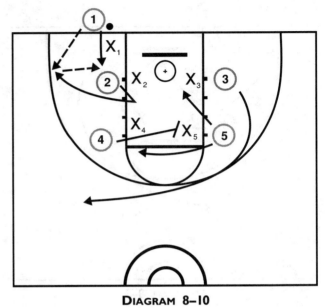

DIAGRAM 8–10

the lane or into the middle of the lane, while serving as a secondary pass receiver. The safety valve is provided by ③, who has moved out beyond the top of the key in the left wing area.

Sideline Out-of-Bounds Plays

Sideline Attack #1 The sideline in-bounds play begins when both ④ and ⑤ move toward the ball, as shown in Diagram 8–11. It is the responsibility of ⑤ to set a (legal) blind screen against X_2, thereby freeing up ② to break for the basket and the lob pass.

Another option is for the in-bounds pass to be made to ④, who darts toward the sideline. If this takes place, ② simply posts up in the low post slot and waits for the relay from ④. The third option, and the safety valve, of this attack is created by ③, who initially moves away from the ball and then quickly cuts back for the outlet pass.

Sideline Attack #2 A second variation of the sideline in-bounds attack is shown in Diagram 8–12. Although this attack is similar to that described in Diagram 8–11, there is a significant difference. The difference is that it is the in-bounds passer, ①, who streaks toward the basket around the screen set by ⑤, once the ball has been put into play. A quick return pass from either ④ or ② results in a crib shot for the offensive team.

End Line Out-of-Bounds Plays: Offensive Back Court

Although it is unusual to attempt to score from an in-bounds situation in the offensive back court, it is not impossible. However, usually such an effort is only successful if the defenders are applying full-court pressure defense, especially against the in-bounds pass. Chapter 7 presented the long bomb attack as an effective weapon in attacking full-court man-to-man pressure tactics. The long bomb attack also serves as an efficient in-bounds play from the offensive back court.

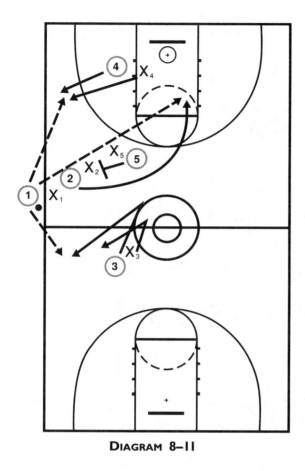

DIAGRAM 8–11

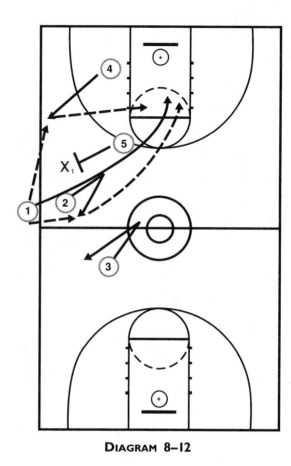

DIAGRAM 8–12

Yet another out-of-bounds play that is effective against full- or three-quarter court, man-to-man pressure is illustrated in Diagram 8–13. The goal in this situation is not to score immediately on the actual in-bounds pass. Rather, the immediate objective is to move the ball up the floor via one or two passes to a position where a high percentage shot can be taken. In this instance, the in-bounds pass can be made to ②, ③, or ④.

A direct pass may be possible to ④ following the screen set by ⑤. In this eventuality, the offensive action involves two against two, ④ and ⑤ against X_4 and X_5. However, if either ② or ③ receives the in-bounds pass, it is the responsibility of the in-bounds passer, ①, to streak immediately down the floor. This is done in the hopes of getting a step ahead of X_1 and receiving a return pass. If this happens, the ball can now be advanced via the dribble straight up the middle of the floor. As ① dribbles toward the basket, both ④ and ⑤ move to either side of the lane, thereby opening up the floor for the traditional three against two fast-break situation and the resulting high percentage shot.

If the defenders are playing a full-court, three-quarter court, or half-court zone defense, it is unlikely that any full-court out-of-bounds play (from the offensive team's back court) will be successful on the first pass. It just is not going to happen. Thus, the offense will have to be satisfied with getting the ball in bounds from the end line of the back court and then advancing the ball up the floor as quickly as possible. It is a mark of a wise coach (and player) to

Coaching Hint 167
Offensive teams frequently have to take what the defense is willing to give them—don't be foolish and attempt to force the situation.

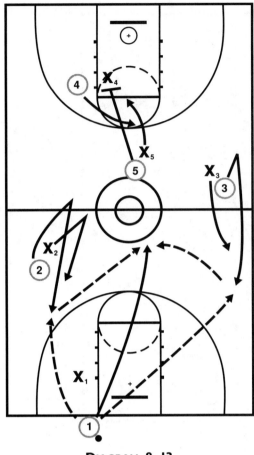

DIAGRAM 8–13

recognize what is possible and what is fanciful, and to make the appropriate decision.

GETTING EXCELLENT LAST-SECOND SHOTS

There will be innumerable times during every season when a team will be facing a situation in which a field goal is an absolute necessity. Perhaps the most common situation is at the end of the contest at which time point production is imperative to emerging victorious. It is the responsibility of the coach to prepare the athletes so that they are ready to meet such a challenge, not only by being able to create a high percentage shot but also making it.

Two Schools of Thoughts on Creating Last-Second Shots

There are two schools of thought when it comes to attempting the last-second shot. Some coaches develop a *special play* (or plays) that results in high percentage shots being created. Other coaches subscribe to the philosophy or theory that their players should just execute a familiar quarter-court offensive attack and take the high percentage shot that would normally be created. Either way, it is important for players to practice creating and executing last-second field goal attempts, both from the two-point range and the three-point range, under a variety of time restrictions and defensive situations.

Of course, excellent last-second shots can be created from most out-of-bounds situations. This is especially true when the in-bounds pass is being executed under the offensive team's own basket or from the sideline in the front court. However, what about when the ball is already in play with the clock ticking away—with 15, 10, 5, or fewer seconds remaining in the game (or half)? What are some excellent scoring attacks that will result in very high field goal attempts? What is a good last-second play against zone defenses? What is a good last-second play against a man-to-man defense?

A Last-Second Play against Zone Defenses

> **Coaching Hint 168**
> Coaches must preplan last-second field goal attempts—don't wait until the game to decide how the team is to create a good shot.

When a coach thinks about creating a last-second shot against the zone, the first question that must be answered is: Does the high percentage field goal need to be a two-point or a three-point shot? That is, does the shooting team need a close-in shot or will a long-distance attempt (generating three-points) be best? The last-second play illustrated in Diagram 8–14 possesses the advantage of creating both types of field goal opportunities at the same time.

The offense is set up in its normal attacking formation—in this case, a 1-3-1 alignment, with a low post on the right side of the lane. The offensive team should attempt to get off a shot with 2 to 3 seconds remaining. This is because if the initial field goal attempt is unsuccessful, there will still be sufficient time for an offensive rebound or a tip-in by a teammate. Similarly, if the initial shot is unsuccessful, there will be insufficient time for the defense to rebound and advance the ball the length of the floor to get off a high percentage field goal attempt before time runs out.

Initiating the Last-Second Play   In this last-second play, with 6 to 7 seconds remaining on the clock, the ball is passed to the left wing player. The purpose of this pass is to get the zone players to shift to the left side of the court in response to this pass. As the defenders shift to the left side, the ball is passed back to the point guard, who immediately relays the ball to the right wing player, ②.

As soon as the ball has been returned from the left wing back to the point guard, the passer, ③, cuts diagonally through the lane on the way to the opposite corner area. Simultaneously, ④, who has been stationed in the right corner, moves toward the basket area in an attempt to set a face screen against X_4, as shown. This screening action frees ③ to cut out to the corner for a possible pass from ② in the right wing. If the team is in need of a two-point field goal, then ③ can stop, turn and shoot as soon as the ball is received. However, if a three-point shot is necessary to tie or to win the game, then ③ must travel out beyond the three-point line and take the jumper from there.

However, there is more to this last-second play than just the attempt to free ③ for a jumper along the baseline. Notice that ⑤, following the screen set for ③, remains stationed in the low post slot (on the "block") on the right side of the lane. By being in this location, ⑤ is in an excellent position to receive a direct pass from ② should X_4 be successful in fighting through or over the momentary screen set by ④. If ⑤ should get the ball while in the low post slot, any number of post moves will result in a close-in two-point shot attempt, and maybe a foul by the defense to boot.

Additionally, as soon as the ball has been relayed to the right wing area, the point guard takes a few steps inside the key area, near the free throw line. It may be possible for ① to actually move to the edge of the free throw line. This maneuver by ① exploits a weakness in the zone should X_5 vacate the middle of the lane in an effort to provide defensive help against ⑤ in the low post slot. The right wing player now has a third scoring option available, a pass to ① standing near the free throw line.

Thus, the offensive team has several scoring opportunities, both two-point and three-point shots. All of these maneuvers can take place within 3 to 4 seconds. The key to the success of this last-second play is the decision-making ability of the right wing player, ②, who must decide when and to whom to make a scoring pass. There are actually four scoring passes that ② can elect to complete, two primary and two secondary.

The *two primary scoring passes* involve getting the ball either to the left wing player as ③ comes around the screen set by ④, or to ⑤, who is open for a direct pass as soon as X_4 leaves the low post area in an effort to guard ③. There are also *two secondary scoring passes*— either to the corner area as ③ crosses the three-point line, or to the point guard as ① steps toward the free throw line.

A Last-Second Play against Man-to-Man Defense

When attempting to create a high percentage shot against the man-to-man defense, it is important to remember two very important rules. First, keep the defenders spread out on the court so as to prevent an easy double-teaming situation. Second, keep the ball in the hands of the best shooter and ball handler.

Diagram 8–15 reveals the initial alignment of the offensive personnel with two players stacked next to each other on the side of the lane. A third player, ③, serves as a rover running around the double-stack screen (in any direction) in an effort to rub off the defensive player, X_3. The remaining two players are on the right side of the court, as shown.

The ball handler, ①, is stationed to the right side of the top of the key and has the entire right side of the floor in which to dribble against a long defender, X_1. The fifth offensive player, ②, is positioned near the baseline, thus clearing the whole right side of the court while serving as an outlet pass for ① if such a pass is necessary. It is important that ② be close enough to the basket that

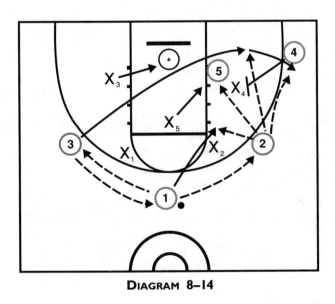

DIAGRAM 8–14

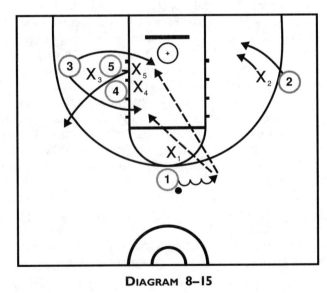

DIAGRAM 8–15

should X_2 leave the defensive assignment and attempt to double team the ball handler, a quick pass to ② will result in a high percentage shot.

Using the Double Stack   This attacking formation provides several scoring opportunities for the offense, depending on the game situation and the amount of time remaining on the clock. One option is to attempt to get the ball into ③ as this rover cuts back and forth around the double-stacked screen, ④ and ⑤. A second option is for the bottom player on the stack, ⑤, to use ④ as a stationery screen and cut out to the left wing area—and a possible scoring pass. Of course, the ball handler may elect to merely retain the dribble and back into scoring position against the lone defender.

Drive toward the Basket and Dish Off to the Outside   Still another option is for the ball handler, depending on the type of defense played by X_1, to blast by the defender and drive directly to the basket. In this situation, should X_2 attempt to sag off and provide defensive help, an outlet pass to ② can result in either a two-point or a three-point field goal attempt.

Reaction to Double-Teaming Action by the Defense   Of course, if the defense attempts to double team ①, it is imperative that the ball handler give the ball up as soon as it is obvious that defensive help is on the way. Rarely will the defensive help be X_2, because a release or outlet pass to ② would simply break the back of the defense. More likely, double-teaming help will come from one of the two defenders, either X_4 or X_5, who are guarding the double stack. If this happens, and both ④ and ⑤ remain stacked together in the low post, one of these offensive players should move up the lane toward the free throw line to receive the outlet pass. This safety valve pass should be possible since one defender cannot adequately guard both ⑤ and ④ in this situation. However, if ⑤ has already cut to the left wing, it is highly unlikely that either X_5 or X_4 will be involved in double-teaming action against the point guard.

STALLING OR FREEZING THE BALL

Being able to protect the ball while retaining possession of it and yet still being capable of scoring should the opportunity present itself are very important capabilities in any team's arsenal. In order to stall or freeze the ball, it is imperative that the defense is prevented, or at least discouraged, from successfully implementing any double-teaming efforts. This is frequently accomplished by keeping the players spread on the half-court area. However, there have been effective and efficient stalling tactics that have violated this concept. For example, the double-stack attack or formation in Diagram 8–15 has been used as a foundation for a stalling or freezing strategy.

Stalling players should not be so reluctant to take the "gimmie" shot that they place themselves in a vulnerable situation. If the pressing defenders know that the offensive team will not take any shot, regardless of how good it is, nothing will prevent the defenders from taking extreme risks in their efforts to force a turnover and seize possession of the ball.

Indeed, there are times and situations that call for absolutely no shot to be taken, regardless of how wide open the ball handler might be. However, on the other hand, there are many situations when the stalling players place themselves at a decided disadvantage in giving up the obvious crib shot. It is up to the coach to ensure that the stalling players know how to differentiate when to take the shot from a stalling pattern and when to pass it up.

Coaching Hint 169
Offensive players driving to the basket must always be on the alert for sagging defenders.

Coaching Hint 170
Stalling implies that the offensive team will keep the ball unless an obvious easy shot is created.

Coaching Hint 171
When stalling, don't be afraid of taking the "gimmie" shots if that is what the defense offers.

Coaching Hint 172
Freezing the ball means putting the ball away in a "deep freezer" with no shots taken—regardless of how wide open or close to the basket the shooter might be.

Using the Regular Offense as a Stalling or Freezing Attack

Some coaches have experienced significant success in their stalling efforts by merely running their regular offense but not taking any shots other than the obvious lay-up. This tactic has been successful for three major reasons:

1. The opponents might not realize that the offensive team is actually stalling for some time. In this event, the stalling team gains valuable seconds or even minutes.
2. The offensive players would have had great experience in executing their regular offensive series. The only difference between the regular offensive attack and the stalling attack is that in the latter case, nothing but "gimmie" shots are to be taken.
3. The offensive alignment is such that the players are spread out on the offensive end of the court and/or the attack involves a lot of cutting moves, thus making double teaming efforts very difficult.

The Box Stall

The box stall (see Diagram 8–16), is an example of excellent floor balance in a stalling attack. The ball handler, ①, is isolated in the middle of the court while the remaining teammates are spread out in each of the four corners. The movement of the offensive players are simplistic yet very effective.

Keeping the Ball in the Middle of the Offensive Court

It is the responsibility of the ball handler to move to and remain in the middle of the half court all the while threatening to drive to the basket. The two players on each side of the floor move to exchange positions with each other, as shown, so as to be free to receive an outlet pass from the ball handler. Beginning with the 1993 basketball season, the 5-second count on the dribbler who is closely guarded was abolished. As a result, it is now possible for the ball handler to continue merely to dribble in the open middle area of the court without fear of being called for a 5-second violation. This has great implications for the stalling tactics of any team.

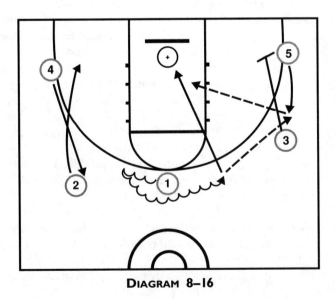

Diagram 8–16

Getting Rid of the Ball Once the Ball Handler Stops Dribbling

Once the ball handler, ①, stops dribbling, a pass must be quickly but safely completed to a teammate on either side of the court. Once such a pass is completed, the passer immediately cuts toward the basket for a possible return pass and a quick score. If this return pass to ① is not possible, the new ball handler dribbles into the now vacant middle area of the half court and continues to dribble while protecting the ball. ① now takes up the position along the side of the court that the new ball handler has just vacated. Thus, the initial alignment of the stalling attack is once again established.

JUMP BALL SITUATION

Today, there are only a few instances in any amateur basketball game where there are actual jump ball situations in which an official tosses up a ball between two opposing players. This is because of the rule change that now provides for alternative possession of the ball, once the game starts, whenever a jump ball is called by the officials.

However, coaches would be making a serious mistake to neglect the jump ball situation altogether. Instead, they would do well to pay attention to and work on mastering or controlling the jump ball toss. This is because every possession is important, especially when a lost possession can result in a score against you while a possession gained can result in a score for you. How many games are lost by a basket? Too many.

There are essentially two factors or situations that alter how players and coaches view the ball being tossed by an official in the center circle: first, when one's own players have a decided advantage (height or jumping ability) when the ball is tossed, and second, when one's opponents have the obvious advantage when the official throws up the ball.

> **Coaching Hint 173**
> Do not neglect the jump ball situation.

The Jump Ball: When One Has the Advantage

When a team has a height or jumping ability advantage in the jump ball circle, the players can be aligned as shown in Diagram 8–17. In this scenario, ⑤ attempts to tip the ball over X_5, to teammate ④. As soon as the ball is tipped in the air, ③ streaks for the offensive basket in anticipation of a quick pass from ④ and the easy crib shot. Nothing can demoralize an opponent more than a quick, easy score right off the bat from the jump ball circle.

Even if the quick pass is not possible, the team still remains in possession of the ball. At that point, the players may then realign in their regular half-court offensive set. Of course, the jumper may also elect merely to play it safe by tipping the ball back towards the back court, to a waiting teammate, either ② or ③. In this event, the possession of the ball is secured, although an immediate scoring opportunity would not be created.

The Jump Ball: When One's Opponents Have the Advantage

When the opponent's center jumper possesses an obvious advantage in terms of height or jumping ability, coaches would do well to take steps to prevent being exploited. One strategy to prevent the opponents from scoring off of the toss involves stacking the players as depicted in Diagram 8–18, with ④ stationed

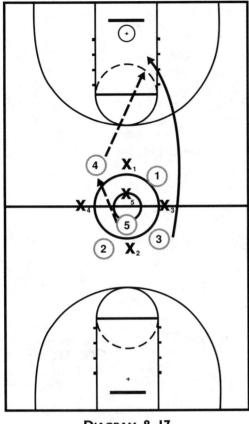

DIAGRAM 8–17

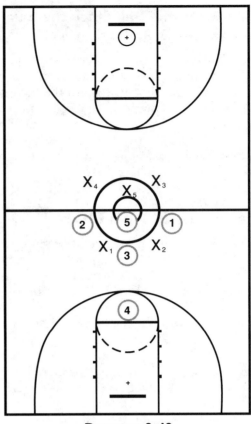

DIAGRAM 8–18

under one's own basket. The other teammates—①, ②, and ③—are aligned at midcourt, but on their side of the circle.

This type of positioning forces or encourages the opponents to tip the tossed ball back toward their own basket. In this eventuality, the defensive players will have time to react, adjust and move to defend their own basket. However, the opponents are not able to execute a quick scoring play right off of the jump ball situation.

SPECIAL STUNTING QUARTER-COURT DEFENSES

Several special stunting defenses can be used to throw a wrench into the opponent's normal offensive attack. These stunting defenses involve a combination where some defenders play zone defense while one or two other defenders are assigned to cover an offensive player man to man. These special defenses include (a) the triangle and two, (b) the box and one, and (c) its variation, the diamond and one.

The box-and-one and the diamond-and-one defenses are especially effective when opponents have only one exceptionally strong scoring threat while the remaining players are only so-so shooters. The triangle-and-two stunting defense is called for when the opponents have two exceptionally effective scorers while the remaining offensive players are mediocre.

All three of these stunting defenses can be equally effective in disrupting an opposing team's regular, methodical, and rather staid offensive patterns. This is because the stunting maneuvers involved in all three of these special defenses are so unique that the so-called regular or normal offensive ploys are usually not very effective in generating high percentage scoring opportunities.

When an opponent traditionally executes a very structured offense and suddenly finds itself up against an usual or stunting-type defense, the regular offensive maneuvers in that team's repertoire may not be adequate. The result is a breakdown in the effectiveness and efficiency of the regular offense attack(s). In short, an offensive team is frequently at a disadvantage when threatened with something that is out of the ordinary, such as one of these stunting defensive attacks. This is especially true in pressure-packed game situations.

> **Coaching Hint 174**
> Stunting defenses can play havoc with opponents' offensive attacks because of the uniqueness of the defensive maneuvers.

The Triangle and Two

This defense has three players playing a zone defense while aligned in a triangle formation (see Diagram 8–19). The remaining two players are assigned man-to-man coverage against the opponent's top offensive threats.

Individual Defensive Assignments in the Triangle and Two   The two roving defenders, X_4 and X_3, who have the responsibility for guarding the top two scorers, ④ and ③, must maintain tight man-to-man coverage against their respective assignments. These two defenders do not sag off their assignments unless ③ and ④ move out of their normal scoring ranges. At all other times, the two roving defenders play belly to belly against their offensive opponents.

The three remaining defenders coordinate in playing a zone with X_1 having responsibility for guarding the top of the key area while both X_2 and X_5 zone their respective wing areas as well as the middle area.

The Box and One

The box and one is a special defense in which a lone offensive player, ③, is targeted for special man-to-man defense pressure (by X_3) while the remaining four defensive players play a modified zone defense (see Diagram 8–20). The zoning action is initiated from a box formation, with two players, X_2 and X_1, stationed

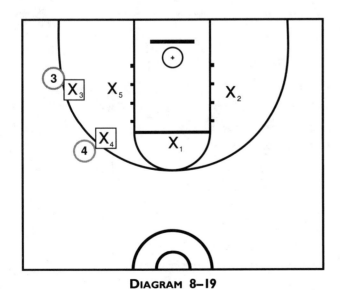

DIAGRAM 8–19

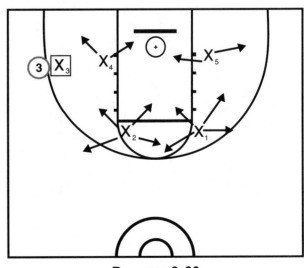

DIAGRAM 8–20

on either side of the lane near the top of the key. The remaining two defenders, X_4 and X_5, are situated on both sides of the free throw lane, each in a low to medium post area.

Individual Defensive Responsibilities   The two defensive guards have primary responsibility for the areas of the floor near and beyond the free throw line extended, including the wing slots. The remaining two defenders, X_4 and X_5, are responsible for the lane and their respective wing areas, including the low post slots and along the baseline.

The Diamond and One

Like the box and one, the diamond and one is especially effective in attempting to put the clamps on an opponent's "top gun." However, in this stunting defense, the remaining defenders align themselves in a diamond formation and execute their various defensive coverages from this configuration (see Diagram 8–21).

Individual Defensive Responsibilities X_1 must be able to cover a great deal of territory since this defender has responsibility for the key area. The two wing players, X_2 and X_4, must guard their respective wings as well as be prepared to slide into the middle of the lane when the ball is on the opposite side of the floor. The fourth defender, X_5, in the diamond formation, has responsibility for the low to midpost area inside the free throw lane. Additionally, X_5 is accountable for both low post slots on either side of the lane.

ATTACKING THE SPECIAL OR STUNTING DEFENSES

Coaching Hint 175
Remain calm, cool, and collected in the face of any stunting or special defense.

The first rule in attacking stunting or special defenses such as the triangle and two, the box and one, and the diamond and one is to remain calm, cool and collected. Two of the major objectives of any stunting defense are to cause confusion and to force the offensive players to make rash decisions, resulting in errors. Thus, it is important to take one's time and not fall into the trap that the defenders are attempting to create.

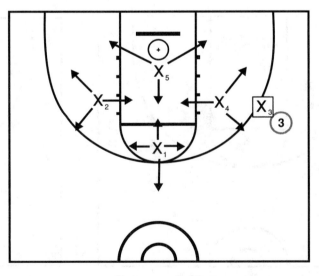

Diagram 8–21

Execute the Regular Half-Court Zone Offense

Sometimes, it is best just to run the regular zone attack against the stunting defense. Since the offensive players are most familiar with their regular zone offense, they should have no difficulty in simply executing it against any of these stunting defenses.

Use the "Top Gun" as a Screener against the Stunting Zones

Many offensive teams have experienced success in using the offensive player (who is usually the "top gun") being guarded in a man-to-man mode as a *screener* against the defenders who are playing the stunting zone. In this situation, the offensive team is sacrificing the scoring potential of its best scorer but it gains high percentage shots for other players.

Use Individual Zone Defenders as Interference against Opponents Playing Man to Man

Instead of using the "top gun" as a screener to run interference for teammates, some coaches prefer to do just the opposite. That is, the offensive player being played man to man maneuvers so that the zone defenders inadvertently become screens. That is, the positioning of individual zone defenders (as well as other offensive players) interfere with the efforts of the defender attempting to enforce man-to-man coverage.

CONCLUDING COMMENTS ABOUT PLANNING FOR GAME SITUATIONS

Coaches would do well to anticipate the worse possible case scenario in terms of what will or could happen in actual game competition—and then prepare their charges to meet such challenges. Planning in advance for special situations not only helps the athletes learn and master specific skills but such planning also helps to create confidence among the players and the coaches. This is because they are aware that they are preparing for actual game competition. Hopefully, nothing the athletes face in future games will come as a complete shock to them, having prepared, well in advance, in practice, for such eventualities.

Coaching Hint 176
It is frequently better to perform or execute what one is familiar with rather than attempt to improvise in the heat of battle.

Coaching Hint 177
It should not make any difference who scores, as long as the team is able to score—do not force the team's big gun to score when facing stunting defenses.

9 The Proper Use of Drills

THE IMPORTANCE OF DRILLS

Drills are an indispensable aspect of coaching basketball. No coach today would attempt to teach the skills (individual as well as team skills) involved in the dynamic and fast-paced sport of basketball without utilizing drills. Drills should be an essential component of almost every practice session. The major challenge facing each and every coach is to determine (a) what type of drills to use, (b) when to use them, and (c) how much time to devote to each individual drill.

What exactly are drills? *Drills* are physical and mental repetitive exercises in which athletes are able to rehearse those skills and competencies, within a practice session, that are required to be mastered and performed in actual game situations. The purpose of any drill is to facilitate the learning and improving of both mental and physical skills required in the performance of both fundamental and elite skills in the sport. Drills should be viewed as a means to an end—that is, the learning and mastery of those skills necessary to be competitive in the sport.

SELECTING APPROPRIATE DRILLS

Not only must appropriate drills be selected by the coach, but it is important that the drills adopted be used in an appropriate manner. Drills must be suitable for the age and interest level of the athletes as well as the youngsters' current skill levels and experience. There is also an appropriate time and place for the greatest benefit to be derived from the use of individual drills. Of course, drills should not be overused or abused. Too much of a good thing can be boring, distracting, and even damaging to the learning process.

> **Coaching Hint 178**
> Drills are indispensable in the teaching, learning, practicing, and mastering of both simple and complex skills and competencies.

> **Coaching Hint 179**
> Drills are a means to an end.

> **Coaching Hint 180**
> The selection and use of drills should be made in light of the skill level of the athletes.

COMPONENTS OF MEANINGFUL DRILLS

There are several criteria that can be used to judge the effectiveness and efficiency of individual drills. Some of these include:

1. Drills should be designed, if possible, so as to allow athletes to work simultaneously on more than one skill at a time.
2. Drills should be simple and easily understood.
3. Athletes should have confidence in and understand the purpose of the drills.
4. Drills should actually accomplish the objective(s) for which they are being used.
5. Drills should be an essential part of the total teaching process.
6. There should be an obvious connection between the drill itself and the skill(s) needed in competition—and the athletes should be aware of same.
7. In the introduction and teaching of drills, there should be progression from the simple to the complex.
8. Simple drills should be capable of being combined with other more complex drills to produce a more meaningful whole.
9. Drills must be economical in terms of time spent, space used and energy expended.
10. Drills should utilize as many athletes as possible and keep "down time" to an absolute minimum (athletes learn little by standing around).
11. Drills should reflect game conditions and require players to make game-like decisions under game-like situations.

> **Coaching Hint 181**
> The justification for the use of any drill is whether the drill actually facilitates the learning process.

Justifying the Use of Drills

In the selection and use of drills, it is very important that the drills actually accomplish what they purport to accomplish. That is, the drills must actually facilitate the learning of various skills, whether simple or complex. Coaches must have rationales for using specific drills; they should not practice a drill just to be drilling in practice. Indiscriminate use of drills is not only foolish and wasteful of energies and time but it is also counterproductive.

Players should also be fully aware of the purpose of the drills. Naturally, for some types of drills, it is quite obvious. However, it cannot hurt and can be a big help to periodically remind the athletes why time is being spent in the practice of specific drills. When athletes understand why a particular drill is part of the workout, the practice experience can become more satisfying and even enjoyable. The consequence is that the drilling routine is much more likely to be truly productive, both for individuals and for the team as a whole.

> **Coaching Hint 182**
> Athletes should understand the rationale behind the use of individual drills.

SIMPLE AND COMPLEX SKILLS

Drills can help train athletes to perform and master simple as well as complex skills. Some drills involve the entire skill, such as shooting a specific number of free throws and then moving off of the line before resuming shooting additional free throws. Other drills might involve only a component or small part of a larger movement series or a portion of a pattern of movement that must be mastered. An example of such a drill could involve individual athletes moving from behind a stationary screen, taking two steps along the baseline, in an effort to receive a pass, and then executing a 15-foot jumper.

This move off a screen, combined with receiving a pass and the subsequent field goal attempt, *is only part of the total offensive series or pattern* that must be mastered. In this example, the overall offensive pattern or series is broken down into several of its component parts and each part is practiced piecemeal by the athletes. After players have practiced small segments of a total offense, they then attempt to put all of the pieces or segments together. They can then practice the total skill—in this case, the entire offensive series that can consist of numerous screens, cutting movements, and passes by any number of offensive personnel.

Coaches would do well to devise drills that would help athletes learn more than a single skill. Thus, truly effective and efficient drills are those that do, indeed, "kill two or three birds with one stone." There are innumerable examples of so-called combination drills. Essentially, these combination-type drills are really nothing more than a uniting of several aspects of individual drills into a single drill.

Coaching Hint 183
In using drills, "kill two or three birds with one stone."

EXAMPLE OF A SINGLE-PURPOSE DRILL: "RUNNING THE LINES"

An example of a single-purpose drill is having the athletes "run the lines." This is a drill where players dash from one end line to the nearest free throw line and back again to the end line. They then immediately dash up the floor to the half-court line and back to the same end line. Then, they run to the furthest free throw line and back again to the same end line. Next, they retrace this pattern and run full court to the opposite end line and return. Then, once again, they run to the far free throw line and back, and then to the midcourt line and back, and, finally, to the nearest free throw line and back. This so-called running the lines can be repeated any number of times. If this drill involves nothing more than athletes running back and forth between the various lines on a court, then this can be said to be a single-purpose drill (the mission being to have the individual players work on their physical conditioning).

EXAMPLE OF A COMBINATION DRILL: PIGGY-BACKING ON RUNNING THE LINES

The same drill may be utilized with an added wrinkle to create a combination-type drill. For example, instead of just having individual players run back and forth between the lines, as they run between one end line and the other, provide each player with a basketball and ask the athletes to dribble the ball while running the lines. Plus, the athletes can then be asked to practice taking either crib shots or field goals (with score being kept) from a variety of spots on the floor, as they reach each basket at either end of the court.

The consequence of this piggy-backing of additional skills to the original drill is that the players are able to work on more than one thing at a time. Athletes have multiple opportunities to perform several skills at the same time—skills that are necessary in the heat of the competitive battle, in an actual game. For example, they run and dribble down the floor. They change direction when they reach each line. They practice eye-hand-foot coordination. They shoot on the run. They shoot while under pressure. They shoot while being physically challenged and tired.

All drills should provide easy cross-over from the practice site to the actual game site. In other words, actual game conditions (pressure, physical challenges

Coaching Hint 184
Drills in practice should be as close to actual game situations as possible.

and decision making opportunities) should be simulated in performing drills in practice. Consider shooting free throws as an example. There can be justification for a player to sometimes shoot 50 free throws in succession. Doing so is an example of attempting to develop and *overlearn* correct shooting techniques. There is, indeed, a time and place to have athletes practice in such a fashion.

However, shooting 50 shots in a row does not help the individual athlete practice the skill of free throw shooting *in an actual game-like atmosphere*. Only rarely will an athlete be asked to shoot more than two free throws at a time in a game situation. And only rarely will a player go to the free throw line without having just been involved in intense physical exertion on the floor, in a pressure situation.

A REALISTIC FREE THROW DRILL

Individual athletes should be encouraged to practice free throw shooting by actually shooting two (maybe three) shots at a time before then stepping off of the line. The athlete can then return to the free throw line to attempt an addition set of two or three free throws. To make the situation even more realistic for the athlete, encourage the individual, after taking the two or three free throws, to run around the gymnasium (or to dribble the ball around the court or around obstacles) before returning to the free throw line.

Requiring the athlete to step up to the free throw line in a competitive or pressure situation, immediately after the individual has been physically challenged by the trek around the floor, creates a more realistic situation in which to attempt the free throw(s). This is exactly the type of situation the athletes will find themselves in when they go to the line in an actual game.

It is very rare that an athlete will take shots from the line after coming directly from the bench. Most likely, the free throw shooter would have been actively engaged in strenuous physical activity on the floor and will be sweaty, a little or very tired, and mentally stressed (pressured). Thus, this is how an athlete should practice shooting free throws—sweaty, a little or very tired, and mentally stressed.

Additional Tactics to Make Free Throw Shooting More Realistic

There are several other tactics or strategies that can result in the free throw shooting practice being more game-like. For example, game-like realism can be created by placing pressure on the individual shooters by having contests between individual free throw shooters as well as groups of players.

An even more realistic game-like situation can be created by placing offensive and defensive players on the sides of the free throw lane, just as in a game. This allows both offensive and defensive players to practice rebounding missed free throw shots and involves the shooter in a real game-like situation. If offensive players grab the missed shot, they are to immediately attempt to put the ball back on the glass. If the defensive players secure the rebound, they practice initiating the fast break by throwing the ball to a teammate streaking toward the sideline.

Asking a player to serve as an "official" who hands the ball to the free throw shooter completes the realistic drill. This "official" hands the shooter the ball just as an official would in an actual contest and starts the 10-second count on the shooter. Keeping score and making a contest of this and other drills adds to the realism of the learning experience. The result is a truly realistic game-like situation—one that will prepare the athlete to perform at a high level in actual competition.

Coaching Hint 185
Practice free throw shooting while tired, sweaty, and mentally stressed (under pressure).

BREAKING DOWN THE OFFENSE INTO A SERIES OF DRILLS

Typically, offensive patterns or plays are broken down into their component parts. Players are then given opportunities to practice these "parts" of the whole. Then the parts are combined to more closely resemble the execution of the total offensive series or pattern in a game situation.

Using the Whole-Part-Whole Method of Coaching/Teaching

A coach might introduce the entire offensive attack or pattern (the "whole") to the athletes by having the players walk through the various options. Or a coach might show a film or video tape of the offense being successfully executed either in a practice session or in an actual game.

Then, the essential components of the total offense can be broken down and practiced individually (the "parts") as drills in various practice sessions. After the various segments of the offense are practiced, improved on, and hopefully mastered, the coach can allow the players to combine the parts into the total offensive pattern (the "whole" again). Thus, the coach has progressed through the whole-part-whole stage of teaching (coaching) the offensive attack in question. The same concept holds true when teaching defensive skills and tactics.

TYPICAL TYPES OF DRILLS USED IN PRACTICES

Drills are typically used in such areas as rebounding and blocking out; field goal shooting (stationary, on the run, dribbling, cutting off a screen); free throw shooting; dribbling; passing and catching; screening; fighting through, over or around screens; conditioning; defensive stance; initiating the outlet pass for the fast break; and concluding the fast break, just to mention a few.

Following are some very specific drills that have proved to be most successful in facilitating the teaching, the learning, and the mastery of the fundamentals involved in basketball. Many of these drills can be equally effective with the elite athlete as well as the neophyte. This is because both the beginning and the more experienced basketball player must demonstrate competency in the fundamentals if they are to play the great sport of basketball successfully.

Each of the drills presented here have been designed to help the individual athlete, regardless of skill level, master these fundamental skills. The ultimate objective is for the basketball player to perform these skills as if the skills were second nature to the individual. The physical performance of fundamentals need to be performed without consciously thinking of the physical acts themselves. That is why drills are performed almost on a daily basis, to assist in the *overlearning* of such skills.

Three-on-Three Drill

Athletes are able to practice many of their individual offensive and defensive skills in a three-on-three situation. In Diagram 9–1, both teams of three players each start near the midcourt line. At the slap of the ball, the three offensive players attempt to score against the three defenders. This simple drill requires the defenders to regroup quickly in response to the offensive players putting the ball into play. Also, if the attacking team cannot score a quick basket off the break

> **Coaching Hint 186**
> When teaching a complex task or complicated physical activity, break down that which is to be mastered into its component parts and practice the parts separately—then combine the parts into the integrated whole.

> **Coaching Hint 187**
> Athletes need to overlearn fundamentals.

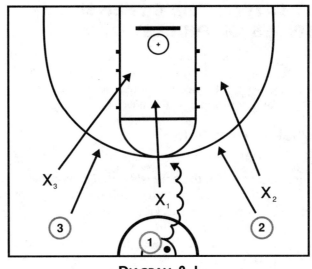

DIAGRAM 9–1

situation, both teams then work on their quarter-court offensive and defensive skills.

An adaptation of this drill involves moving the six players to the opposite end of the court and beginning the same drill at that distance. This creates an opportunity for both defenders and the offensive personnel to adjust and run the entire length of the court in an effort to score or to defend the basket.

Yet another modification of this simple drill has one of the defenders, X_1, being required to wait at the end line until the offensive players reach midcourt. Only at that time can X_1 begin to rush up the floor to render assistance to the two teammates attempting to defend against the three offensive attackers (see Diagram 9–2). This tactic allows the offensive players to practice executing the fast break. Thus, attackers must attempt to score quickly before the defensive trailer, X_1, can arrive and help defend the basket. Also, this drill gives the defensive players opportunities to practice stopping or at least delaying the quick score, especially when outnumbered.

Most importantly, this drill teaches the defensive trailer, X_1, the importance of hustling up the floor to provide help to teammates. The defenders will quickly learn that it takes only a few seconds of delaying tactics to provide sufficient time for X_1 to hustle up the floor to provide effective defensive assistance against the fast break. As a result, both offensive and defensive players not only are able to *practice and perfect* various offensive and defensive maneuvers and tactics but also to *understand* why such tactics and skills are necessary for the successful basketball player and team.

Circle Lay-Up Drill

The circle lay-up drill is a multipurpose exercise that allows the players to work on a large number of offensive skills—including dribbling, passing, and shooting—while at the same time improving physical conditioning. The players line up in four lines, as shown in Diagram 9–3. The player ③, in front of line A, and the player ⑨, in front of line D, each have a basketball.

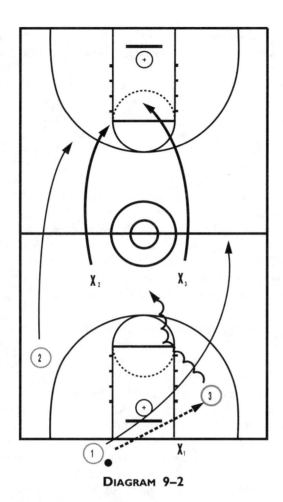

DIAGRAM 9–2

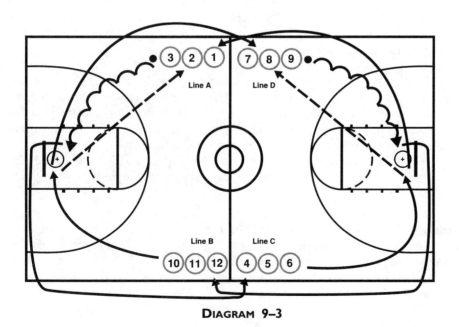

DIAGRAM 9–3

Running (Circling) around the Court   At the start of the drill, each player runs around the court in a circle, either clockwise or counterclockwise. Those players in line A dribble to the basket and attempt a lay-up. They then continue to run around (counterclockwise) the outer edge of the court and take up a position in line C and become rebounders. The players in line D also dribble to their basket and attempt a left-hand crib shot and then continue clockwise to take a position in line B.

Those in line B start out as rebounders. These athletes retrieve the ball and throw it to the next player in line A before advancing along the sideline (clockwise) to assume a position in line D as a shooter. Similarly, those players in line C are rebounders first and then become shooters when they run the length of the floor and join line A.

The result is that the athletes are running in a circle around the court. Some are moving clockwise while others are moving counterclockwise. Each player becomes a shooter while at one end of the court and assumes the role of a rebounder (retriever) and passer at the opposite end. Boredom is prevented because no one player is a rebounder all the time.

Using More Basketballs   Initially, only two balls are used, one in line A and one in line D. However, this soon becomes too simple. To make it more challenging, add another basketball in line A and another in line D, and allow the athletes to continue the drill. Subsequently, after the players are adept at the drill while using two balls in line A and in line D, the coach may allow three basketballs in these two lines. The addition of a third ball in line A and in line D creates much more of a challenge for all of the athletes.

Coaching Hint 189
Require the athletes to run close to the sideline as they circle the floor—to do otherwise defeats the purpose of the drill.

It will not take long for the players to realize that they can cut out a great deal of running as they circle the court by moving away from the sideline and toward the center of the floor. However, this defeats one of the major objectives of this drill—to increase *aerobic conditioning*. The players must keep close to the sideline as they make their circular pattern around the court.

Far too often, athletes become lackadaisical in their lay-up attempts, especially in practice, and doubly so in drills. This is to be avoided at all costs. Whether it is a lay-up in practice or a crib shot in a game, with the score tied and only seconds remaining, the athlete should approach the shot with equal seriousness and determination.

Coaching Hint 190
Emphasize the importance of players always being serious in practice as they shoot lay-ups—never take a crib shot for granted.

Actually, the shooting aspect of this drill, not to mention the dribbling and passing components, serve two very important purposes. First, the shooting, rebounding, and passing opportunities enable individual athletes to practice and improve upon these all important fundamental skills while performing at full speed. Second, and equally important, shooting, dribbling, and passing make the drill itself more enjoyable by diminishing the monotony usually associated with such aerobic conditioning and skill development exercises. The fact remains, athletes must view all of the components of the circle lay-up drill with equal relevance.

Forbidding Rebounds from Hitting the Floor   Another tactic that can place an additional challenge for those players who are rebounders in this drill is to require that they get to the rebounds prior to the ball hitting the floor. This places greater pressure and higher expectations on the rebounders. As a consequence, these athletes must concentrate even more on getting to the ball quickly.

Shooting Jumpers   Once the players are able to successfully and correctly execute the circle lay-up drill with three balls at both baskets, the coach can think about further enhancing the sophistication, the scope, and the degree of difficulty of the drill. This is accomplished by having the shooters attempt 10- to 15-foot jumpers in the wing area, along the baseline or near the free throw line, rather than the usual lay-ups. This creates a whole new dimension for the drill. The drill becomes much more challenging.

Now, instead of lay-ups being attempted, field goals are the norm. Field goals—at varying distances—can be attempted by those players in line A and line D. However, the players must shoot the field goals after they have been running—not an easy feat, even in practice. Although this creates a game-like situation, it also makes it much more difficult to make the shot.

As a consequence, those players while in lines B and C, serving as the rebounders and retrievers, will have a much more difficult time rebounding the missed shots. These rebounders will have ample opportunities to exercise and develop judgment in terms of where missed shots will bounce so that they can be quickly retrieved and the ball passed to the next person in the shooting line.

It is frequently better to spend too short a time on a drill than too much time on the same drill. Coaches should be able to ascertain whether the drill is becoming a bore. One sure sign that athletes have had enough of the exercise is when they start to make obvious mistakes or miscues. Another sign that it is time to do something else is when the players have lost their concentration and intensity and become lethargic and indifferent. Hopefully, the competent mentor will end the drill before it comes to this. Nevertheless, the concept of not overdoing any drill situation is an important one for all coaches at all levels.

A related concept that is equally important is to attempt to conclude a drill on a positive note. Ending any exercise or drill in an atmosphere of failure is self-defeating. Coaches need to be sure that the athletes view the drill experience as a positive one—even if it has been physically and mentally tiring and challenging.

Toward this end, concluding or ending a drill when the athletes are unhappy and disgruntled or when they are failing to execute the exercise properly only creates a bad taste in their mouths. Instead, coaches should pick an opportunity when the players are generally performing well, or at least at an acceptable level, to conclude that particular drill. Hopefully, when the players are asked to perform that same drill the next time, they will not associate the drill with failure or negativity.

> **Coaching Hint 191**
> Do not overdo any drill, and do not wait until the athletes are tired or bored to death before switching to another activity.

> **Coaching Hint 192**
> Attempt to end a drill when the players have been successful in its implementation.

THE ALLEY-OOP DRILL

This is an excellent drill with which to conclude a practice. Coach Buddy Bremmer, former head coach of Rockhurst College and later St. Louis University, used this drill while coaching the Rockhurst team to the NAIA championship in 1964. This drill is as simple as it is effective and efficient, and *it is fun*. It will lift up the players' spirits and allow them to enjoy themselves. It involves a unique and unorthodox way to play basketball in a recreational type environment.

All the players on the team are divided into two equal groups. It is irrelevant as to how many players there are. The drill can be executed with 10 players or 20 players or even 30 players. With the two teams selected, all of the available baskets on the court are used to play a whole-court game. However, the uniqueness of this drill is that members of either team can score at any of the baskets.

> **Coaching Hint 193**
> There is much to be said for allowing one's players to let their hair down and just have fun in a practice situation.

There may be only 2 baskets involved or as many as 10 or more baskets involved.

Diagram 9–4 illustrates the situation in which there are 10 different baskets surrounding the court, including a portable set of four baskets in the middle of the floor. When the coach throws the ball into play (anywhere on the floor), both teams scramble to gain possession of the ball.

Simplistic Rules for the Alley-Oop Drill

The rules of this drill are very simple. The objective is to have fun and relax while playing a modified version of basketball. The few simple rules include:

1. A score *can be made at any basket*, anywhere on the court.
2. All field goals are worth two points.
3. There are no 10-second violations.
4. There are no 3-second lane violations.
5. There are no out-of-bounds violations.
6. A player who scores may regain possession of the ball as soon as it goes through the net and can score again, immediately, without giving an opponent a chance to score.
7. The first team to score 15 or more points wins the game.
8. Personal fouls result in 2 foul shots—players line up as in a game (each foul shot worth 1 point).
9. All other rules of the game are applicable.

Coaching Hint 194
Too much of a good thing can lessen or even destroy the effectiveness and benefit of an otherwise worthwhile drill or exercise.

Although the Alley-Oop drill can be used every day as well as at any time during practice, it is best not to overdo a good thing. In terms of when this drill should be used in a practice setting, it is suggested that the Alley-Oop be incorporated as a concluding (positive) experience in a given practice. It should also be used sparingly in terms of the number of times during a week.

Do not use this drill every day in practice or even every week. Overusing the Alley-Oop will kill its effectiveness. Save it for the day when the players really

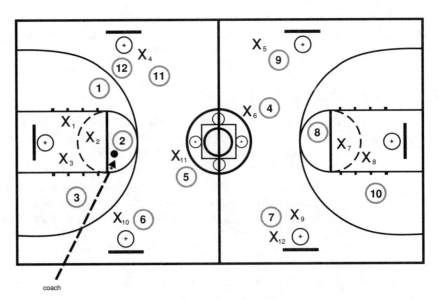

DIAGRAM 9–4

need a pick-me-up or save it as a reward for hard work or another achievement; save it for the day when it will have the greatest positive impact on the players.

If this drill is used too frequently, its effectiveness tends to diminish. In fact, sometimes the effectiveness deceases in direct proportion to the number of times it is used. Thus, keep the youngsters eager in their anticipation of this unique and fun drill. They will anticipate and enjoy it all the more.

11-PLAYER DRILL

The 11-player drill is aptly named because the exercise requires a minimum of 11 players to run. The drill is designed to provide realistic, game-like experience in exploiting a fast-break situation. The drill also provides opportunities for the players to practice defending against the fast break (two against three) as they rotate from an offensive to a defensive mode in the normal course of the *continuous* exercise.

This particular drill (as well as the 10-second drill explained later in this chapter) requires players to make numerous split-second decisions. Such decisions are made in realistic game-like situations against opponents who are equally motivated to negate such decisions. These decisions are absolutely critical if the athletes are to be successful in implementing the defensive or offensive maneuvers required in this drill.

An added benefit of the 11-person drill is that the exercise provides for *continuous movement and full-court execution* of essential skills by the athletes running the drill. In the case of the 11-person drill, athletes are intimately involved with all aspects of the fast break, both offensively and defensively. Some of the specific skills and attributes (both mental and physical) that can be developed or enhanced through the use of this drill include:

> **Coaching Hint 195**
> Effective and efficient drills duplicate game-like situations in which athletes must make split-second decisions in the heat of battle.

1. Passing the ball in bounds after a made basket by the opponents
2. Defensive rebounding and blocking out under the basket
3. General ball-handling skills
4. Advancing the ball up the court via the pass
5. Advancing the ball up the court by dribbling
6. Passing the ball from the sideline to the middle of the floor, thereby advancing the ball to the offensive front court
7. Attacking two defenders with three offensive players
8. Attempting to stop a score when the defenders are outnumbered
9. Executing a scoring pass against two defenders
10. Creating appropriate shot selection
11. Shooting the lay-up or a short jumper on the run
12. Offensive rebounding and second-shot attempts (including tip-ins)
13. Increased physical conditioning and stamina

The drill begins with 11 players situated on the court, as depicted in Diagram 9–5. Players ①, ②, and ③ begin the drill by advancing the ball against the two temporary defenders, X₄ and X₅. Two other athletes, X₇ and X₆, also take up momentary defensive positions at the opposite end of the floor, as shown.

The remaining four players—⑧, ⑨, ⑩, and ⑪—take up positions in areas A, B, C, and D, *outside* the sidelines, as shown. These players are ready to step into the court and the action once the drill has progressed. However, in the meantime, the players who are stationed in these areas remain out of bounds and out of the play.

> **Coaching Hint 196**
> Follow the KISS recipe in creating drills: keep it simple and straight-forward.

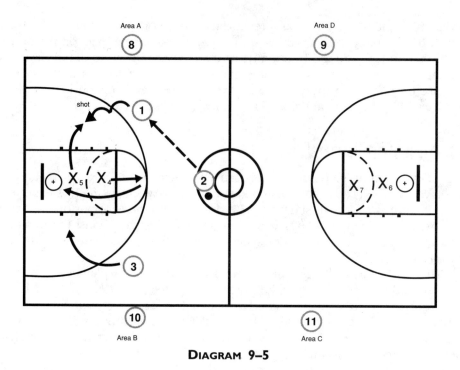

DIAGRAM 9–5

The drill is simplistic in its nature and straightforward in its execution. The initial three offensive players attempt to score against the two defenders. If the field goal is missed and rebounded by one of the offensive players, the ball remains in play and a second (or third or fourth) shot can be taken, in a three against two situation.

Initiating the Fast Break

If a basket is made, in this case by ①, the defender (X₄), who retrieves the ball from the net, steps out of bounds to initiate the in-bounds pass to the sidelines, to ⑩, who now steps onto the court. Similarly, if the field goal is unsuccessful and a defender garners the defensive rebound, an immediate pass should be attempted to the sidelines in an effort to initiate the fast break at the other end of the court.

Both ⑧ and ⑩ step in bounds onto the playing floor as potential pass receivers from X₄ (see Diagram 9–6). As soon as the release pass is completed to the wing, to ⑩, it is imperative that the passer, X₄, fill the vacant lane as shown. Thus, there are now three new offensive players—⑧, ⑩, and X₄—moving the ball and advancing toward the opposite end of the court in an effort to score against two defenders, X₆ and X₇.

At the other end of the floor (areas A and B), there now remains four players who need to move to specific areas of the court in order for the drill to continue uninterrupted. The two former offensive players who did not take the shot—② and ③—now assume new positions on the court as defenders. Simultaneously, the former scorer,①, and the sole remaining defender, X₅, now position themselves out of bounds along the sideline, in area A and area B, respectively. Both X₅ and ① now become future offensive threats (see Diagram 9–7) as the drill continues.

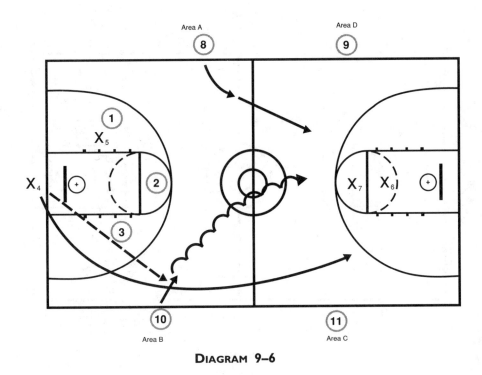

DIAGRAM 9–6

The Drill Continues

The drill continues (Diagram 9–7), with ⑧ attempting the shot, missing, and X_7 garnering the defensive rebound. Both ⑨ and ⑪ step in bounds, with ⑪ receiving the outlet pass from the rebounder. The ball is then dribbled into the center of the court while X_7 fills the now vacant lane along the sideline. Thus, there are now three new offensive players moving the ball down the floor to attack the two defenders, ③ and ②, at the opposite end of the court.

Once the ball has reached the 10-second line, the four players remaining in the now offensive back court reposition themselves according to the rules (outlined earlier). The two offensive players, X_4 and ⑩, who did not attempt the field goal, become defenders of the basket at which they had attempted to score. The player who attempted the unsuccessful field goal, ⑧, and the remaining defender, X_6, split and move out of bounds to take up positions at areas B and C.

Thus, this drill can be continued by the 11 players, without stop, as long as desired. It is important to note that any number of players can be used in this drill. Extra players can merely be lined up behind those who are stationed out of bounds in areas A, B, C, and D. Thus, these athletes merely wait their turn to step in bounds and advance down the floor as part of the three-pronged offensive attack against two defenders.

It is very important, however, that there not be too many athletes in line waiting their turn to become involved in this or any drill. Too much time doing nothing by too many leads to boredom and valuable time wasted. Thus, the maximum number of athletes suggested for this drill is 15, with 2 players stationed out of bounds along the sideline, in each of the areas A, B, C, and D.

All the athletes executing this drill will have ample opportunities to play *all* positions on the court, offensive and defensive. The fact that the players are

> **Coaching Hint 197**
> Drills that have athletes standing around, doing nothing but waiting their turn, are ineffectual and inefficient.

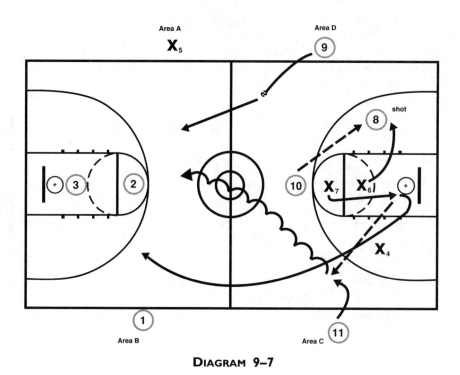

Diagram 9–7

asked to make the adjustments from defense to offense is one of the major advantages in this specific drill. Each of the players will have numerous opportunities to make critical decisions—decisions that must be made against substantial and vigorous opposition, in the heat of battle.

10-PLAYER DRILL

The 10-player drill, like the 11-player drill, has numerous inherent advantages. First, the drill is a continuity exercise—that is, it can be continuously executed until the drill is halted. Thus, a more realistic and beneficial workout is created. Second, the drill enjoys the advantage of providing realistic, game-like experiences for the players. Third, the activity enables the players to work on both offensive and defensive aspects of full-court presses. Fourth, this stratagem provides the opportunity to practice the offensive and defensive skills involved in the fast-break (three on two) situation. And, finally, the 10-player drill has numerous experiences that facilitate players making wise decisions in light of an ever-changing environment on the court.

The initial alignment of players in this exercise is depicted in Diagram 9–8. The drill involves two teams of five players each. Three players from each team are on opposite ends of the court facing two defenders from the opposite squad. Thus, ①, ②, and ③ are pitted against X_4 and X_5 on court A while on court B there are three offensive players—X_1, X_2, and X_3—aligned against two defenders, ④ and ⑤. It is required, as least initially, that the players *not cross* the 10-second, midcourt line.

Starting the Three against Two Scoring Thrust

The drill begins with the coach tossing the ball to ① and the three offensive players attempting to score. If a score is successful, the two defenders, X_5 and X_4,

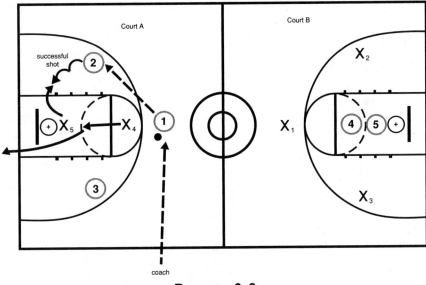

DIAGRAM 9–8

must attempt to get the ball in bounds against the three players who had just scored.

However, in this situation, there are now three players attempting to guard against the in-bounds pass and prevent the movement of the ball to the other end of the court (see Diagram 9–9). Thus, the out-of-bounds passer, X_4, being guarded by ②, must work very hard to get the in-bounds pass safely to the lone pass receiver, X_5. Likewise, X_5 is being guarded by *two* defenders, ③ and ①. Much work and hustle is required of X_5 to work free in order to receive the in-bounds pass safely.

A special rule is in effect for this drill that prevents either X_4 or X_5 from merely passing the ball the entire length of the court to a teammate in court B. This rule enhances the learning experience for the participants. Without this rule,

> **Coaching Hint 198**
> Adapt game rules to enhance the learning experience for the athletes.

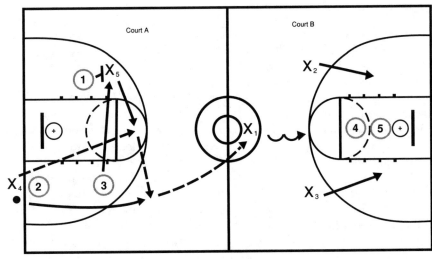

DIAGRAM 9–9

it would be too easy for the players to circumvent the purpose for which this drill has been created.

This rule simply states that *there must be at least one pass made from within the offensive back court (court A) after the in-bounds pass has been completed into this area of the floor.* Thus, before X_4 or X_5 is allowed to pass the ball across the 10-second line, one additional pass must be made *back* to the in-bounds passer, who has now stepped onto the court after the in-bounds pass has been completed. As a result, both X_4 and X_5 must work exceedingly hard not only to get the ball in bounds but also to protect the ball against continuing defensive pressure in their efforts to advance it past the midcourt line.

This situation presents the three defenders—①, ②, and ③—with an excellent opportunity to work on double teaming the potential pass receiver as well as harassing the in-bounds passer. Additionally, the two offensive players, X_5 and X_4, now can practice in-bounding the ball against extreme pressure. The potential in-bounds receiver must also be adept at faking, feinting, and maneuvering so as to become free to get the ball. Once the ball is in bounds within the back court, a second, return pass must be made to the in-bounds passer who has stepped into play. If the defenders—①, ②, and ③—intercept the ball, a shot can be immediately taken and the drill continues as before.

All of this creates an excellent realistic game-like atmosphere in which athletes must make split-second decisions as well as execute various offensive and defensive (team and individual) skills.

Once the ball is passed across the midcourt line to one of the other offensive players—X_1, X_2, or X_3—the "shoe is on the other foot," so to speak. Now these offensive team members—X_1, X_2, and X_3—attempt to score against two defenders, ④, and ⑤. If the offensive team scores a basket, the drill continues as already explained.

What happens if the offensive threesome is unsuccessful in scoring—that is if the two defenders, ④ and ⑤, either gain possession of the ball through a turnover or a defensive rebound? The special rule cited states that *there must be at least one pass made from within the offensive back court (in this case, court B) after the inbounds pass has been completed.* Since the ball is already in the offensive back court, only one pass must be made between ④ and ⑤ before passing the ball back across the time line to their teammates. The drill continues until the coach elects to stop it.

A Stunting Move

A stunting move that helps emphasize to all the players on the floor the importance of hustling and the value of quick action is the use of the "rover." In this modification or adjustment, the offensive player X_2 has been designed as the "rover" (see Diagram 9–10). A rover is a designated player who is able to play the entire length of the floor. Thus, X_2 can play offense while on court B as part of the threesome with teammates X_1 and X_3.

Additionally, once the ball has been passed across the half-court line to court A, this rover can attempt to render defensive assistance to teammates X_4 and X_5 by running the length of the floor. If X_2 really hustles up the floor quickly enough, it is indeed very possible (if not highly likely) to be able to be of real defensive help to X_4 and X_5. This is especially true if these two defenders can force the offensive players to overpass, thus providing more time for the rover to move up the floor and help out.

Both the offensive and defensive players soon learn the importance of scoring quickly on the fast break. For the offensive players, it becomes obvious

---

Coaching Hint 199
Modify drills to make them more challenging and demanding, thus making the exercises more beneficial and valuable for the participants.

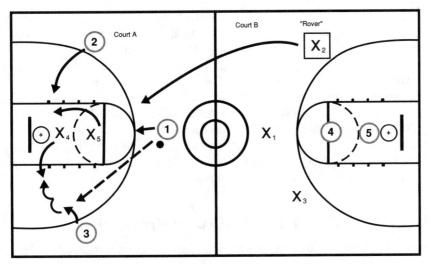

DIAGRAM 9–10

through the use of this drill that if they can get off a high percentage shot with a minimum of passing, they can score before the rover or extra defensive player can arrive to render meaningful assistance to the outnumbered defenders.

On the other hand, the defenders quickly grasp the importance of delaying, through sound defensive tactics and strategies, the time it takes for the offensive personnel to get off a good shot. Thus, it is important to rotate the designation of rover among all of the players so that each can experience what it is like to run the full length of the court to provide assistance to fellow defenders.

> **Coaching Hint 200**
> Alternate the "rover" among the offensive players so that each can benefit from the experience.

TIPPING AND REBOUNDING DRILL

This drill is very simple but its simplicity should not discourage coaches from incorporating it in their repertoires. Players line up, as in Diagram 9–11, on either side of the basket, with the first player in both lines with a basketball. Upon the signal to start, the first player in each line tosses the ball onto the glass and

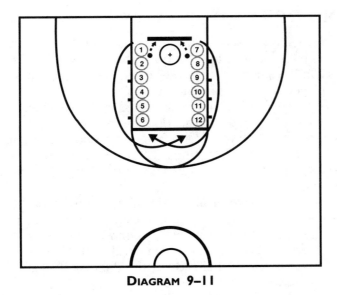

DIAGRAM 9–11

moves to the end of the opposite line, as illustrated. The second and subsequent players in each line keep the ball "alive" on the glass by tipping the ball once against the glass and then also moving to the end of the opposite line.

When all of the players have gone through both lines, the player who initially tipped the ball against the glass now tips the ball into the basket. Then, the two players who were second in their respective lines when the drill began can take the front position and the drill is executed once more. The drill is repeated until each of the players in each line has had a turn initiating the drill by tossing the ball against the glass and concluding the drill by tipping the ball in the basket. If at any time a miscue is made, the players in that line merely toss the ball back onto the glass and the drill continues.

FREE THROW AND REBOUNDING DRILL

Another drill involving free throws, in addition to the examples provided earlier in this chapter, has one player on the line and two players on the side of the lane. The shooter is allowed to shoot two free throws, if the initial attempt is successful. If the shooter misses either the first or second shot, the ball is "in play" and up for grabs by any of the three players. Whoever grabs the rebound can immediately attempt a *field goal* from that very spot or another area on the court while being guarded by the remaining two players. Whoever scores the field goal goes to the free throw line to attempt to make two shots in succession.

Score is kept, 1 point for a free throw and 2 points for a field goal. The drill/game is continued until one player scores 15 points. If the free throw shooter makes both free throw attempts, the shooter rotates off of the line and exchanges places with one of the two players on the lane who has the least number of points.

Basketball is made up of many simple facets. In fact, the game of basketball itself is rather simplistic. However, coaches frequently fail to provide opportunities for their players to practice and perform those very simple and rudimentary skills, tasks, and tactics that can often spell the difference between success and failure—between winning a game and ending up on the short side of the score.

Coaching Hint 201
If there is a secret in basketball, it is paying attention to details, to the little things in the sport.

SPEARING DRILL

How many times have you seen a defender attempting to come up from behind a dribbler in an effort to steal the ball or, at the very least, hit (spear) it out of the dribbler's hand? No doubt, numerous times. But how many coaches actually provide their players with opportunities to practice such a tactic? Not many.

The spearing drill is one example of attempting to pay attention to the small details in the sport of basketball. This drill involves nothing more than having several lines of defensive players just in front of the end line, facing the opposite end of the playing area (see Diagram 9–12). In front of each line of defensive players are dribblers who take up a position just a few feet in front of the free throw line extended.

On a signal, each dribbler is allowed to move to the top of the key before the first defender in each line starts to chase down the dribbler in an attempt either to steal the ball or to spear it away from the offensive player. It is important that the chaser, the defender in each line, really hustle up the floor and position himself or herself on the ball side of the dribbler so that the ball can be swatted or speared away.

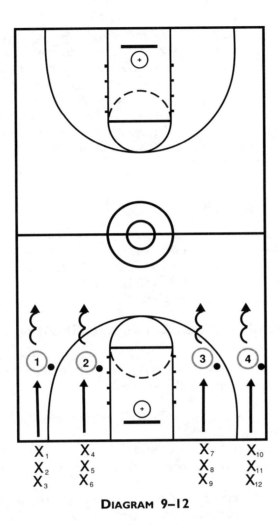

DIAGRAM 9–12

"PICK UP THE HANKY" (BALL) DRILL

This drill is similar to the childhood game of pick up the hanky that many have played. However, in this version, the hanky is a basketball and the purpose of the drill is to help teach players to gain possession of the ball while an opponent also strives to get the ball.

With two opposing players stationed some 5 to 6 feet apart, the coach places a ball on the floor between the two combatants. On the signal, both players must attempt to gain possession of the ball without fouling each other. This drill allows the players to practice and improve their reaction time, quickness, and retrieval techniques.

A stunting adaptation involves having the player who does gain possession of the ball make a move to the nearest basket in an attempt to score against the opponent. Naturally, the opponent must defend against such a move. Another adaptation is to use four players in the drill.

"CUT-THROAT" DRILL

This drill is just what its name implies, the one against two game of basketball. In this drill, the shooter initially attempts to score either from the free throw line or from another designated spot, either from 2-point or 3-point range. This attempt is uncontested. If the field goal is successful, the shooter gets another chance and continues to have uncontested shots as long as the attempts are successful.

If the field goal is missed, the rebounder now becomes the lone offensive player attempting to score immediately against the two opposing players. If such a score is successful, the shooter now moves to the free throw line (or other designated spot) for the uncontested shot. The drill or game continues until one of the three players reaches 21 points.

SHOOTING DRILLS

There are innumerable variations of shooting drills. Suffice to say that athletes need to practice their shooting, both free throws and field goals. It behooves coaches to create opportunities for their players to practice shooting from the general area of the court where shots will be taken in a game. Thus, the phrase, *spot-shooting drills* has been popularized.

Things to Remember When Conducting Shooting Drills

When attempting to construct and implement productive shooting drills, it is important to remember the various conditions and situations under which field goals can be taken in a game—for example:

1. Standing still in possession of the ball, without dribbling the ball, and then shooting from that spot
2. Standing still, receiving a pass, and then shooting from that spot
3. Standing still, receiving a pass, and then dribbling and shooting from a designated spot
4. Cutting off the screen, receiving a pass, and immediately shooting
5. Cutting off the screen, receiving a pass, dribbling, and then shooting
6. In possession of the ball, dribbling off of a screen, and then shooting
7. With one's back to the basket, receiving the ball, and working for a high percentage shot

Repetitive Spot Shooting

One type of spot-shooting drill involves repetitive shooting, one shot after another. The shooter stands in a specific spot and is passed one ball immediately after another, as soon as he or she is able to launch a carefully aimed field goal. The biggest danger in this type of drill is for the shooter to become careless or lackadaisical in the act of shooting. It is therefore essential that each player pay the strictest attention to correct shooting technique. However, this does not diminish the fact that the shooter will be given 15 to 20 to 50 opportunities, one after the other, to make a field goal, from a specific position on the floor.

Spot Shooting under Game-Like Conditions

Offensive players should be provided opportunities to work against defenders in their efforts to score from specific spots on the floor. At first, such defenders can be instructed not to actually attempt to block the shooter's shots. Rather, the defenders merely attempt to distract and otherwise harass the shooter. Later, the defenders can be allowed to exert full-blown defensive pressure against the shooter.

> **Coaching Hint 202**
> Pay strict attention to the mechanics of field goal attempts in all spot-shooting drills.

Players with the ball can be provided with stationery screens over which the offensive players may shoot behind or dribble past and then elect to initiate the field goal attempt. Additionally, offensive players without the ball can be instructed to cut off a stationary screen in anticipation of a pass and then attempt the shot, with or without dribbling the ball once the pass is completed.

Paired Shooting

Pairing two team members together and allowing one of the players to shoot the ball while the other rebounds is a common practice. However, a stunting variation calls for the rebounder not to let the ball bounce on the floor, whether the field goal is successful or not. Additionally, immediately after retrieving (rebounding) any missed field goal, the rebounder immediately becomes a shooter from that very spot and attempts to put the ball in the basket. The original shooter then assumes the role of the rebounder, with the same responsibilities the other player had. This drill places great pressure on both the shooter and the rebounder to execute their respective tasks in an appropriate and timely fashion.

CONCLUDING COMMENTS ABOUT DRILLS

Drills are an absolute essential ingredient in the teaching and coaching of basketball. Do not overlook the importance of adequate drills used at the appropriate time and for the proper length of time. Regardless of the talent level of the participants, athletes need to practice drills in order to learn, improve, master, and retain both fundamental and advanced skills. Drills should be viewed as tools, as a means to an end. That is, drills are the tools by which coaches teach their players and are the means by which the athletes are able to increase their understanding and physical performance of the integral components of the sport as well as the game as a whole. Without adequate drills, participants would be operating under a severe handicap—a situation that should never exist if there is adequate coaching available. Good coaches, skilled coaches, experienced coaches have an understanding of when, where, and how to utilize drills in the overall scheme of coaching.

10 The Psychological/ Mental Dimensions of Coaching Basketball

For the most part, earlier chapters dealt with the technical aspects of coaching basketball—that is, the Xs and the Os of the sport. However, as alluded to previously, there is another equally important dimension involved in the coaching of any competitive sport in which coaches must be knowledgeable. Specifically, basketball coaches must also be familiar with and competent in dealing with the mental or psychological realm of teaching (coaching) and learning.

In order to be consistently successful as a coach in any competitive sport, one must be a quality teacher of both skills and knowledge to one's athletes. In order to be such a quality coach/teacher, one must possess an understanding of (a) exactly what motivation is as it relates to sports; (b) what motivates or prompts athletes to make the sacrifices and commitments necessary to master that which must be learned; (c) how an athlete actually learns, improves, and masters physical and cognitive skills; and (d) what facilitates or hinders the learning process associated with the acquisition of knowledge and mastery of physical skills.

A basketball coach, at any level of competition, would be making a very serious mistake, indeed, if he or she concentrated on the technical Xs and Os of the sport while neglecting the mental or psychological dimension. The purpose of this chapter is to provide a basic framework and understanding of the mental and psychological dimension of coaching basketball. In reality, this aspect of coaching is not only equally important as the physical but is often more difficult to deal with both by the inexperienced as well as the experienced mentor.

> **Coaching Hint 203**
> Do not overlook the importance of the mental aspect of coaching basketball.

THE ROLE OF MOTIVATION IN SPORT

The purpose of this book is not to delve into all the intricacies of motivation and sports, nevertheless, there are some general principles or coaching hints regarding motivation that will be presented in this chapter that will help both the inexperienced and experienced mentor.

A key component associated with the psychology of coaching is the factor of motivation. It is always easier to coach and teach a youngster who is motivated, whether the person is extrinsically or intrinsically motivated. The challenge for any basketball coach is to have the individual athlete, as a member of a team sport, appropriately motivated so that the athlete is able to learn and perform at that person's potential—or near potential—on a consistent basis.

However, not everyone can be motivated equally or in a similar manner. Thus, it is important for coaches to be skilled communicators and adept in motivating their charges. Toward this end, success can be further facilitated if coaches are successful in selecting individuals to be on the team who are coachable, that is—those who are or can be motivated to work hard, to learn and to perfect those skills necessary for success in the fast pace sport of basketball.

Student athletes, especially seniors who are not starting or who are not receiving a great deal of playing time, can be a hinderance to the progress of the entire team. Such seniors can turn into deviants rather than serve as positive role models when they are insufficiently motivated and/or have not bought into the "team concept" of basketball. Thus, the team selection process that takes place at the first of the season can have a significant effect on the motivational activities and efforts that will be necessary as the team progresses throughout the season.

Individual and Team Motivation

Different strokes for different folks is an coaching adage that has some basis in the motivational scheme for basketball coaches. Each athlete needs to be motivated as an individual. Yes, coaches can still motivate the team, as a whole, but the emphasis should remain on individual motivation. Specifically, coaches need to attempt to find out what the individual and collective needs of the players are and attempt to meet those needs.

Perhaps two of the greatest challenges facing any basketball coach is (a) to sufficiently motivate athletes of all ages to attempt to do their best as well as actually doing their best, both in practice and in actual competition; and (b) to have the athletes actually learn, improve, and perfect that which is necessary to excel in the sport of basketball.

Thus, motivation can be viewed from two perspectives. First, a coach can think of motivation as a tool or tactic that can help an athlete and/or a team want to try harder, want to excel, want to produce, want to perform at a high level, and be willing to make sacrifices in order to achieve these objectives. Thus, in this context, motivation has to do with effort, wants, and desire. However, a second perspective of motivation deals with actually facilitating or enhancing the learning process itself—both in the cognitive and psychomotor domains. Basketball coaches need to concern themselves with both perspectives of motivation. Doing so will pay big dividends for the team and for the coach.

What causes an individual athlete to act or not act in a certain way? What are the "hot buttons" or motivational triggers of would-be athletes and athletes? What motivates youngsters to behave in appropriate ways that will enhance and facilitate the elite-level performance by these individuals? How can an athlete and the team as a whole be motivated, be encouraged, be helped to learn and hopefully master the knowledge and skills necessary for success in the competitive world of sports?

The answers to these and other related questions are very important for would-be successful coaches. If mentors can answer these questions, they will

---

Coaching Hint 204

It is easier to coach and teach a highly motivated individual.

Coaching Hint 205

Emphasize the team concept: Team members are like wooden matchsticks—when together they are difficult to break (defeat).

Coaching Hint 206

A key to successful coaching is being able to motivate one's players not only to want to do their best but also to actually do their best—consistently.

Coaching Hint 207

Discover the "hot buttons" or motivational triggers of one's athletes.

be way ahead of the game in terms of preparing their youngsters to perform within the physical and the mental (psychological) world of competitive basketball.

Intrinsic and Extrinsic Motivation

There are two types of motivation with which basketball coaches need to be familiar: intrinsic and extrinsic. *Intrinsic motivation* is that impetus or incentive for action or decision making that comes from within the individual athlete rather than from external sources. Intrinsic motivation is self-motivation that comes from inside the athlete. *Extrinsic motivation*, on the other hand, is when the stimulus for action is generated externally to the individual, by the promise or threat from outside the individual. This type of motivation is generally provided by the coach or others associated with the basketball program.

Intrinsic motivation is associated with an internal belief or conviction that particular behavior is worthwhile in and of itself. For example, an athlete who is intrinsically motivated either to do something or not do something is persuaded to action because of that person's own belief that such behavior and the inherent consequence(s) of such behavior is (are) of value and worth. In this instance, the individual is not motivated by external factors. Rather, the motivation comes from within the individual in question. In short, a person is intrinsically motivated to act because of an individual's intuitive and natural inclination to do what that person feels should be done—the source of the action or inaction is within the individual.

Positive versus Negative Motivation

Motivation can be either positive or negative. *Positive motivation* involves the potential for receiving a reward—something of value, something desirable, either tangible or intangible—as a result of some action or inaction. *Negative motivation* involves a promise, fear, or threat of a loss of something of value—or something undesirable, unpleasant, or distasteful actually happening to the athlete.

Examples of positive motivation are a letter award, a championship ring, or a plaque. On the other hand, positive motivation can be as simple as a compliment, an approving nod of the head, or general words of encouragement. Additionally, positive motivation might involve that good feeling that an athlete has during and/or following competition or reaching one's objective or goal.

On the other hand, examples of negative motivation can include punishment (or the threat of punishment) of some kind, either physical or psychological. Physical punishment can encompass running laps, being made to perform specific kinds of physical exercises, being denied the privilege of playing, or even being removed from the team.

Psychological punishment can take the form of being browbeaten, embarrassed, humiliated, ostracized, and so on. Playing so-called mind games with athletes seems to be all too prevalent in today's basketball circles, at all levels of competition. Such a negative approach to coaching and learning should be avoided at all costs.

Coaches need to lead and coach through example. They must be motivated, enthusiastic, and optimistic. It is difficult, if not highly unlikely, for athletes to be motivated to work hard and to make sacrifices when they see their coaches failing to take a leadership role in this area.

Coaching Hint 208
Poor motivation or lack of motivation can seriously hamper or impair learning.

Coaching Hint 209
Coaches motivate through example—one must be motivated, enthusiastic, and optimistic.

What Motivation Is Not

Motivation is not a cure-all for a multitude of ills facing today's coaches. Motivation is not the answer to all coaching problems. It is more than mere gimmicks, slogans, and screaming. If properly utilized and understood, motivational techniques and skills can help the competent mentor become an even better coach by being able to persuade, stimulate, and inspire athletes to meaningful and purposeful action.

Dangers of Motivational Efforts

There is a very real danger of too much of a good thing. Some coaches mistakenly think that motivation is all about "rah-rah" tactics geared to make the individual athletes and the team, as a whole, sky high and ready to take on all comers. Nothing can be further from the truth. Although there is a place for the isolated stereotypical, motivational locker-room speech, such attempts at getting athletes highly motivated for individual games can frequently backfire.

For example, with a basketball team of 15 players, there may be 5 or 6 athletes who are already too highly motivated (over motivated). These athletes may be so sky high that their performance will be impaired by their present motivational state. Another group of 4 or 5 athletes might be just right in terms of being motivated. And, a third group of players might really need to be motivated for optimum performance. Attempts to treat all of the basketball players identically could result in the majority of the team members being too highly "charged" to perform satisfactory.

Another problem associated with motivation is that players and teams—following extreme motivation such as that associated with being sky high for a specific game or competition—frequently come crashing down to earth following that specific contest. Having climbed to the mountain of motivation, these same athletes come tumbling down the valley afterwards.

That may be why there are so many "upsets" when teams are flat against a supposedly weaker opponent following a big or important contest against a much stronger opponent. It may have been the result of being highly or super-motivated for the previous opponent only to have a subsequent let-down for the next contest. The end result is often a less than stellar performance, resulting in a loss to a less worthy opponent. Thus, coaches need to be alert to the dangers of getting their players too excited, too sky high, too motivated, less they come crashing down afterwards.

Gimmicks in Coaching Basketball: Fluff versus Substance

Should basketball coaches use gimmicks such as slogans, posters, signs, awarding of special weekly honors or recognition to players, and so on. Yes and no. There is nothing inherently wrong with the use of so-called gimmicks if they are used judiciously and appropriately. Naturally, such gimmicks should be in good taste, used in moderation, and be effective. Do not overdo it, however. Such tactics should be used sparingly in order to be effective. Again, be aware of the principle that *too much of a good thing destroys its usefulness and effectiveness.*

It is a matter of substance versus fluff. The fluff may be considered the little add-ons, and the substance might be considered to be major motivational factors such as the existence of a truly big game. The fluff might be slogans hanging in the locker-room and the rally held the afternoon of the big game. The substance might be in willingly making sacrifices, being dedicated, and being committed to hard work, and in feeling the pride and increased self-esteem following doing

---

Coaching Hint 210
Do not overdo the motivation thing—too much of anything can have negative consequences.

Coaching Hint 211
Treat each athlete as an individual—don't expect to motivate all team members the same way.

Coaching Hint 212
Beware of mountains and valleys when it comes to motivation.

Coaching Hint 213
Use the motivation style that works in one's own situation.

one's best or reaching worthwhile objectives and goals. In the case of the so-called big game, probably no special motivational (gimmicks) tactics are even called for, since the approaching game itself is frequently all the motivation the players need to be up for that specific contest.

MOTIVATING TACTICS AND STRATEGIES

There are innumerable motivation tactics and strategies that are appropriate for basketball coaches at all levels. Provided here are some of the tactics that coaches might want to consider when exploring how to appropriately motivate their youngsters.

• *Emphasize doing one's best—do not constantly harp on winning.*

If the emphasis is placed on doing one's best, the individual athletes will be better able to keep in focus their primary responsibility—to perform to their potential. The winning will take care of itself. Athletes should concentrate on performance, the process—not on winning. To do otherwise is to place a great deal of pressure—and in some cases, too much pressure—on the individual athlete and on the team itself.

• *Publicly acknowledge and compliment athletes and the team on their efforts, achievements, and accomplishments.*

Nothing can have a more positive effect on an athlete (or coach, for that matter) in terms of motivation than being complimented or acknowledged in public for one's efforts and accomplishments. Coaches should take advantage of such opportunities to highlight individual and team activities and achievements, whenever appropriate. Such public acknowledgments can be made in the confines of one's practices as well as in any number of public forums, athletic luncheons, in the newspaper, at the team banquet, and so on.

• *Emphasize team achievements over individual achievements.*

Although acknowledgments of achievements are important, it is imperative that coaches remember that team achievements should always be emphasized over individual achievements. Nevertheless, individual accomplishments and successes can and should be recognized and emphasized when such feats serve as motivation for the individuals and for the team.

• *Use game statistics and records sparingly to help motivate and stimulate athletes.*

Although records and statistics can serve as motivational tools for both individuals and for the team, there is always the danger that game and practice statistics can have the opposite effect. That is, making public some statistics or records might create problems within the team in terms of creating undesirable competition or resentment among players (and members of their families).

One statistic that the author suggests not to make public (although the coaching staff should certainly have access to such information) is the amount of individual playing time of each individual athlete. It is not so important how much playing time an individual athlete receives—rather, it is how effective and efficient the individual is when the athlete actually is on the court. Far too often, individual athletes become frustrated if they do not receive the playing time that they or their parents think they deserve. Nevertheless, keeping practice and game records (statistics) can serve as a positive motivational practice in that such

> **Coaching Hint 214**
> Do not emphasize or publicize individual game statistics such as playing time.

records provide much needed feedback to the individual athletes and the team as a whole. Such feedback is beneficial since it enables team members to have a snapshot of their performance while also serving as motivation to improve or elevate their performance to the next level.

• *Appropriate use of scrimmages can be highly motivating.*

If there is one thing in basketball that almost all athletes enjoy, it is being able to go full court in a scrimmage, either against other members of the team or against outsiders. The use of competitive scrimmages can be a great motivational tool in that such activity is not only enjoyable but the athletes are given opportunities to demonstrate or show off their skills and competencies to the coaching staff. From the coaches' perspectives, scrimmages similarly serve two purposes. First, they provide opportunities to see how athletes perform (individually and as a team) in competition, which is often as close to real game situations as possible, and second, they create an environment or atmosphere in which the athletes can enjoy themselves.

• *Keep practices brief, to the point, well planned, and well executed.*

Practices should not only be kept brief but athletes should be kept busy (in a meaningful way) all the time. Time wasting during practice is one of the fastest ways to break down motivation among the players. Practices should be stimulating, interesting, and demanding—certainly not dull or monotonous. Practices that are mundane, predictable, and repetitious are not only tedious for the athletes but create motivational and moral problems as well.

Coaches would do well to remember to keep practice activities on task—that is, to have athletes practice those things that will facilitate individual and team improvement. To do otherwise not only hurts the motivational level of the players but hinders the learning process—a double whammy that coaches could well do without.

> **Coaching Hint 215**
> Being organized facilitates learning and helps motivate team members.

• *Never have athletes leave a practice or a game with a bad taste in their mouths—always conclude on a positive note.*

Basketball coaches make a serious mistake when they allow individual athletes to leave a practice or a game in a negative atmosphere or mood. For example, when a coach kicks a youngster out of practice or when the coach punishes an athlete or the entire team, and then immediately concludes practice, the end result is a sour taste in the mouths of those affected athletes. The mental or psychological dimension of coaching can be devastated when such occurrences are commonplace. The general rule of thumb for practices is that each practice session should end on a positive note to provide for appropriate carry-over to the next practice or game. To do otherwise is nonproductive at best and counterproductive at worst.

• *Coaches should be patient and understanding of their players.*

It is a responsibility for coaches to be both patient and understanding of their athletes. Patience is indeed a virtue for the modern-day basketball coach. It is frequently easy for coaches to be highly motivated—after all, that is a big part of their livelihood. For athletes, it is a different matter. There are many other attractive nuisances vying for their time, effort, and dedication.

For athletes, participation on a basketball team may not be the most important thing in their lives. Athletes face many and varied challenges and problems in their lives, some associated with the sport but many having no connection with basketball at all. Thus, coaches should try to walk in the shoes of their athletes in an effort to better understand them and the challenges that face them both on and off the basketball court. Doing so makes the coach a better coach and teacher.

• *Develop a positive interpersonal relationship with the players.*

Coaches need to cultivate and develop a positive relationship with their athletes and their parents. Being honest and forthright with the youngsters can go a long way to developing a positive interpersonal relationship and establishing an appropriate learning atmosphere, on and off the court. Really caring about the players, being a mentor and counselor for one's athletes, being there in the "thick and thin" for the athletes, is a mark of a quality coach.

One sign of a coach who really cares about youngsters is the coach who goes out of his or her way on behalf of a youngster even if the individual can no longer participate on the team. Being recognized as such a caring and concerned mentor can be highly motivating to all current and potential basketball players.

FACTORS ASSOCIATED WITH HOW AN ATHLETE LEARNS, IMPROVES, AND MASTERS PHYSICAL AND COGNITIVE SKILLS

There are many factors that can have a positive effect on an athlete's ability to be a successful basketball player. Coaches must realize that they have a major role in helping their athletes learn, improve, and master a wide range of skills and competencies.

• *Athletes need to know how they are performing.*

Athletes can more easily and effectively learn, improve, and perfect physical and cognitive skills if they have a sense of how they are currently performing. This involves feedback. *Feedback* is the giving to the performer information as to how the performer is doing. Without adequate feedback, the learner is at a severe disadvantage. For example, in shooting a field goal, if the shooter is blindfolded, it becomes extremely difficult not only for the individual to make the first shot but also to improve on the chances of making subsequent shots. However, the situation is immediately altered when the blindfold is removed and the athlete can see the results of one's efforts in attempting the shot.

This is true with any skill. The learner must be able to receive information relative to how he or she is performing. Without such feedback, the learner is helpless. Coaches should make extra effort to ensure that their athletes are never in the position of not knowing their status in terms of their performing specific skills. Similarly, athletes need to know of their status with the team in terms of performance level, the pecking order of the players, starting potential, and so forth. Knowing one's status and one's potential within the team can greatly facilitate the learning process.

• *Athletes need to receive positive reinforcement in terms of their efforts and achievements.*

Not only do athletes need feedback in terms of their performances but they also need positive reinforcement when they perform adequately, both in terms of effort and in respect to actual performance. Coaches need to provide positive verbal and nonverbal reinforcement for individual athletes and for the team when the performance and/or the effort(s) is such that such reinforcement is warranted. However, coaches should not fall into the trap of providing praise for every little thing. Too much praise or inappropriate accolades decreases the effectiveness of providing praise.

Proper use of feedback significantly lessens the prospects of repeat errors. Athletes must be informed of any mistakes they are making and what specifically needs to be changed. Finally, coaches would do well to specify the positive results that will emanate from correcting specific mistakes.

Also, timely constructive feedback prevents athletes from continuing to practice skills incorrectly. Nothing is more disheartening for a coach than to have to attempt to correct errors that have been perfected by the uninformed athlete. Reteaching an individual to stop doing something that has become a habit and to change to do something else is very, very difficult. That is why it is imperative that athletes not be placed in a situation in which they can practice and learn a skill incorrectly. Immediate feedback can play a major role in reducing this unfortunate situation.

> | **Coaching Hint 216**
> When pointing out errors of athletes, be explicit in what needs to be changed and what the results will be if the changes are made.

• ***Athletes must be physically and mentally ready to learn that which must be mastered.***

Coaches do themselves a disservice when they do not take the time to ascertain the current level of proficiency or skill of their athletes. Youngsters must be ready to learn if they are to be proficient in learning. Not being ready could be due to physical factors such as being too tired, injured, and so on. It could also be due to a maturation factor—that is, the youngster is not physically (or mentally) capable of learning the particular skill. For example, a youngster in the eighth grade might not have the physical strength or coordination to master the jump shot from 15 feet away from the basket.

One of the worst times to attempt to have athletes learn a new skill or new concept is when they are tired (physically and/or mentally). At the end of a hard practice session is not the ideal time for the coaching staff to begin to introduce a new offense or defense or variation thereof. By that time, the players are most likely physically exhausted and mentally drained. That which will actually be effectively and efficiently learned and retained is minuscule compared to what could be mastered if these same athletes were mentally alert and physically refreshed. As the adage goes, there is a time and place for all things. Trying to teach new things to tired athletes is neither the time nor the place if one is expecting true learning (and retention) to take place.

Not being ready to learn could also be attributed to mental or psychological factors such as worrying about things at home, being concerned about one's academic progress, being troubled by finances, disturbed by a boyfriend or girlfriend, or just being mentally tired or burned out, just to mention a few. Not being ready to learn could be due to any number of reasons or to a combination of factors.

It is important to recognize that not being ready to learn might be a matter of concern only on a particular day or it could involve weeks or even months. The point to remember is that forcing players to learn that which they are not ready to learn, for whatever reason(s), is foolish and inefficient. It also creates more problems than it solves. Coaches need to recognize when to back off and try again another day.

> | **Coaching Hint 217**
> Do not introduce new concepts or skills when athletes are tired.

- *Meaningful practices involve the opportunity to physically as well as mentally practice that which is to be mastered—psychological skills training can enhance learning.*

Psychological skills training involves the athletes mentally "seeing" themselves as they perform their physical skills, both simplistic and complicated skills. Stier (1995) lists six advantages of psychological skills training:

1. It can be practiced almost anywhere.
2. It is time efficient.
3. It is not physically demanding or fatiguing.
4. The mind frequently cannot tell the difference between reality and day dreaming (imagery).
5. It can be effective and efficient (i.e., successful).
6. It can serve as a motivational factor for the individual player.

In mental practice, the viewing in the mind's eye of the physical performance (past or future) is referred to as *mental imaging*. In a simplistic example, it involves athletes, while in a state of complete or near relaxation, consciously thinking or "day dreaming" or picturing themselves successfully shooting field goals during a competition or successfully rebounding missed field goals while in critical situations.

One of the keys to psychological skills training is allocating the appropriate amount of time to be devoted to such mental practice and imagery. Meaningful practice activities and time spent on task are two critical elements underscoring successful mental practice. The athletes must be able to commit to concentrating on the task at hand—that is, on mentally creating an image of themselves successfully performing every aspect of a physical skill, even one as complicated as shooting a field goal or free throw. These athletes must be able to feel—to "see" in their mind's eye—themselves actually performing the physical skills while, in reality, being in a relaxed state, such as lying down on a couch or sitting comfortably in a chair in a quiet room.

- *Learning plateaus are to be expected in mastering physical and mental skills.*

There will be times when the players will reach a learning plateau—that is, they seemingly cannot improve in spite of concerted efforts to do so. A learning plateau is when an individual reaches a point in the development and refinement of a skill where progress seems to stop. In some instances, learning can actually regress. Further refinement and improvement of the skill ceases in spite of all efforts to the contrary. This is sometimes to be expected. Do not immediately suspect that the athletes are slacking off in their efforts to enhance their physical and mental competencies. Usually, quite the contrary is occurring. Provide them with encouragement and make them aware of the possibility of such learning plateaus that can affect individuals as well as entire teams.

To counteract these temporary road blocks, athletes and coaches need to be patient, focused, and confident. Sometimes, athletes need to walk away or take a day or two off from the normal grind or hustle and bustle of practice. In other instances, the athletes must "tough" it out by being persistent, focused, and committed in their efforts to improve and be willing to continue to work at the skill(s) in spite of no apparent progress (or actual regression). Sometimes, this involves a day or two of rest or alternate practice activities.

FACTORS THAT FACILITATE OR HINDER THE ACQUISITION, LEARNING, AND PERFECTION OF PHYSICAL AND MENTAL SKILLS

Basketball coaches need to be cognizant of the fact that not only are they held responsible for enhancing the learning experience for their players but they can also play a major role in impeding or hampering the learning process. Whether or not the learning process is hindered or enhanced can be the direct result of either something not being done that should be or something taking place that should not.

- *Athletes must have appropriate opportunities to practice, practice, and practice—in an appropriate setting and circumstances and within an appropriate time frame.*

    Meaningful practices involve teaching activities where athletes are able to use multiple senses to analyze and synthesize that which is to be learned, practiced, and perfected. Complex skills need to be broken down into their component parts for the players to master in a whole-part-whole teaching scheme.

    Teaching skills usually involves learning simple concepts and simple physical movements prior to attempting to master more complex concepts and skills. That is why drills can play such an important role in coaching basketball. A wide range of drills should be employed in an effort to provide opportunities for the athletes to overlearn the skills to be mastered. Athletes do not perfect skills without appropriate practice opportunities.

- *Fear and intimidation tend to hinder learning.*

    Contrary to popular opinion, the use of fear and intimidation by coaches is not necessary nor advisable in order for athletes to learn satisfactorily and to perform up to expectations. In fact, the presence of such negative teaching or coaching tactics can have a negative effect on the level of performance and on the athlete's ability to learn and master physical skills and cognitive knowledge. Far too many coaches attempt to coach through fear and intimidation, and the end result can be catastrophic. Perhaps one of the reasons why some coaches use this negative style of teaching and coaching (fear and intimidation) is because some high-profile collegiate coaches employ this style and have been successful in the win/loss column.

    However, coaching through intimidation is not appropriate, either from the learning perspective or the humanistic perspective. Just because a famous (or infamous) college coach has a reputation for being a screaming, intimidating dictator, this does not mean that other coaches should attempt to copy that coach's antics. In reality, the mentor who coaches through intimidation (fear) might be even more successful without browbeating athletes.

    Athletes should never be humiliated or shamed by their coaches, either publicly or in private. First of all, there is no sound, rational reason for such behavior. Second, the consequences can be negative, both for the athlete and for the coach (in terms of negative perceptions of the coach by the athlete and others). Such actions on behalf of coaches are examples of negative motivation as well as examples of ineffectual teaching strategy. In fact, such tactics can seriously hinder the learning process. Coaches should treat each player as if the youngster was his or her own child.

- *Athletes should not be fearful of making honest mistakes—as long as they make an earnest effort and learn from their experience.*

Coaching Hint 218
Make drills an integral part of almost every practice session.

Coaching Hint 219
Do not humiliate athletes—allow players to maintain their dignity.

Basketball players who are afraid of making mistakes, for whatever reason, on or off the court, are working under an inappropriate burden that can seriously impede learning. Athletes need to feel comfortable, not apprehensive, in taking calculated risks that can result in mistakes. A mistake does not really become an error unless it is repeated. Allow athletes the freedom to take reasonable risks without the threat of castigation.

If athletes become hesitant in practice or competition for fear of what their coaches might say or do, there is a very real danger of the players becoming too conservative in their ability or willingness to take appropriate risks. Coaches need to develop an atmosphere of trust with their players and encourage them to explore and expand their limitations, both physically and mentally.

> **Coaching Hint 220**
> Coaches need to develop an atmosphere of trust between themselves and their players.

• *Be poised and give the impression of competence—perceptions of expertise and proficiency enhance trust and assurance and facilitate learning on behalf of the athletes.*

Perceptions are very important for any basketball coach. Those coaches who give the impression of competence facilitate their athletes' learning curve. Athletes need to have confidence in their coaches. They need to believe in their mentors. Without such confidence or faith, the players' learning process can become stagnant. Coaches who are calm, cool, and collected while presenting an image of competency create a positive learning atmosphere—an environment in which individual athletes are better able to learn as well as perform.

• *Athletes learn better when they know their coaches have confidence in them as athletes.*

Coaches would do well to show confidence in their athletes. This is especially important for those individual athletes who are attempting to improve their skill level or seeking to demonstrate their performance capabilities. One reason it is important for coaches to show confidence in players is that such an expectation by the coaching staff can often turn out to be a self-fulfilling prophecy.

• *Coaches should be willing to take risks by providing opportunities for athletes to demonstrate their skills and competencies in both practices and games.*

An important aspect of showing confidence in one's players involves the willingness on behalf of coaches to provide opportunities for players to demonstrate what they can actually do, both in practice and in games. Yes, this involves some risk taking by coaches, especially in game situations. However, athletes deserve to have such opportunities. Otherwise, some individual players may be forever relegated to assume roles on the team that may not take advantage of their full potential.

In too many instances, coaches indicate that players cannot get more playing time or cannot earn a starting spot until the athletes can demonstrate that they are capable of assuming such a big responsibility. And then, these same coaches fail to give these athletes opportunities to prove themselves, to demonstrate that they, indeed, are capable of doing more or assuming a greater role on the team.

• *Athletes need to set reasonable but obtainable goals for themselves.*

A helpful element associated with enhancing learning is goal setting. Athletes should be encouraged to set goals for themselves. These goals should be both reasonable and obtainable. It is imperative that these goals not be so lofty or distant that they cannot be achieved. Nothing discourages young athletes more than having goals established that are unreasonable and out of reach.

Coaches should encourage their individual players to establish numerous small goals that are within each person's grasp, with an average amount of hard work and dedication.

• *Coaches should be seen more and heard less in practice.*

Coaches have a tendency to talk too much in practice. Far too often, basketball coaches spend entirely too much time conversing with their athletes when these youngsters should be spending their valuable time physically performing, practicing, and perfecting skills. This is especially true when coaches have their players interrupt practice to stand or sit for long durations, listening to someone speak, only then to have these same athletes attempt to strenuously exert themselves again in practice without adequate warm-up activities.

No, it is not being suggested that coaches should not talk during practice. Rather they should "walk silently and carry a big stick" in terms of how much they say during practice time so that they do not waste valuable time and create artificial barriers to student learning. In short, coaches should be succinct in their verbiage. Practice time is too valuable for idle talk.

• *Don't assume anything in practices—be exact in directions and expectations.*

Another problematic area involving the learning process revolves around the directions given by coaches. Directions must be explicit, with no potential for misunderstanding, misinterpretation, or confusion in terms of what the coaching staff said or meant. Toward this end, it is suggested that coaches do not assume anything while keeping their communication efforts brief and to the point.

Experienced teachers and coaches do not assume that the individual athlete understands what has been communicated. Instead, these mentors go to extra lengths to ensure that there is no miscommunication between themselves and the players. One example of going the "extra mile" is to ask the individual player(s) to reiterate what has been said. Another tactic is to observe closely the individual player to determine whether the athlete is performing or acting as expected or directed.

• *Tell athletes why they are being asked to do something—such knowledge enhances learning.*

Athletes need to know *why* they are being asked to do something, whether it pertains to learning a physical skill or merely relates to the existence of a rule or regulation or some expectation of behavior. Such knowledge can greatly facilitate the entire learning process because (a) it helps to motivate the individual athlete and (b) it often creates insight into the skill to be learned, thus facilitating learning that skill. If a player understands the rationale behind a specific drill, a conditioning rule, an offense tactic, or a defensive strategy, that individual is much more likely to be motivated to work successfully to achieve the objective or goal. It also helps the player make the connection between what is done in practice and what is expected in game situations. In modern-day basketball, the players deserve to be told the *why* of what they are expected to do or not do. As a result, these athletes are able to internalize and justify the hard work and sacrifices frequently associated with practices and actual game competition.

• *Use technological tools in practices, games, and during planning sessions.*

Basketball coaches are teachers. As teachers, modern basketball coaches must take advantage of the wide range of technological tools that can effectively

Coaching Hint 221
Coaches need to stay focused during practice—don't waste players' time.

Coaching Hint 222
Utilize all the available technological resources and teaching tools in the conduct of one's practices.

and efficiently enhance the teaching and learning situation. Such tools include a wealth of audiovisual machines as well as exercise and conditioning devices.

The use of films, overhead projectors, videotapes, audio tapes, computers, and computer software is commonplace in today's planning and practice sessions. The modern-day basketball coach cannot ignore the availability of such technological resources, which are not only plentiful but have proven to be of great assistance in the teaching of the skills associated with the sport of basketball.

> **Coaching Hint 223**
> Take advantage of audio-visual tools to teach skills and concepts as well as to reinforce learning.

CONCLUDING COMMENTS ABOUT THE MENTAL SIDE OF COACHING

The effective basketball coach today must remain aware of the mental or psychological side of coaching. However, being merely aware of this dimension of coaching is not enough. Rather, the successful mentor must be actively involved in dealing with this dimension of the sport. This means being able to recognize how young athletes actually learn mental and physical skills as well as what tactics and strategies can be successfully used to facilitate the mastery of these skills.

Finally, the ultimate test for the successful mentor is to be willing to utilize the psychological principles and hints outlined in this chapter. In today's world of sports, as coaches know all too well, "the proof is in the pudding." Talk is cheap. Actually "doing it" is what counts.

REFERENCE

Stier, Jr., W. F. (1995). *Successful coaching—Strategies and tactics.* Boston: American Press.

Index